Oppenheim Toy Portfolio
Award Rating System

O₀₀₀₀₀ Rating system for quick reference!

₀₀₀₀₀ An outstanding product, not to be missed.

₀₀₀₀ A very good worth-the-money product.

₀₀₀ Good, not fantastic. Will have limited appeal, but not for everyone.

₀₀ Good idea, poorly executed; or great execution, terrible idea.

₀ Thumbs down, or "What were they thinking?"

What They Win

₀₀₀₀₀ 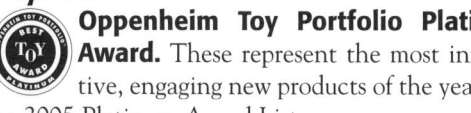 **Oppenheim Toy Portfolio Platinum Award.** These represent the most innovative, engaging new products of the year. See the 2005 Platinum Award List.

₀₀₀₀ **Oppenheim Toy Portfolio Gold Award.** Given to outstanding new products that enhance the lives of children.

₀₀₀–₀ Nothing.

Other Notable Awards

 **Oppenheim Toy Portfolio Blue Chip Classic Award**—Reserved for classic products that should not be missed just because they weren't invented yesterday. Products must be in the marketplace for five years to be considered for this award.

 Oppenheim Toy Portfolio SNAP Award—Given to products that can be used by or easily adapted for children with special needs.

Applauding Manufacturers. We applaud the manufacturers that submitted products to our review knowing that we write about the good, bad, and otherwise. Unlike many other toy testers, we don't charge fees to submit products. We don't take ad dollars. We don't sell any products. Our editorial independence means we can say what works and what doesn't. No manufacturer refused to send us products for review. (We will keep you posted if that changes!)

Praise for

OPPENHEIM
TOY PORTFOLIO

As seen on NBC's TODAY Show, Oprah, and CNN

If thoughts of holiday shopping have you fretting about what to buy for the little ones, help is on the way... the Oppenheim Toy Portfolio is just out... recognizing the year's best new toys.

—*USA Today*

...cuts through the confusion and offers the consumer sound information about what's good—and not so good.

—*Associated Press*

Sane comprehensive survey... absolutely worth the price.

—*Miami Herald*

Put away the aspirin, because there's a new book... that should make your toy-buying decisions smart and easy.

—*Houston Post*

Definite parental appeal.

—*Booklist*

The authors of the Oppenheim Toy Portfolio have yet again answered the call of parents who are tired of guessing which are the best toys and products for children—they've published a book.

—*New York Family*

The Oppenheim Toy Portfolio tells parents which are the best and dumbest toys.

—*Business Week*

OPPENHEIM TOY PORTFOLIO

2005 Edition

The Best Toys, Books, Videos,
Music & Software For Kids

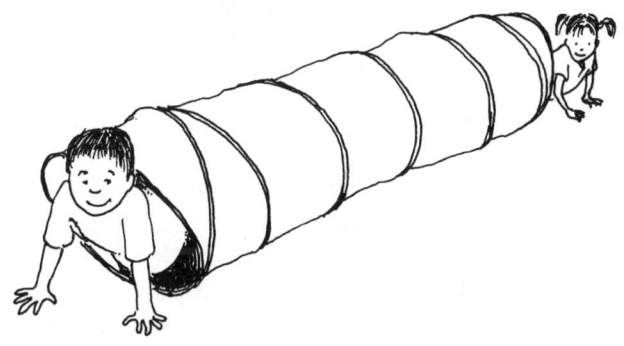

Joanne Oppenheim
and Stephanie Oppenheim
with **James Oppenheim,** *Technology Editor*

Illustrations by **Joan Auclair**

With thanks to our family and the many other families who helped us test for the best.
—Joanne, Stephanie, & James

This book may be purchased for educational, business, or sales promotional use. For information contact: Stephanie Oppenheim, Publisher, Oppenheim Toy Portfolio, Inc., 40 East 9th St., Suite 14M, New York NY 10003 or call (212) 598-0502 or e-mail stephanie@toyportfolio.com.

Designed by Joan Auclair

ISBN: 0972105026

Contents

Introduction

Our Twelfth Edition

We have spent the past year sifting through the hundreds of new toys, books, videos, audios, and software that you will be considering for the children in your life. Whether you are a new parent or grandparent, or an uncle, aunt, or family friend, you will find reviews in these pages that can help you bring home memorable and engaging products that will entertain and fit your child's developing needs. That is what we do for you.

Why a guide to children's media? Anyone who has walked the aisles of a giant toy supermarket or tried to sift through the mountains of books, videos, audios, and software designed for children appreciates how hard it is to know what to buy. Our goal is to take the guesswork out of choosing products that are not a waste of your money or your child's time.

Over the last two decades of reviewing products targeted to kids, we've noted that the expectations of what a toy does have changed radically, although not always to the benefit of children and their play lives. So, too, has the nature of videos and computer software directed toward children changed.

Quick Rating at a Glance. In addition to awarding products with a Platinum, Gold, or Blue Chip rating, we have also marked products with "play balls" right after the price to give you a quicker read on what worked and what didn't. You'll find our lists of this year's award-winning and top-rated products in the opening pages of this book. In addition to our PLATINUM AWARD Winners list, you'll find lists of outstanding products for group play, parent-child interactions, and office quiet time; top-rated science, educational, special needs, and gender-free products; our top picks for Under $10, $15, and $20; as well as Break-the-Bank (grandparent!) gifts.

You'll find full descriptions of these as well as other excellent new products, along with shopping information, in each of the age-appropriate chapters of the book. As always, we've included our Blue Chip classics, since we believe it would be a shame for kids to miss such products just because they weren't invented yesterday.

Children's products have a short shelf life. In fact, over 60 percent of this year's book is entirely new content—a response to the thousands of new choices introduced this year (6,000 new toys alone).

As always, we tested plenty of products that just didn't work or live up to our expectations. Yet as the process moved along, we were relieved and ultimately delighted with the range of wonderful choices available to consumers this year.

What Are the Trends for 2005?

Notable Trends

Potty Dolls. If toys are a reflection of societal interests and values, then it seems as if a good part of our culture is focused on toilet training! We have never seen so many drink-and-wet dolls. The good news is that the competition has inspired choices at different price points—you can even buy a doll that only tinkles when she's placed on her special potty (works with magnets, and is actually pretty neat). Even Elmo has gotten into the potty doll competition.

Plug and Play. A new category that isn't so new. Remember Pong? Before your child is ready for the serious gaming platforms (XBox, Playstation 2, and GameCube), three companies are hoping that you'll buy one of their gaming systems for younger kids. We're not sure that sooner is better, but the three contenders: InteracTV (Fisher-Price); ETO (Ohio Arts) and V.Smile (VTech). See page 239 for our reviews.

Castles. Perhaps thanks to the great success of Lord of the Rings, castles are big this year. You can build your own plastic version or buy one of several impressive wooden structures for your own medieval adventures.

Knit One, Purl Two. The hot adult craft trends of knitting and scrapbooking have also found a new younger audience.

Orange Alert Toys. Perhaps one of the most telling trends is the new batch of security toys including Hazmat action figures. Or how about the family game, Bounty Hunter, the Hunt and Capture Game: "Be the First to Capture the World's Most Wanted Fugitive and Take Him to Justice!"

Aquapets. We don't know if these new voice-activated imports will take off this season, but they are very cute. Like their predecessors of the '90s, these electronic pets need virtual food and affection… but they don't die!

Generational Markers. Transformers, Weebles (remember? "They wobble but they don't fall down"), GI Joe (40 years old), Carebears, and Dream Pets are all trying for a comeback with a new generation of kids.

On the Up Side

Fewer Stupid "Smart" Toys. Toys that claim to teach babies school skills before they can talk are thankfully on the decline.

Mini Dramatic Play Power. There's a miniature play setting for every interest: a pirate ship, a zoo, an amazing crane, a fire station, and a treehouse are just some of the great props for pretend that made our top list.

Colonel Mustard in the Billiard Room with the Candlestick. Classic games, as well as a new crop of innovative games, are among the best choices in toyland. Most kids will jump at a chance to play any truly "interactive" game with their folks. Games are also a no-tears way of developing math, language, geography, and reading skills, and gamesmanship, too. They give families an opportunity to share some important values (being a good sport, for example) and also time to talk while the game's being played.

Volume Controls Are In! Perhaps to bolster parental sanity, toy makers have added volume controls to their electronic wonders (and even the revolutionary option of playing with the sound off). We usually find that less noise means more play value in the long run.

Who's the Boss? Thank goodness there seem to be fewer intrusive toys that dictate how kids are to play. Indeed, play is one of the areas where kids can and should be empowered to use their own creative powers.

On the Down Side

Bad trends

Gross Toys Are Back. Last year we reported a happy decline in the gross toy market. It was a short-lived break. Leading the pack are Stink Blasters. These collectibles include B. O. Brian: "just squeeze the head and …peee uu!" There's also Toe Jam Jimmy, Burpin' Buddy, Butt Breath Bob, Barfin' Ben, and Porta Potty Paul.

Gross Books, Too. How about the following titles: Zombie Butts from Uranus, The Day My Butt Went Psycho! Pee-Ew! Is That You, Bertie? (a picturebook about a child with a flatulence problem) and we had three different books on the origin of poop (not that there's anything wrong with exploring a natural body function, but we were taken aback by the amount of attention this particular function was receiving. We guess this is the ultimate bathroom reading.

Who needs a body? What's In Ned's Head? In this game, players pull things out of Ned's head (e.g., a lab rat, a loose screw, etc.). Or how about the video, George the Head, where the character has a great family and nice toys—one problem, he has no body. Or Mattel's newest collectible doll line, Shorties: "Just pop off the Shorties heads and snap on a different body…"

Well, Excuse You! Last year we complained about the abundance of flatulence jokes in movies. We wondered whether there was a public relations campaign under way by the Flatulent Society of America. This year, forget flatulence. How about a movie about an animated doggie poo? (no, joke).

Talk to the Hand. With the new behavior modification toy Qwesty, you wear a large fabric covered question mark to signal to your child that they have to wait before they speak to you. Good luck with that one!

Back to the Mall Girls. We got a new crop of games where the game play is to be the best shopper at the mall or, with a nod to architectural design, build your own mall. We also got a diary where you speculate on who you will marry, how many children you'll have, and, our favorite question, how many pairs of shoes you will own.

Hurry Up, Baby! The marketing message to new parents is clear. Their "smart toys" will help your baby learn faster and achieve more. They don't mention that developmentally, babies learn best through real-life experiences and that too many lights and sounds can stimulate babies to distraction. Babies and toddlers are not ready for symbolic learning. The fact that a toddler can recite the alphabet is nothing more than a great parlor trick—ask the same toddler what "l-m-n-o-p" means and see what happens. There is no one magic toy that will guarantee an Ivy League acceptance (or even a spot in your city's competitive preschools)!

The Ultimate Downside. All of this rushing gives kids the unfortunate message that learning is hard and that maybe they're not very good learners. The most important thing parents can do is provide an environment that helps develop their children's confidence and a positive sense of themselves as learners. Many of the academic skills will be learned with much less difficulty later on, when children are more developmentally ready.

Trust your instincts and relax; the misguided "sooner is better" mentality is not a view shared by the majority of child development experts. Your toddler does not need to know how to spell *cat* or five words that rhyme with *star*. For children at every stage of development, toys that match their emerging abilities can best foster learning.

Talk, read, play with, and enjoy your child. Children learn language when people talk and listen to them. Literacy grows from the pleasures discovered in sharing books with meaningful stories and memorable illustrations. It is not served by rushing babies and toddlers with letter and sound drills. During early childhood the everyday discoveries of life have more educational value than any quiz machine you can bring home. Interactive people are far more important to learning than interactive machines!

Just Toys—What Difference Do They Make?

So what's the harm? After all, this is the 21st century. This is the age of technology, and even the Consumer Product Safety Commission is considering adjusting its age guidelines.

But pushing kids to do things that are developmentally inappropriate delivers a powerfully negative message that colors how kids think about themselves as competent, able doers. Parents, bombarded with the "smart toy, smart child" message, may also wonder if there's something wrong with their toddler who's incapable of rhyming in three languages or spelling *unicorn* by age three!

We used to "invest" in our toys. A favorite doll would be your companion in good times and bad (real and pretend), and our toys grew with us. Preprogrammed toys do not have the same lasting play value, however. For the most part, they are the Toyland equivalent of a one-trick pony.

Pretend No More. Pretend play is not merely something cute that children do while they are waiting to grow up. It's through pretending that children begin to think symbolically, letting one thing stand for another. The ability to make their own symbols, by turning a mud pie with sticks into a birthday cake with candles, provides the underpinnings for more abstract symbolic systems.

Changing Expectations. Play is also one of those wonderful states where kids can step into roles of control—even if it is pretend. So playhouses with sound effects that tell kids it's raining—"shut the window"—or small trucks with drivers who run the show with voice commands, steal words from the mouths of babes. As more and more tech toys invade Toyland, the expectations of what a toy does seem to be changing in the minds of children as well as adults. As toys become more literal, children also become more passive observers; the true value of play is turned upside down, with children reduced to pushing buttons and reacting to what the toy does instead of being active players. Kids end up moving around the play schemes dreamed up by adults—and being robbed of the power of play.

We're all for technology, but not when it is used to strip the value and fun of play from children.

Expanded Coverage

We have included reviews of the best products we tested this year as well as highlighting some notable losers. Unfortunately, there isn't space for all the products we review—so be sure to visit our website, www.toyportfolio.com, where our database of reviews is available. We'd like to thank all the families that contributed to this book. As always, we welcome you, our readers, to give us your feedback on the selections. For new readers, you'll find our review process and criteria for our award program below.

Happy playing!

How We Select the Best

We shop for children year 'round—only we get to do what most parents wish they could do before they buy. We open the toys, run the videos, read the books, play the music, and boot up the software. We get to compare all the toys that may look remarkably similar but often turn out to be quite different. For example, we put the toy trains together and find out which ones don't stay on the tracks.

How We're Different

We don't sell products. We don't take fees for looking at products. The **Oppenheim Toy Portfolio** was introduced in 1989 as the only independent consumer review of children's media. Unlike most other groups that rate products, we do not charge entry fees or accept ads from manufacturers. When you see our award seals on products, you can be assured that they are "award-winning" because they were selected by a noted expert in child development, children's literature, or education, and then rated by the most objective panel of judges—kids.

The Real Experts Speak:
Kids and Their Families

To get a meaningful sampling, we deal with families from all walks of life. We have testers in the city and in the country, in diapers and in blue jeans, in school clothes and in tutus. They have parents who are teachers, secretaries, lawyers, doctors, writers, engineers, doormen, software programmers, editors, psychologists, librarians, engineers, business people, architects, family therapists, musicians, artists, nurses, and early childhood educators. In some instances we have tested products in preschool and after-school settings where we can get feedback from groups of children. Since all new products tend to have novelty appeal, we ask our testers to live with a product for a while before assessing it. Among other things, we always ask, Would you recommend it to others?

Criteria We Use for
Choosing Quality Products

- What is this product designed to do and how well does it do it?

- What can the child do with the product? Does it invite active doing and thinking or simply passive watching?

- Is it safe and well designed, and can it withstand the unexpected?

- Does it "fit" the developmental needs, interests, and typical skills of the children for whom it was designed?

- What message does it convey? Toys as well as books and videos can say a great deal about values that parents are trying to convey. For example, does the product reflect old sexual stereotypes that limit children's views of themselves and others?

- What will a child learn from this product? Is it a "smart" product that will engage the child's mind or simply a novelty with limited play value?

- Is it entertaining? No product makes our list if kids find it boring, no matter how "good" or "educational" it claims to be.

- Is the age label correct? Is the product so easy that it will be boring or so challenging that it will be frustrating?

Rating System

Outstanding products, selected by our testers, are awarded one of four honors:

 Oppenheim Toy Portfolio Platinum Award— These represent the most innovative, engaging new products of the year. See the 2005 Platinum Award List.

Oppenheim Toy Portfolio Gold Seal Award— Given to outstanding new products that enhance the lives of children. Products listed with four playballs have received a Gold Seal Award.

Oppenheim Toy Portfolio Blue Chip Classic Award—Reserved for classic products that should not be missed just because they weren't invented yesterday. Products must be in the marketplace for five years to be considered for this award.

Oppenheim Toy Portfolio SNAP Award—Our Special Needs Adaptable Product Award is given to products that can be used by or easily adapted for children with special needs. All products reviewed in that chapter are recommended; the most outstanding are SNAP Award winners.

Using This Book

Each section begins with a play profile that tells you what to expect during each developmental stage and what "basic gear" will enhance learning and play. We also give you suggestions for best gifts for your budget and, perhaps most importantly, a stage-by-stage list of toys to avoid.

Because we know how busy people are these days, our reviews are purposely short and provide information on how to get your hands on the product.

A word about prices: Our award-winning products are not all high-ticket items. We have selected the very best products in toy supermarkets, as well as those that you will find in specialty stores, museum shops, and quality catalogs. We have listed the suggested retail prices, but they will vary tremendously depending on where you shop.

Telephone numbers: Where available, we have given a customer service number in case you have difficulty locating the product in your area. For some educational products, you'll find a catalog number for ordering, and in the Computer Software chapter you'll find consumer websites.

Child's Play—More Than Fun!

For children, playing is more than a fun way to fill the day. It's through play that children learn and develop all sorts of important physical, intellectual, and social skills. Like musicians, children use well-chosen toys, books, and music to orchestrate their play. As they grow and develop, so does their need for more complex playthings that challenge and enhance their learning. Toys and stories with the right developmental fit help create a marvelous harmony for learning and fun. The **Oppenheim Toy Portfolio** is a resource book you can use to make that kind of mix.

OPPENHEIM TOY PORTFOLIO PLATINUM TOY AWARDS 2005

INFANTS

Sleepyhead Bunny* (North American Bear Co.)/
Turnaround Froggie* (Mary Meyer), p. 3
Harold Hound Teether Rattle (Mamas & Papas), p. 11
Itty Bitty Bugs Rattles (Gund), p. 11
**Tap & Twirl Top*, Crawl-Along Wobbler* & Swirlin'
Saucer*** (Fisher-Price), pp. 17, 20, 21, 259, 260
Babipouce Collection* (Corolle), p. 24/
Tutti Frutti 5" Collection* (Gund), p. 25

TODDLERS

Dudley Musical Pull-Along Duck (Mamas & Papas),
p. 36
Lego Quatro (Lego Systems), pp. 45, 261
Retro Rocket (Radio Flyer), pp. 35, 62
Musical Stack & Play (Tiny Love), pp. 43, 261
**Musical Pop-tivity Table* / Pop 'n' Twirl Building
Table*** (Fisher-Price), pp. 43, 261
My First Madeline (RC2/Learning Curve), p. 49
Potty Elmo (Fisher-Price), p. 71

PRESCHOOLERS

Rocking Horses (Mamas & Papas), p. 95
Ryan's Room Adventures Ahoy (Small World Toys),
p. 76
Lego Duplo Block-o-Dile (Lego Systems), p. 83
Get Real Gear (Aeromaxtoys), p. 67
Lila (Corolle), p. 69
**Groovy Girls Bombastic Bunk Beds and
Supernova Sofa** (Manhattan Toy), p. 71

indicates a tie in the category

PRESCHOOLERS (*cont.*)

Deluxe Tumble Treehouse (Maxim Enterprises), *p. 77*
Rugged Riggz Trucks (Little Tikes), *p. 77*
Collapsing Bridge (Brio), *p. 80*

Games & Puzzles
Color Pixter (Fisher-Price), *p. 104*
Cookin' Cookies (Fundex), *p. 84*
Duck Duck Goose (Milton Bradley), *p 85*
Letter Factory Game (LeapFrog), *pp. 85, 265*
Richard Scarry's Busy House* (Mudpuppy Press) /
Puzzibilities Sound Puzzles* (Small World Toys),
   pp. 88, 263

EARLY SCHOOL YEARS

Construction
Castle of Morcia (Lego Systems), *p. 110*
Crane and Zoo (Playmobil), *p. 109*
Big Air Ball Tower (K'nex), *p. 116*

Doll
American Girl Nellie O'Malley (American Girl), *p. 112*

Remote Controls
Mgears Remote Control Racers
   (Learning Resources), *p. 114*
Robosapien (WowWee), *p. 115*
Tyco R/C RollCage (Mattel), *p. 115*

Games
Balloon Lagoon (Cranium), *pp. 120, 266*
4-Way Spelldown! (Cadaco), *p. 120*
There's a Moose in the House (Gamewright), *p. 122*
Who? What? Where? (Pazow), *p. 122*

Crafts
Crayola Gadget Headz Car Factory (Binney &
   Smith), *p. 133*
My Jewelry Box Kit (Balitono), *p. 131*

*indicates a tie in the category

PRESCHOOLERS *(cont.)*

Babar's Book of Color (Brunhoff, Abrams), *p. 162*

Four Friends in Autumn (dePaola, Simon & Schuster), *p. 157*

I Am Too Absolutely Small for School (Child, Candlewick), *p. 164*

Mister Seahorse (Carle, Philomel), *p. 163*

Little Brown Bear and the Bundle of Joy (Dyer, Little, Brown), *p. 186*

Pie in the Sky (Ehlert, Harcourt), *p. 164*

The Pigeon Finds a Hot Dog! (Willems, Hyperion), *p. 158*

Watch Out! (Fearnley, Candlewick), *p. 160*

You're All My Favorites (McBratney/Jeram, Candlewick), *p. 160*

EARLY SCHOOL YEARS

Fiction

Apples to Oregon (Hopkinson/Carpenter, Atheneum), *p. 169*

Baby Brains (James, Candlewick), *p. 165*

Ella's Big Chance (Hughes, Simon & Schuster), *p. 169*

Detective LaRue: Letters from the Investigator (Teague, Scholastic), *p. 166*

Eddie: Harold's Little Brother (Koch, Thaler/Warhola, Putnam), *p. 168*

The Giant and the Beanstalk (Stanley, HarperCollins), *p. 170*

Ish (Reynolds, Candlewick), *p. 178*

Perfectly Martha (Meddaugh, Houghton Mifflin), *p. 167*

Photographer Mole (Haseley/Kangas, Dial), *p. 168*

Toot & Puddle The New Friend (Hobbie, Little Brown), *p. 167*

The Trial of Cardigan Jones (Egan, Houghton Mifflin), *p. 168*

EARLY SCHOOL YEARS *(cont.)*

OPPENHEIM TOY PORTFOLIO SPECIAL NEEDS ADAPTABLE PRODUCT AWARDS 2005

Crawl-Along Wobbler (Fisher-Price), *p. 259*
Tap & Twirl Top (Fisher-Price), *p. 260*
Musical Stack & Play (Tiny Love), *p. 261*
Lego Quatro (Lego Systems), *p. 261*
Beginner Pattern Blocks (Melissa & Doug), *p. 262*
Fridge Farm Magnetic Animal Set (LeapFrog), *p. 263*
Puzzibilities Sound Puzzles (Small World Toys), *p. 263*
Letter Factory Game (LeapFrog), *p. 265*
Balloon Lagoon (Cranium), *p. 266*
Leap Pad Plus Writing Learning System with Dr. Seuss books (LeapFrog), *p. 267*
Story Reader with Beatrix Potter books (Publications International), *p. 268*
Fairy Woodkins (Pamela Drake), *p. 276*

OPPENHEIM TOY PORTFOLIO PLATINUM SOFTWARE AWARDS 2005

Due to the late release dates of children's software, the complete Oppenheim Toy Portfolio Platinum Software Awards 2005 List will be posted on our website, www.toyportfolio.com.

OPPENHEIM TOY PORTFOLIO PLATINUM AUDIO AWARDS 2005

Beethoven's Wig 2 (Rounder Kids), *p. 231*

Mike Mulligan and his Steam Shovel (Simon & Simon), *p. 233*

Nancy Cassidy's Kids' Songs (Klutz), *p. 227*

Number the Stars (Listening Library), *p. 234*

Sing Along with Putumayo (Putumayo Kids), *p. 227*

OPPENHEIM TOY PORTFOLIO PLATINUM VIDEO AWARDS 2005

Miffy's Springtime Adventure (Sony), *p. 205*

What's the Name of That Song? (Sony Wonder), *p. 202*

The Miracle (Disney), *p. 211*

Cheaper By the Dozen (Fox), *p. 210*

Harry Potter and the Prisoner of Azkaban (Warner Bros.), *p. 210*

Skrek2 (Dreamworks), *p. 211*

Kids are by nature social beings and enjoy few things more than being with other kids. Still, learning to share and play together can be rough going. We kept an eye out this year for toys that work especially well with groups of kids. For kids who are still at the "it's mine" stage, the key is to find toys with enough multiple pieces to go around. We also looked for products that lend themselves to cooperative play—whether it's a board game or activity kit that more than one child can enjoy together or simply side by side. We often talk these days about interactive toys, but here are some wonderful products for interactive kids.

Cranium Hullabaloo (Cranium), *pp. 84, 267*
Colossal Barrel of Crafts (Chenille Krafts), *p. 100*
Finger Painting Party (Alex), *pp. 100, 279*
Jump 'n Splash (Wham-O), *p. 139*
Lego Quatro (Lego Systems), *p. 45, 261*
My Playhouse (Alex), *p. 98*
Naturally Playful Clubhouse Climber (Step2), *pp. 38, 62*
Wooden Trains/Unit Wooden Blocks
  (various makers), *pp. 78–82*

Whether your kids are getting top grades or the other kind, there are playful ways you can help. Here are some of our highlighted favorites that give school skills a boost without your having to break out the flashcards.

Reading, Storytelling, Listening, & Language Skills
4 Way Spelldown (Cadaco), *p. 120*
I Spy Word Scramble (Briarpatch), *p. 121*
Letter Factory Game (LeapFrog), *pp. 85, 265*
PowerTouch Learning System (Fisher-Price), *pp. 127, 239*
Story Tapes & Player, *p. 232–235*

Prewriting/Fine-Motor Skills
Lacing Games (various makers), *pp. 90, 264*
Leap Pad Plus Writing System (LeapFrog), *pp. 127, 239, 267–68*
Operation Shrek (Milton Bradley), *p. 121*

Math, Logic, & Visual Perception
I Never Forget A Face Memory Game (eeBoo), *p. 87*
Rumis (Educational Insights) *p. 120*
Talking Math Mat Challenge (Learning Resources), *p. 126*
There's a Moose in the House (Gamewright), *p. 122*

Staying Power & Problem Solving
Bead Kits (various makers), *pp. 134–135*
Construction Toys (various makers), *pp. 44–46, 80–83, 109–110, 116–119*
Magnetic Building sets (various makers), *p. 118*
Puzzles (various makers), *pp. 42–43, 87–90, 128–129, 262–263*

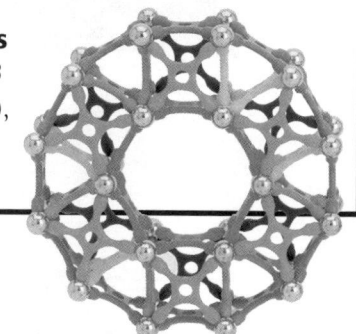

TOP-RATED OFFICE TOYS 2005

Whether your office is in a complex or in a corner of your home, when kids come to visit, having a few quiet toys can make the time more enjoyable for everyone. Besides a pack of crayons and paper, here are some top choices:

TODDLERS AND PRESCHOOLERS

Crayola Color Wonder Paper & Markers (Binney & Smith), *pp. 56, 99, 277*

Lego Duplo Bucket (Lego Systems), *pp. 44, 273*

Doodle Pro (Fisher-Price), *pp. 104, 278*

Fairy Collection Woodkins (Pamela Drake), *pp. 105, 276*

EARLY SCHOOL YEARS

Bead Kits (The Bead Shop), *p. 134*

Crunch Art (Hands On Toys), *pp. 135, 278*

Gameboy Advance SP (Nintendo), *p. 146*

Lacing Puppets (Lauri), *p. 114*

Make Your Own Cards (Made By Hands), *pp. 131, 280*

Scratch & Sparkle Deluxe Kit (Scratch Art), *p. 132*

While it's important for kids to know how to play independently, games and cooperative projects provide the raw materials for interactions that can be rewarding for adult and child. Without taking over, adults can help kids get started and be there as "consultants," giving kids strategies for working in an orderly fashion. Making time to do such things together gives you a chance to play and experiment together—a chance to solve problems, think creatively, and even have fun learning together.

Here are some of our favorites:

PRESCHOOLERS

Duck Duck Goose (Milton Bradley), *p. 85*
Letter Factory Game (LeapFrog), *pp. 85, 265*
Puppets & Puppet Stage (various makers), *pp. 73–74, 113–114, 273–274*
Puzzles (various makers), *pp. 42–43, 87–90, 128–129, 262–263*
Wooden Trains (various makers), *pp. 78–79*

EARLY SCHOOL YEARS

Construction sets (various makers), *pp. 109–110, 116–119*
Crayola Gadget Headz Car Factory (Crayola), *p. 133*
Hanging Bird House & Feeder Kits (TWC of America), *p. 142*
There's a Moose in My House (Gamewright), *p. 122*
Sir Steps-A-Lot (imadethat), *p. 100*
Zoo (Playmobil), *p. 109*

Many of the toys, books, and videos you bring home may have a built-in Gender Agenda™—products that reinforce stereotypes and shape your child's self-image. It often begins innocently in the nursery with pastel color coding, but quickly moves on to a glut of products with themes of hair-play for girls and gunplay for boys. The gender issue is not just one that is important to girls. The overly aggressive and violent-themed toys and video games directed at boys are even more alarming to us than the dating games or lavender blocks that come with blueprints for a shopping mall.

Can you avoid all gender-specific toys? Probably not. These are often the products kids want the most, not only because they are heavily promoted on TV, but also because children tend to sort the world out in the simple and absolute terms of right or wrong, hard or easy, boy or girl. There are, however, positive choices you can make—where a gender-free product will work for both boys and girls... and products that break gender stereotypes.

Balloon Lagoon (Cranium), *pp. 120, 266*

Deluxe Tumble Treehouse (Maxim Enterprises), *p. 77*

Dudley Musical Pull-Along Duck (Mamas & Papas), *p. 36*

Lamaze Sing & Spin Bugs (RC2/Learning Curve), *pp. 19, 260*

Retro Rocket (Radio Flyer), *pp. 35, 62*

Richard Scarry's Busy House (Mudpuppy Press), *p. 88*

Swirlin' Saucer (Fisher-Price), *pp. 17, 260*

Trikke 5 (Trikke Tech), *p. 141*

Wooden Kitchen Appliances (Small World Toys), *p. 54*

MAKE A GIFT LIST 2005

Teaching kids to give, not just get, can be fun with any one of these craft kits. These are just a few of our favorite kits that make a finished product that kids can give with pride to family, friends, or teachers.

Beeswax Candles (Creativity for Kids), *p. 133*

My Jewelry Box (Balitono), *p. 131*

Potholders & Other Loopy Projects (Klutz), *p. 136*

Ribbon Plates (Alex), *p. 132*

Tutti Frutti Safety Pin Bracelet (The Bead Shop), *p. 134*

Wake Up! Alarm Clock (Creativity for Kids), *p. 133*

TOP-RATED SCIENCE PRODUCTS **2005**

One of the best ways to excite kids about science is to make it a hands-on experience. Here are our favorite picks of this year's top science toys. Many require some adult involvement—providing a chance to make discoveries together. Be sure to check our science books, videos, and software recommendations.

Box of Rocks (GeoCentral), *p. 141*
Crayola Gadget Headz Car Factory
(Binney & Smith), *p. 133*
Dig Kits (Action Products), *p. 142*
Discovery Awesome Avalanche Kit
(Discovery Kids), *p. 141*
Kids' Sundial Kit (Milestones), *p. 137*
Magnetic Building Sets (various makers), *p. 118*
My Birdhouse Kit (Balitono), *p. 142*
Tabletop Greenhouse (Creativity for Kids), *p. 137*
Telescopes (various makers), *p. 143*

TOP-RATED PRODUCTS UNDER $25 *2005*

Duck Duck Goose (Milton Bradley), *p. 85*
Knitting (Klutz), *p. 136*
Musical Pop-itivity Table (Fisher-Price), *pp. 43, 261*
Musical Stack & Play (Tiny Love), *pp. 43, 261*
Super Saver Teaching Bank (LeapFrog), *p. 111, 270*
Wooden Shoe Wanna Paint These? (The Bead Shop), *p. 133*

TOP-RATED BIG TICKET LIST *2005*

American Girl Nellie O'Malley (American Girl), *p. 112*
Color Pixter (Fisher-Price), *pp. 104, 146*
Leapster (LeapFrog), *pp. 144, 238*
Lila (Corolle), *pp. 69*
Little Brewster (Mary Meyer), *p. 72*
Retro Rocket (Radio Flyer), *p. 35*
Tyco R/C Rollcage (Mattel), *p. 115*
Robosapien (WowWee), *p. 115*
Rocking Horses (Mamas & Papas), *p. 95*
Ryan's Room Adventures Ahoy (Small World Toy), *p. 76*
Super Art Table (Alex), *p. 130*
Wooden Blocks/Trains (various makers), *pp. 78–82*

I • Toys

1 • Infants
Birth to One Year

The Horizontal Infant

What to Expect Developmentally

Your Role in Play. To your newborn, no toy in the world is more interesting than you! Babies are more interested in people than things. Your smiling face, your gentle touch, the sound of your voice, even your familiar scent make you the most perfect plaything. Don't worry about spoiling your newborn with attention. Responding to your baby's needs now will make him less needy later. Playing with your baby is not just fun—it's one of the most important ways babies learn about themselves and the world of people and things!

Learning Through the Senses. Right from the start, babies begin learning by looking, listening, touching, smelling, and tasting. It's through their senses that they learn about the world. In this first remarkable year, babies progress from gazing to grasping, from touching to tossing, from watching to doing. By selecting a rich variety of playthings, parents can match their baby's sensory learning style.

Reaching Out. Initially, you will be the one to activate the mobile, shake the rattle, squeeze the squeaker. But before long, baby will be reaching out and taking hold of things and engaging you in a game of peekaboo.

Toys and Development. As babies develop, so do their needs for playthings that fit their growing abilities. Like clothes, good toys need to fit. Some of the toys for newborns will have short-term use and then get packed away or passed along to a new cousin or friend. Others will be used in new ways as your child grows. During this first year, babies need toys to gaze at, listen to, grasp, chomp on, shake, pass from one hand to another, bang together, toss, chase, and hug.

BASIC GEAR CHECKLIST
FOR THE HORIZONTAL INFANT

✓Mobile   ✓Crib mirror
✓Musical toys   ✓Activity mat
✓Soft fabric toys with differing sounds and textures
✓Fabric dolls or animals with easy-to-grab limbs

🚫 **Toys to Avoid**

These toys pose choking and/or suffocation hazards:

✓Antique rattles
✓Foam toys
✓Toys with elastic
✓Toys with buttons, bells, or ribbons
✓Old wooden toys that may contain lead paint
✓Furry plush dolls that shed
✓Any toys with small parts

Crib Toys: Musical Toys, Mobiles, and Mirrors

Few toys are as soothing to newborns as a music box with its quiet sounds. Today, most musical toys for infants don't come as boxes but as plush toys. We prefer some of the newer pull-down musical toys to dolls with hard metal wind-up keys that older babies may chew on or get poked with by accident.

Musicals

■ **Bethany Butterfly Musical Activity Toy** 🎇*2005*

(Mamas & Papas $19.99 ●●●●½) Hang this brightly colored velour and patterned butterfly in the crib or on a stroller for gazing. Plays "Somewhere Over the Rainbow." New for **2005**, **Munch Giraffe** ($19.99 ●●●○): a gentle pull on her tail and she plays "Hush Little Baby"— very soothing. (310) 631-2222.

■ Lamaze Jester Music Box

(RC2/Learning Curve $19.99 ●●●●●) Twist this brightly patterned music box and the colorful antennae move to the music. Black-and-white graphics and velour balls have interesting textures, plus crinkle and jingle sounds that invite investigating. PLATINUM AWARD '02. (800) 704-8697.

■ Lizzie Light Up Musical Toy **2005**

(Gund $22 ●●●○) Pull Lizzie down from the leaf she's attached to, and she plays "Somewhere Over the Rainbow" (the quality of the music is close to an old-fashioned music box). Lizzie has a big smile and a colorful palette (mostly yellow and blue) that would be appropriate for both boys and girls; her wings light up a bit when the music plays. (800) 448-4863.

■ Lyrical Lion

(Sassy $14.99 ●●●●●) It's hard not to smile back at this cheerful yellow lion who has polka-dotted paws, of course. He has a thick ribbon mane that surrounds a clear face for baby to look at while resting in her crib. Plays "Babes in Toyland" with a lovely old-fashioned sound. PLATINUM AWARD '03. (800) 323-6336.

■ Sleepyhead Bunny **2005** PLATINUM AWARD

(North American Bear Co. $29 ●●●●●) Pull the long blue-and-white sleeping cap on this floppy pastel bunny, and it plays "Beautiful Dreamer" Music with an old-fashioned musical sound. Also comes in pink. (800) 682-3427.

■ Turnaround Froggie **2005** PLATINUM AWARD

(Mary Meyer $12 ●●●●○) Wind up the polka-dotted green velour froggie and it turns slowly on its platform, playing "You Are My Sunshine." (800) 451-4387.

■ Whoozit Pull Musical *2005*

(Manhattan Toy $19.95 ●●○○) Fans of the zany Whoozit line will consider this pull-down musical a must-have for the crib. A little Whoozit face pulls down from a collection of brightly colored stars, and plays "Twinkle, Twinkle, Little Star" with a lovely sound quality. (800) 541-1345.

Mobiles

A musical mobile attached to crib rail or changing table provides baby with fascinating sights and sounds. During the first 3 months, infants can focus only on objects that are relatively close. Toys should be between 8" and 14" from their eyes. Before you buy any mobile, look at it from the baby's perspective. What can you see? Many attractive mobiles are purely for decoration and do not have images that face the baby in the crib. **Mobiles to Avoid:** pastels (since baby won't be able to see them very well) and mobiles where the images are not directed at baby.

Here are our favorites (all gender-free):

■ Learning Patterns Changing Sensations Mobile

(Fisher-Price $19.99 ●●●●●) One of the best mass-market mobiles we've seen in a long time. The animals are properly tilted down so baby can see their faces as well as the patterns of the dancing critters. This plays four melodies, including "The Lion Sleeps Tonight." PLATINUM AWARD '03. (800) 432-5437.

■ Nursery Verse Mobile

(North American Bear Co. $50 ●●●●●) A charming mobile featuring a cast of well-known nursery stars including Humpty Dumpty, the Cat and the Fiddle, the Baker's Man, and Mother Goose. Done in bright colored felt with characters properly tilted so baby can see their faces. Plays "Humpty Dumpty." PLATINUM AWARD '03. (800) 682-3427.

■ Shine On Me Musical Mobile

(RC2/Learning Curve $50 ●●●●●) A cheerful mobile with a bright smiley sun face tilted down for baby to see. A bird, a butterfly, and some friendly bugs spin as the mobile rotates. Plays jazz, classical, and Latin music that can be activated with a remote control. PLATINUM AWARD '04. (800) 704-8697.

■ Symphony in Motion Deluxe

(Tiny Love $49.95 ●●●●●) How do you make a good thing better? Add a remote control and new animals to this clever musical mobile with innovative motion. Small shapes slide on the arms of the mobile, making a clicking sound as the mobile turns. The sound quality is better than most and it plays several classical selections. PLATINUM AWARD '02. (800) 843-6292.

■ Wimmer-Ferguson Infant Stim-Mobile
BLUE CHIP

(Manhattan Toy $20 ●●●●●) Newborns will be fascinated with the black-and-white, high-contrast patterns of the ten vinyl 3" discs and squares that dance and dangle on this non-musical mobile. Not as cute looking as other mobiles, but babies do react to the visual stimulation of this crib toy. Updated classic with new graphics. (800) 541-1345.

☞ **SAFETY TIP: Mobiles should be removed by the time baby is 5 months old, or whenever baby can reach out and touch them, to avoid the danger of strangulation or choking on small parts.**

SMART BABY TRICK: Monkey See, Monkey Do. Here's the first really neat trick your baby will be able to do. Almost from the start your baby will be able to imitate your expressions. Try sticking your tongue out and see what happens! Who says you need words to "talk"?

SMART PARENT TRICK: Babies stop looking at things that are always there, just as you stop looking at a vase that's always in the same place. Changing things to gaze at will interest babies more. Also, it's hard to focus on too many objects at once. So less may be more.

Crib Mirrors

Even before your baby can reach out and touch, a crib mirror provides her with ever-changing images. It will be a while before baby knows whose face and hands she sees. In time, she'll be babbling to that face and studying the reflection of her hands.

■ Earlyears Crib Mirror

(International Playthings $16.99 ❍❍❍❍) Best choice for newborns, this 14½" x 11" black-and-white, high-contrast graphic will attract baby's attention. Reverse it and you have an infant-safe, distortion-free mirror with colorful trim. (800) 445-8347.

■ Me in the Mirror

(Sassy $14.95 ❍❍❍❍) This large (9½") mirror has interesting toys attached for gazing, and even a place for adding your own photo. Great for tummy time on the floor, or you can attach it to the side of the crib. (800) 323-6336.

■ Soothe & Amuse Crib Mirror *2005*

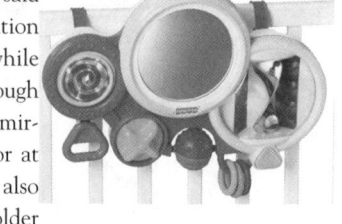

(Fisher-Price $19.99 ❍❍❍) We had mixed reviews on this product. One parent said that there was too much stimulation for her five-month-old baby, while another thought it didn't do enough and preferred a simpler, bigger mirror. With a large circular mirror at its center for early gazing, this is also an activity toy for the crib for older babies. There are clacking rings, a lever to pull down, and a clicking dial; parents can set the toy to play ten minutes of music to go along with the moving spiral (with some lights). (800) 432-5437.

☞ **SAFETY TIP:** Many catalogs and picture books show baby cribs overflowing with quilts, pillows, and toys. These are pretty to look at, but totally unsafe!

BABY TRACKING GAMES

Following a moving object is no small feat for the new baby. Use a boldly patterned soft toy with quiet rattle or squeaky sound to get baby's attention. Give it a shake and move it slowly from side to side in baby's line of vision. In time baby will reach out to touch, but for now, looking and listening is the name of the game. Remember, newborns can't focus on objects more than 8–14 inches from their eyes.

Everything That Goes Up: Here's a little baby science lesson. Hold your hand up in the air in baby's sight line, saying: "Everything that goes up comes down, down, down!" (Gradually spiral your hand down, down, down 'til you gently tickle baby under the chin or on the tummy.) Before long baby will anticipate the tickles, and giggle before your fingers touch!

Equipment for Playtime

Babies are such social beings that they are often happiest when they are in the midst of the action. Many of the following products have serious safety issues that you should be aware of before you buy:

☞ **SAFETY TIP:** Swings, baby seats, playpens, and saucers are often recalled because they can tip or collapse with frightening consequences. Be sure to check the Consumer Product Safety Commission website if you have inherited a product or find one at a yard sale.

👉 **SAFETY TIP:** Never place any type of baby carrier on a table, bed, or counter. Even though the baby has never done it before, there's no way of predicting when he will make a move that can tip the carrier.

👉 **SAFETY TIP:** Many parents find the back-and-forth action of a swing a soothing diversion for a restless infant. However, we find it difficult to recommend any infant swings because they can entrap limbs and necks, or even collapse. If you choose to use one, we urge you not to leave the room. Use it only with constant supervision.

👉 **SAFETY TIP:** While stationary entertainment units are safer than the walkers most of us had as kids, you should know that they do not build muscles for walking and the time in these seats should be limited and supervised. Babies do need to crawl before they walk!

SMART PARENT TRICKS
You Don't Say! Some new parents feel awkward about speaking to a baby who can't talk yet. What can you talk about? Anything. Talk about what you are doing, even if you are changing a diaper. Imitate baby's coos, gurgles, and squeals. In the beginning you'll do most of the talking . . . but before long baby will be answering. Pause, so baby can take turns! Before long you'll be having real "chats." Research indicates that babies who are fre-

quently talked to have almost 300 more words by age 2 than tots who are rarely spoken to.

Puff 'n' Pop. Puff your cheeks. Then use your hands to pop them to make a funny noise. Soon, baby will reach out to pop your cheeks for you.

Playmats/Activity Gyms

As a general rule, avoid playmats and blankets that have lots of doodads, which pose a choking hazard. We found many expensive quilts with ribbons, buttons, and fuzzy trims that are unsafe. Also avoid mats with activities all over and no really comfortable place for baby to lie down on.

Best in Category

■ Gymini Super Deluxe Electronic Lights & Music 3-D Activity Gym

(Tiny Love $59.95 ●●●●●) This mat remains the all-time favorite of our tester parents and babies. The music is soothing, with a choice of classical or nursery tunes. Like the original, this has two arches and dangly toys for gazing at and batting. We also recommend the less expensive version without the lights and music. PLATINUM AWARD '03. (800) 843-6292.

Contenders

■ Lamaze 2-in-1 Drop & Pop

(RC2/Learning Curve $60 ●●●●) A reversible playmat with high-contrast red, black, and white on one side, and bright colors on flip side. Closes up easily with a Velcro closure. Comes with three hanging toys for early gazing. (800) 704-8697.

■ Starlight Symphony Play Gym *2005*

(Kids II $39.99 ●●) This large mat got high marks for the dangling mirror and the music, and for being extremely well padded. The flashing "disco" lights on the arched bars, however, were way too stimulating for our testers. Less would have been more. (770) 751-0442.

■ Whoozit Gym to Go

(Manhattan Toy $50 ○○○) Handsome playmat with signature Whoozit design but smaller than both the Gymini and Lamaze versions, folds up with a small handle that our tester found not as easy to carry as the Gymini, which she preferred. (800) 541-1345.

> ☞ **SAFETY TIP: With any gym you use, total supervision is required. Gyms are also not for babies who are beginning to pull themselves up. We prefer fabric playmats to most plastic gyms, which can be accidentally kicked over.**

First Lap and Floor Toys: Rattles, Sound Toys, and More

Infant toys can help adults engage and interact with newborns. A bright rattle that baby tracks visually, a quiet music box that soothes, or an interesting doll to gaze or swipe at, are ideal for getting-acquainted games. These toys can be used on the changing table or for lap games during playful moments after a feeding, before a bath, or whenever.

■ Lamaze First Mirror BLUE CHIP

(RC2/Learning Curve $19.99 ○○○○○) A fabric-covered wedge with a mirror is covered in eye-grabbing bold black-and-white patterns with red piping. The distortion-free mirror is now padded and, like the original, can be removed and hung in the crib. PLATINUM AWARD '98. (800) 704-8697.

■ Peter Rabbit Musical

(Gund $25 ○○○○○) Peter Rabbit moves his head very slowly as he plays Brahms' Lullaby. The old-fashioned music box gives this a very special quality—a welcome relief from so many electronic sounds. He's ultra soft, and the key for winding him up is hidden in his white tail. PLATINUM AWARD '04. (800) 448-4863.

■ **Visual Cards** BLUE CHIP

(Sassy $7.99 oooo) New babies enjoy gazing at
these cards with high-contrast images and licks
of primary colors on all four sides. Flip them
from time to time for a change of visual interest and stand them on the changing table.
(800) 323-6336.

Rattles

Many rattles are too noisy, hard, and heavy for newborns.
While most will be used by adults to get baby's attention, the
best choice for newborns is a rattle with a soft sound that
won't startle and a soft finish that won't hurt. During the first
months, an infant's arm and hand movements are not yet
refined. Here are some of the best rattles for early playtimes:

■ **Itty Bitty Bugs Rattles** *2005* PLATINUM AWARD

(Gund $5 ooooo) If you have a preemie, these
lightweight rattles will be a better choice as your
baby's hand strength grows. They are covered with brightly colored terry and have a
hole in the middle, making it easier for little hands to grasp. Also, **Mini Pro
Grabbies** (Gund $5 oooo) are even
lighter, done in velour, and have a sports
theme. (732) 248-1500.

■ **Harold Hound Teether Rattle**
2005 PLATINUM AWARD

(Mamas & Papas $7.99 ooooo) A col-
orful patchwork velour dog rattle with
floppy ears, striped handle, little noise,
but big eye appeal. Still top rated, last
year's **Molly Moo Teether Rattle**
($8.99 ooooo). (310) 631-2222.

■ **Mommy and Me
Flower Rattle** *2005*

(Dolly $4.99 oooo½) A bright fabric flower has
a smiley face with colorful plastic rings hanging
down from the base, making this a good toy for
teething babies. Our five-month-old tester's mom
wrote, "this is just right for him to hold, not too

heavy, and keeps him busy when we go out." (888) 463-6559.

■ Stars & Sun Rattle 2005

(Sassy $5 ●●●●½) Easy to grab, this polka-dotted ring has stars that clack and a two-sided soft velour sun that smiles on one side and sleeps on the other. (800) 323-6336.

SMART BABY TRICK: If a young baby drops a toy she is holding, she will not look to see where it goes. Developmentally, at this stage, out of sight is out of mind. If she has a toy in one hand and you show her another, she will drop the first and reach for the offered toy.

BABY MUSIC GAMES

Sing, Sing a Song! Okay, it doesn't matter if you sing off key or you don't know all the words. To your baby, you deserve a Grammy! Singing can soothe a crying baby or refresh and surprise a fussy baby. Go ahead! Add his name to the songs you sing and you'll really have a fan! Don't be afraid to do a little dancing—it's a great way to release your tension as well as baby's.

The Vertical Infant

What to Expect Developmentally

Once babies can sit up, they have a new view of and fascination with the world of things. Now they don't just grasp at toys, they can use their hands and mouths to explore and feel objects. At around 9 months, babies gain fuller control of their separate fingers and begin to use their index fingers to point and poke at openings. Now they can activate toys with spinners. It's also at this stage that they can handle two objects at the same time.

Watch how your baby explores any toy, examining every angle. She looks at it, fingers it, tastes it. Using two hands, she bangs two blocks together, or spends many moments passing a toy from one hand to another. This is serious work, a way of discovering how things function and what she can do to make things happen.

During this exciting time your baby will begin to crawl and even pull himself up on his two little feet. Some babies may even take their first steps. In a matter of just a few months, your baby grows from needing others to play a game of patty-cake, to putting out his hands and leading others to play patty-cake with him.

Many of the toys from the horizontal stage will still be used. By now, however, the mobile should be removed from the crib, and other interesting playthings should be added gradually. As new toys are introduced, put some of the older things away. Recycle toys that have lost their novelty by putting them out of sight for a while, then reintroduce them or give them away. A clutter of playthings can become more of a distraction than an attraction.

BASIC GEAR CHECKLIST FOR THE VERTICAL INFANT

✓Rattles and teething toys
✓Manipulatives with differing shapes, sounds, textures
✓Plastic containers for filling and dumping games
✓Cloth or sturdy cardboard books
✓Washable dolls and animals   ✓Musical toys
✓Soft fabric-covered ball   ✓Cloth blocks
✓Rolling toys or vehicles   ✓Bath toys

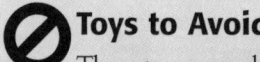 ## Toys to Avoid

These toys pose choking and/or suffocation hazards:
✓Antique rattles
✓Foam toys
✓Toys with elastic
✓Toys with buttons, bells, and ribbons
✓Old wooden toys that may contain lead paint

✓**Furry plush dolls that shed**
✓**Any toys with small parts**

These toys are developmentally inappropriate:
✓**Shape sorters and ring-and-post toys—these call for skills beyond those of an infant**

Rattles and Teethers

Now is the time for manipulatives that encourage two-handed exploration while providing interesting textures and sounds, and safe, chewable surfaces for teething. You can't teach eye-hand coordination, but you can motivate exploration by providing toys that develop baby's ability to use hands and fingers in new and more complex ways.

■ Baby Smiley Face Rattle BLUE CHIP

(Sassy $5.99 ●●●●●) Older babies will enjoy exploring this friendly rattle with a smiling face, jiggly eyes, squeaky nose, and chewy, polka-dotted, handle-shaped ears. It reverses to a distortion-free mirror. (800) 323-6336.

■ Tolo Abacus Rattle BLUE CHIP

(Small World Toys $5.95 ●●●●●) There are lots of moving parts to explore as they clack and move on this colorful plastic rattle for two-handed play. Also, still top rated, the **Tolo Roller Ball** with a small ball inside a larger ball and easy grip openings. Both beautifully crafted in sturdy, primary-colored plastic with interesting action for baby to manipulate. (800) 421-4153.

■ Trinkles 2005

(Gund $10 ●●●●) When your baby is ready to hold a rattle with two hands, this is just the right toy to bring home. The yellow butterfly has floppy pink wings that jingle, and small mirror disks. Easy to grab, the smiling face has stitched features, gentle chiming sound, and lightweight structure that makes this a great choice for older babies to explore. (800) 448-4863.

■ Whoozit Touch & Teethe

(Manhattan Toy $12 ●●●●½) An easy-to-hold, visually exciting rattle. The Whoozit face with a squeaky nose is on one side, and a mirror is on the other. A ring with hearts, stars, and other textured shapes surrounds the face and is ideal for two-handed exploration and teething. Also interesting, **Winkle** ($12 ●●●●); put this in the fridge to chill the plastic loops for teething. This toy has a quiet rattle sound and many loops for easy holding and two-handed play. (800) 541-1345.

SMART PARENT TRICKS: Who's That? Your baby in arms will be amazed to catch sight of herself and you in a mirror. Watch her surprise as she sees you twice—the real you and your reflection. Talk about what she sees and let her touch your face and your reflection. In time, you can play little games of "Where is my nose? Where is baby's nose?" Move baby in and out of the sight line of the mirror, playing yet another variation of peekaboo!

Floor Toys

COMPARISON SHOPPER
First Blocks

We like the **Discover & Play Color Blocks** (Baby Einstein $12.99 ●●●●½) that have interesting textures on each side. One block makes a quacking sound that your baby will enjoy hearing long before she'll be able to make it happen. These are fun for stacking and knocking down. (800) 793-1454. We also still recommend **Earlyears Soft Busy Blocks** (International Playthings $15 oooo½) which have softer sides and corded piping, making them easier for baby to grasp. Colorful graphics and patterns and quiet sounds make these good floor toys for beginners. Also, **Earlyears Sweet Baby Blocks** ($10 oooo). Six soft, squeezable vinyl blocks, easy to grasp, with a colorful single image on each face of the cubes. Fun for stacking, knocking down, and tossing. (800) 445-8347.

■ Lamaze Clutch Cube

(RC2/Learning Curve $12.99 oooo) An updated version of this classic is slightly smaller and lighter for little ones to hold and explore. There's a chime inside the cube that makes a quiet sound as baby investigates the many patterns and differing textures on the four grabbers. A black-and-white target graphic lifts to reveal a black-and-white bear. There's a lot here for sensory feedback and two-handed play. (800) 704-8697.

TWO-WAY BABY GAME Booom! Before baby starts stacking blocks, he'll like knocking them down. Use fabric blocks or a stack of big plastic ones. How high can you stack them before your little playmate makes them go BOOOOOOOOM? Baby loves the powerful feeling of making this happen, especially if you laugh it up.

Filling and Spilling Games

With their newly acquired skills of grasping and letting go comes the favorite game of filling and dumping multiple objects in and out of containers.

■ Baby's First Blocks and Snap-Lock Beads BLUE CHIP

(Fisher-Price $8 & $3.99 ooooo) Babies will enjoy these
toys long before they can do what the boxes promise.
Baby's First Blocks is technically a shape-sorter, but
the 12 blocks will be used to fill, spill, and throw
long before baby can fit them into the four-
place shape-sorter lid of the container. Put the
lid away for now. The same is true of the lemon-
sized **Snap-Lock** plastic beads that will be
enjoyed for chomping on, picking up, toss-
ing, and little games of fill and dump. Putting them together
comes much later. Great for developing fine motor skills and the ability to litter the floor. (800) 432-5437.

■ Swirlin' Saucer *2005* PLATINUM AWARD

(Fisher-Price $12.95 ooooo) Our seven-month-old
tester loved picking up the oversized plastic balls
and dropping them in the saucer. You can turn on
the toy base so that the saucer shakes and makes
noise as the balls drop. A pleasingly easy-to-activate first floor toy. (800) 432-5437.

■ Lamaze Soft Sorter

(RC2/Learning Curve $19.99 oooo) Babies don't
need to know their shapes to use this big colorful fabric cube with a lift-up lid and different geomet-
ric openings on each side. The colorful patterns
on each side match the four soft rattle shapes
that fit into the cube. However, the openings are
big enough to allow baby to put any shape into any
opening. (800) 704-8697.

How Many Socks? Game The Lamaze Soft Sorter is
a perfect prop to fill with all those unmatched socks
you keep saving. Leave the wide door open and let
some stick out of the other openings on the cube.
This is almost as much fun to empty as a box of tissues, and much safer, since tissues fall apart when
they are tasted. Strengthens hands and fingers
while exploring textures, colors, and patterns.

■ Lego Baby BLUE CHIP

(Lego Systems $10 & up ●●●●●)
These colorful big chunky plastic
blocks are ideal for grasping, filling,
spilling, and, eventually, stacking.
Choose a slightly larger set that includes
a wheeled base block for stacking and rolling
back and forth. (800) 233-8756.

■ Put and Peek Birdhouse 2005

(Manhattan Toy $19.95 ●●●●) This cheerful fabric
birdhouse is a parent-intensive toy with lots of
possibilities for hamming it up. You can fly the
four birds into the house (the roof opens wide,
as does one side). Our nine-month-old tester
favored holding (and tasting) the red bird as he
watched his father fly the other ones about. 6 mos.
& up. (800) 541-1345. Preferable to Infantino's **Puppies Playhouse**
(●●●) (same idea, but the animals aren't as nice and the house is
smaller and not see-through).

Toys for Making Things Happen

Some of the best infant toys introduce babies to their first lessons in cause and effect. Such toys respond to baby with
sounds or motion that give even the youngest players a sense
of "can do" power—of making things happen! **What to Avoid:**
toys that do too much. Most are overwhelming to kids and the
they end up "watching" rather than doing.

■ Classical Stacker 2005

(Fisher-Price $10 ●●●●●) This former PLATINUM-
AWARD winning stacker is back with new colors. The
star rings fit on the post in any order (a plus). Post has
magical lights that wink and play music when top is
pressed. Sound quality is not excellent, but it is a
long-term favorite. Says 6 mos. & up, we'd say 9
mos. & up. Brand new this year, **Dance Baby
Dance Buildin' Band** (Fisher-Price $12.99
●●●●½) Easy to activate, this stacking toy has a
small keyboard, tambourine, drum that rattles, and
"snare drum and cymbals" that play with a tap. Plenty of ways to
make something happen! Pass on the **Bouncing Bongo** (●●) from
the same line—it is over-the-top frenetic. (800) 432-5437.

■ Developlay Activity Center

(Tiny Love $44.95 ○○○○○) A two-sided activity center loaded with interesting challenges for the senses. A polka-dotted spinner reflects in a mirror; music plays with a press of the happy face; pull a ring to make a "hammer" rise and fall. Flip it over for musical buttons, knobs to turn, a gentle pop-up, and gears that spin. 9 mos. & up. PLATINUM AWARD '04. (800) 843-6292.

■ Discover Sounds Kitchen 2005

(Little Tikes $40 ○○○○) There are multiple fill-and-spill activities built into the doors and chutes of this mini-kitchen. There are some noises but none that our parents found objectionable. In contrast, the new **DiscoverSounds Workshop** (○○) was noisy, with limited playability. 9 mos. & up. (800) 321-0183.

■ Fascination Station BLUE CHIP

(Sassy $8.99 ○○○○○) Our favorite highchair toy on the market. Little testers can bat at this spinning toy that attaches to a tabletop with a stout suction cup. There is plenty to see, hear, and feel as the balls and clackers with bold graphics and textures turn. 6 mos. & up. PLATINUM AWARD '99. (800) 323-6336.

■ Lamaze Sing & Spin Bugs

(RC2/Learning Curve $24.95 ○○○○○) A must-have toy for the sitting-up crowd. We have not found anything with more appeal than this! Three jolly bugs spin when placed on the colorful musical platform. A single big button activates the music and bug dance and provides a little lesson in cause and effect. This innovative toy develops motor skills, visual tracking, and a powerful sense of being in charge. 6 mos. & up. PLATINUM AWARD '04. (800) 704-8697.

■ Roll & Rhyme Melody Block

(LeapFrog $19.99 ○○○○○) Turn this big fabric block and it either plays music or says a rhyme about the animal featured on the topmost face. The block includes a small mirror, peekaboo leaves that open to reveal a parrot, a polar bear that slides on the snow, a fox that pops in and out of its den, and a lion with a satiny mane. Fun for rolling as well as exploring its textures and sounds. They say birth & up, we'd say more like 6 mos. & up. PLATINUM AWARD '04. (800) 701-5327.

■ **Tap & Twirl Top** *2005* **PLATINUM AWARD**

(Fisher-Price $12.99 ❍❍❍❍❍) "What a great toy!" wrote our tester parent. Kids enjoy hitting the green top that activates the jazzy music, lights, and movement on the saucer-like floor toy that has interesting ribbons on it for little fingers to explore. Great lesson in cause and effect. High marks for adjustable volume level. Takes 3 AA batteries. 6 mos. & up. (800) 432-5437.

■ **Wobble Top** *2005*

(Infantino $15.99 ❍❍❍❍) An easy push on the big purple button sets the balls inside the dome wobbling, spinning, and clacking. Five fabric petals around the dome have interesting texture and patterns. (800) 365-8182. Still top rated, **Tolo First Friends Carousel** (Small World Toys $12 ❍❍❍❍❍)— an easy-to-activate flat-bottomed top with little people that spin inside the see-through dome. PLATINUM AWARD '04. (800) 421-4153.

SMART BABY TRICK: How Big? Here's a good game for changing-table time. While baby is flat on her back, say, "How big is the baby?" Take baby's hands in yours and lift her arms up over her head and say, "SOOO Big!" At first you'll do all the action, but before long, when you ask, "How big is baby?" she'll lift her arms and happily do this smart baby trick!

First Toys for Crawlers

At around 7 months, most babies begin to creep. It takes a few months more before most are up on hands and knees and truly crawling. Rolling toys such as small vehicles and balls can match baby's developing mobility. Toys placed slightly beyond baby's reach can provide the motivation to get moving. But make it fun. Avoid turning this into a teasing time. Your object is to motivate, not frustrate. Games of rolling a ball or car back and forth make for happy social play between baby and older kids as well as adults.

■ Crawl-Along Wobbler **2005** PLATINUM AWARD

(Fisher-Price $12.99 ●●●●●) With a simple bat, the two wobbling disks roll forward, activating some lights and sounds (none of which are overwhelming) and a spinning rattle. The toy plays three jazzy tunes and has two volume levels. The textures on the disks, the ribbons and clacking beads make this a sensory delight. 8 mos. & up. (800) 432-5437.

■ Melody & Motion Activity Toy

(Baby Einstein $9.99 ●●●●½) Smaller-scaled than the **Crawl-Along Wobbler.** Our tester loved batting at this rolling musical toy and making the paddle wheel spin, or crawling after it as it rolled and played "Für Elise." Unlike some of the other musicals in this line, the music is slow and calming, not frenetic. Winding it up calls for adult help, but this is a good choice to motivate baby to get moving. 6 mos. & up. (800) 793-1454.

■ Poppin' Push Car **2005**

(Sassy $6 ●●●●½) Push this little car forward and the popping beads (safely enclosed in the dome roof) make a pleasing sound. Pull the car back and when you let go the car zooms forward. One of the best toys of the season! Just right for floor time play. (800) 323-6336. Also a great choice, the BLUE CHIP **Ambi Baby's First Car** (Brio $10 ●●●●●) A safe and chunky, easy-to-roll car for little hands. **Safety note:** Hot Wheels and Matchbox-styled cars have small parts that pose a choking hazard for kids under 3. (888) 274-6869.

COMPARISON SHOPPER
Fabric Balls

Nothing is more basic for this stage than a soft fabric ball that's easy to grasp, toss, and roll. A perfect toy for crawlers to chase and for early back-and-forth roly-poly social games. Our favorites: **Colorfun Ball** BLUE CHIP (Gund $12 ooooo) A brightly colored ball done in soft velour. (800) 448-4863. Also of interest, **Whoozit Wiggle Ball** (Manhattan Toy $12 oooo) This ball is not solid—it has six satiny arms with bright ribbons that make it even easier for babies to grasp. A black-and-white squeaker attached to the center vibrates when pulled. (800) 541-1345.

SMART BABY GAMES: Roly-Poly Ball. Your sitting-up and crawling baby will love the back-and-forth fun of rolling a ball. Choose a soft fabric ball with jingle inside or a big beach ball that's slightly soft.

I'll Catch You and You Catch Me! Get down on the floor and take turns playing a crawling catch game. Say, "I'm going to catch you!" and crawl after baby. Or play it in reverse, telling baby to "Try and catch me!" Go slowly enough so baby can catch you. This can be a pretty exciting game!

Tub Time

Bathing a baby can be one of the scariest chores for new parents. (After all, once you take off all those layers, they're so small, and that doesn't even take into account the wobbly neck situation!) For your own comfort as well as baby's, make sure you have everything ready before you begin. The key is to remain calm, comforting, and prepared to get wet! For beginners, a small tub will be more comfortable for both bather and bathee. Little ones don't need much in the way of toys, but once they can sit securely, a few simple bath toys add to the fun.

■ Ambi Family Duck BLUE CHIP

(Brio $13.50 ●●●●●) Three little primary-colored plastic ducks and their parent (we make no gender assumptions). Great fun for the bath. The babies store in big duck's body. Also look for Ambi's **Waterball** ($8.50 ●●●●) with two little ducks inside. (888) 274-6869.

■ Musical Bobbing Sprites

(Sassy $6.99 ●●●●) Attach these three suction-cupped "fish" to the bottom of the tub and they stay put while bobbing about as your little one pushes them. Ideal for sitting-up baby to activate but keep in easy reach. Not really musical, more like squeak, rattle, and snappy sounds. (800) 323-6336.

☞ SAFETY TIP: The Consumer Product Safety Commission reports 66 deaths since 1983 associated with baby bath "supporting rings," devices that keep baby seated in the bathtub. Never rely on such devices to keep baby safe. Going to answer the door or phone can result in serious injury, or worse, to babies and toddlers.

■ Splish Splash Bath Puppets

(Gund $6.50 ●●●●) These happy-looking terry cloth puppets come in pairs, so eventually you and your tot can share the fun. For now, you can use one while the other is drying. Use them for little singing games, as in, "Bunny's going to wash your tummy, Bunny's going to wash your tummy!" Making a game and telling baby what you are doing expands both his language and his comfort level. (800) 448-4863.

☞ **SAFETY TIP:** Avoid foam bath toys, which are often labeled in fine print, "Not for children under 3." Babies can choke on bits of foam that break off when babies chew on them.

First Huggables

Babies often receive tons of soft dolls that are too big, too fuzzy, and even unsafe for now. Although they may be decorative and fine for gazing at, fuzzy plush dolls with ribbons, buttons, plastic features that may pull out, or doodads that may be pulled off, are better saved for preschool years.

When shopping for huggables, look for:
✓Interesting textures
✓Easy-to-grasp legs or arms
✓Sound effects sewn safely inside
✓Washable fabric such as velour or terry cloth
✓Stitched-on features; no loose ribbons or bells
✓Small enough size for infant to hold with ease

■ **Babipouce** 🏆2005 PLATINUM AWARD

(Corolle $10 & up ●●●●●) Older babies are fascinated by dolls that look like real babies. The trick is to find dolls that are washable and safe enough for them to handle. Corolle has an assortment of dolls with all-fabric velour rompers in various colors and soft vinyl painted faces. Our favorites this season: **Puppet Blue,** with a tri-knottie hat, or **Puppet Raspberry,** which is easy to grab with an un-stuffed body, or **Miss Grenadine** with a bright red romper. (800) 668-4846.

■ **Molly Moo Activity Toy**

(Mamas & Papas $29.99 ●●●●●) Pull Molly's tail and she plays "Old MacDonald." With her colorful face and soft body, Molly has interesting textures and patterns at the ends of her front two legs, and a dial to spin and a mirror on her back legs—plus a vinyl pocket for a picture you can change. PLATINUM AWARD '04. (310) 631-2222.

■ Tutti Frutti 5" Collection *2005* PLATINUM AWARD

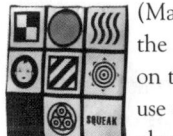

(Gund $8 ●●●●●) From a new collection, this smaller 5"-scaled group (monkey, elephant, bear, turtle, puppy, and frog) are just right for little hands to handle. They are done in extremely soft and brightly colored velour with corduroy on their feet for added interest. (800) 448-4863.

Best Travel Toys for Infants

Having a supply of several small toys can help divert and entertain small travelers, whether you're going out for a day or away for a week. Bring along a familiar comfort toy—a musical toy or doll that's like a touch of home. Pack a variety of toys with different sounds and textures and don't show them all at once; you need to dole them out. Select several very different toys, for example:

✓**Teether**   ✓**Hand-held mirror**
✓**Highchair toy**   ✓**Small huggable**
✓**Musical toy**   ✓**Books and pictures to share**
✓**Familiar quilt/playmat to rest on**

■ Baby Whoozit *2005*

(Manhattan Toy $10 ●●●○) Updated with a defuzzed nose that lifts for a peek-a-boo surprise, this zany smiley face (5½" diameter) has dangling toys to explore. Also fun for peekaboo lap games, the big **Whoozit** ($20 ●●●○) (10½") with lots of dangly toys to tuck in and pull out. New for *2005* from the same company, **Twinkle Turtle** ($20 ●●●●) has multiple distractions: chewy teethers and crinkly petals that light up and vibrate when you pull the turtle's neck. (800) 541-1345.

■ Car Seat Gallery BLUE CHIP

(Manhattan Toy $12 ●●●●●) Hang the four-way pattern pocket chart on the back of the front seat of the car and use either the included graphic cards or your own photos! (800) 541-1345.

■ Clip n Go Musical Mobile *2005*

(Tiny Love $24.95) Designed to attach to baby carriers, strollers, and car seats. This battery-operated mobile plays five classical tunes and has high-contrast images for newborns that parents can later change to bright characters (turtle, bee, butterfly, or bunny). Looked promising, but was not ready for testing. (800) 843-6292.

■ **Jittery Jungle Pals** *2005*

(Infantino $6.99 each ●●●●½) This pull-down patterned elephant or cat with dangly legs jiggles when you pull it and easily attaches to carseat or stroller. Or use the frog- or duck-faced **Peek-a-boo Rattle** (●●●●) with crinkle sounds and teething rings as a welcome distraction. Also nice for take-along gazing, **Tag Along Chimes** ($5.99 ●●●●), two colorful critters with gentle chiming sounds that look down at baby. (800) 840-4916.

■ **Lamaze Traveling Mobile**

(RC2/Learning Curve $14.99 ●●●●½) Three happy fabric critters hang from a ring that can be attached to either an infant carrier or stroller. Has a quiet sound and interesting textures for little hands to explore. (800) 704-8697.

■ **Mane Attraction**

(Sassy $9.99 ●●●●) A bright cheerful smiling (and friendly) lion provides a clear focal point for early gazing. Soon enough baby will enjoy reaching out and exploring the textured mane (made from colorful thick ribbon) and three dangling toys. On the reverse side there is a distortion-free mirror. A good take-along for rear-facing carseats—it will give your baby something pleasant to look at while on the go. Also top rated, this company's **Soft Stroller Bar** ($21.99 ●●●●) At the center of this activity bar there's a snail with a fabric book on his back, squeeze the frog at the end of the story and he ribbits. May buy you a few extra moments at the check-out line! (800) 323-6336. 6 mos. & up.

☞ **SAFETY TIP:** Links should never be made into a loop, or linked across a crib or playpen. We often see baby strollers draped with long lengths of links. Warning labels say that a chain of links should never be more than 12″ long and should be used with adult supervision.

Best New Baby/Shower Gifts

Big Ticket ($40–50)	**Gymini Super Deluxe Electronic Lights & Music 3-D Activity Gym** (Tiny Love) or **Nursery Verse Mobile** (North American Bear Co.) or **Symphony in Motion Deluxe Mobile** (Tiny Love)
Under $40	**Molly Moo Activity Toy** (Mamas & Papas) or **Sleepyhead Bunny** (North American Bear Co.)
Under $25	**Wimmer-Ferguson Infant Stim-Mobile** (Manhattan Toy)
Under $20	**Lamaze Jester Music Box** (RC2/Learning Curve) or **Learning Patterns Changing Sensations Mobile** (Fisher-Price) or **Bethany Butterfly** (Mamas & Papas)
Under $15	**Lyrical Lion** (Sassy) or **Car Seat Gallery** (Manhattan Toy)
Under $10	**Turnaround Froggie** (Mary Meyer) or **Fascination Station** (Sassy)
Under $5	**Snap-Lock Beads** (Fisher-Price)

Toddlers-in-Training Toys

Some of the early walking toys found in the following chapter may be ideal for infants who are seriously working on walking before their first birthday.

Looking Ahead: Best First-Birthday Gifts for Every Budget

Big Ticket ($50 or more)	**Push Cart** (Galt) or **Discover Sounds Kitchen** (Little Tikes)
Under $30	**Musical Pop-tivity Table** (Fisher-Price) or **Lego Baby** (Lego Systems) or **Stride-to-Ride Walker** (Fisher-Price)
Under $25	**Lamaze Nesting Present** (RC2/Learning Curve) or **Read to Me Tot Tower** (eeBoo)
Under $20	**Musical Stack & Play** (Tiny Love) or **Babipouce** (Corolle)
Under $15	**Colorfun Ball** (Gund)
Under $10	**Poppin' Push Car** (Sassy) or **Dudley Musical Pull-Along Duck** (Mamas & Papas) or **Tolo Baby Concerto** (Small World Toys)
Under $5	Cardboard book (see Books section)

2 • Toddlers
Ones and Twos

What to Expect Developmentally

Ones and Twos. There is a tremendous difference between your one-year-old, whose focus is primarily on mastering and enjoying his new-found mobility, and your two-year-old, who is now running, jumping, and making giant leaps with language and imagination. Yet the second and third years are generally known as the toddler years. Many of the toys and games recommended for ones will continue to be used by twos in new and more complex ways. Since some toddlers will be steady on their feet earlier than others or talking and pretending at different times, you'll want to use this chapter in terms of your own child's individual development. This chapter is not arranged chronologically. You'll find toys and games for ones and twos under each of the following main headings: **Active Physical Play, Strictly Outdoors, Sit-Down Play, Pretend Play, Art and Music, Bath Toys, Basic Furniture, Travel Toys,** and **Birthday Gifts.**

Active Exploration. Anyone who spends time with toddlers knows that they are active, on-the-go learners. They don't visit long, because there are so many places and things to explore. Toys that invite active investigation are best for this age group. For toddlers, toys with doors to open, knobs to push, and pieces to fit, fill, and dump provide the raw material for developing fine-motor skills, language, and imagination.

Big-Muscle Play. Toddlers also need playthings that match their newfound mobility and budding sense of independence. Wheeled toys to push, ride on, and even ride in are great favorites. So is equipment they can climb, rock, and slide on. In these two busy years, toddlers grow from wobbly walkers to nimble runners and climbers.

Language and Pretend Power. As language develops, so does the ability to pretend. For beginners, games of make-believe depend more on action than on story lines. Choose props that look like the things they see in the real world.

Toys and Development. As an infant your baby was involved mainly with people. Now, your toddler will spend more time investigating things. Some of the toys in this chapter, such as those for beginning walkers, will have short-term use. However, many of the best products are what we call bridge toys, playthings that will be used now and for several years ahead. While no toddler needs all the toys listed here, 1- and 2-year-olds do need a good mix of toys that fit varying play modes—toys for indoors and out, for quiet, solo sit-down times, and social run-and-shout-out-loud times. A variety of playthings (which may include a plain paper shopping bag or some pots and pans) give kids the learning tools they need to stretch their physical, intellectual, and social development.

Your Role in Play. Playing (and keeping up) with an active toddler requires a sense of humor and realistic expectations. In order to satisfy their growing appetite for independence, select uncomplicated toys that won't frustrate their sense of "can do" power. For example, if your toddler does not want to sit down with you and work on a puzzle now, she may be willing in an hour, or she may be telling you that it's too difficult and should be put away and tried again in a few weeks.

Childproofing:
Setting the Stage for Learning
Childproofing involves more than putting things out of reach. It

involves setting the stage for learning by providing appropriate objects that children can safely explore. To avoid a constant monologue of "No! Don't touch!" remove treasures and objects that may be dangerous to handle. Touching is what toddlers do—it's how they learn. Toddlers who lack the freedom to explore get a negative message about learning. Your goal is to encourage their curiosity about, not set up roadblocks to, the world around them.

Many household items are the most interesting objects to explore. Toddlers need opportunities to discover how things work—knobs to pull, boxes to open, fabrics to feel, and containers to stack. A low cabinet in the kitchen with a stack of paper plates to explore will hold a toddler's interest. Pots and pans with lids to fit on and lift off will keep toddlers occupied while you are working in the kitchen. Toddlers love to take things off shelves. Why not put sturdy cardboard books on a low shelf so they can enjoy them independently?

Enlarging the Circle: Playmates

Your 1-year-old will play mostly with you and the significant people in her life. But 2s are ready to enlarge their social circle. Whether they go to a play group or the park or visit with neighbors, 2s begin to enjoy playing near and ultimately with other children.

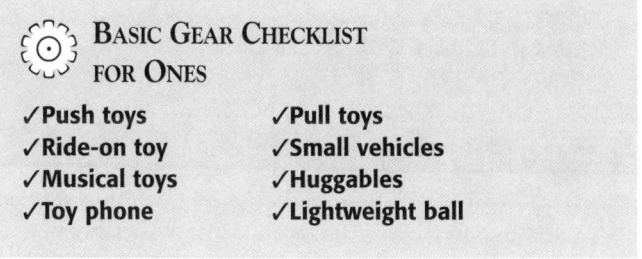

A Word on Sharing. Lacking experience, toddlers live by the philosophy that what's mine is mine and what's yours is mine, too. It's not selfishness so much as not really understanding what sharing means. Toddlers consider their toys almost as extensions of themselves—not for sharing. How can you help? If you are having visitors over, keep visits relatively short. An hour is plenty for 2s—always leave them wanting more!

BASIC GEAR CHECKLIST
FOR ONES

✓Push toys	✓Pull toys
✓Ride-on toy	✓Small vehicles
✓Musical toys	✓Huggables
✓Toy phone	✓Lightweight ball

✓ Fill-and-dump toys
✓ Manipulatives with moving parts

 BASIC GEAR CHECKLIST
FOR TWOS

✓ Ride-on/-in toy   ✓ Pull and push toy
✓ Big lightweight ball ✓ Shovel and pail
✓ Climbing/sliding toy ✓ Art supplies
✓ Big blocks   ✓ Table and chair
✓ Huggables   ✓ Props for housekeeping
✓ Simple puzzles/shape-sorters

🚫 Toys to Avoid

These toys pose choking and/or suffocation hazards:

✓ **Foam toys**
✓ **Toys with small parts** (including small plastic fake foods)
✓ **Dolls and stuffed animals with fuzzy and/or long hair**
✓ **Toys labeled 3 & up** (No matter how smart toddlers are! The label almost always indicates that there are small parts in or on the toy.)
✓ **Latex balloons** (Note: The Consumer Product Safety Commission reports that latex balloons are the leading cause of suffocation deaths! Since 1973 more than 110 children have died from suffocation involving uninflated balloons or pieces of broken ones. They are not advised for children under age 6.)

These toys are developmentally inappropriate:

✓ **Electronic educational drill toys**
✓ **Shape-sorters with more than three shapes**
✓ **Battery-operated ride-ons**
✓ **Most pedal toys**

Active Physical Play

Between 12 and 15 months most babies start toddling. At first, they sidestep from one piece of furniture to another. Soon, with

arms used for balance, they take their first independent steps. In these first months of the second year they grow from those thrilling wobbly
first steps to being sure-footed adventurers. Few
toys lend the kind of security you give as you
extend your hands to assure him you are
there to catch him.

Beginning walkers will get miles of use from a low-to-the-
ground, stable, wheeled toy. The products on the market are
not all created equal. Here are some basic things to look for:

- Wobbly toddlers may use toys to pull up on, and most
  are tippable, so save push toys for true walkers.

- Try before you buy. Some ride-ons are scaled for tall
  kids, others for small kids.

- Toddlers do not need battery-powered ride-ons.
  Encourage foot power, not push-button action!

- Toddlers are not ready for pedals. Few have the coordination to use pedals before 2½. Four wheels and two
  feet on the ground are best.

- Toys with loud and constant sound effects may be appealing in the store, but can become annoying in tight spaces.

Walkers, Wagons, & Ride-ons
for Steady-on-Their-Feet Toddlers

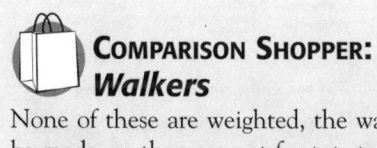

COMPARISON SHOPPER:
Walkers
None of these are weighted, the way they used to
be made, so they are not for tots to pull up on.
Testers gave high marks to two versions:
Musical Activity Walker (Fisher-Price
$19.99 ●●●●) This updated classic now has
some musical features and seems to roll more
slowly than most. Folds for sit-down play with
dials and clackers to spin. 9 mos. & up. (800) 432-5437.
Little Tikes' **Wide Tracker Activity Walker** ($19.99
●●●●) has a wider opening in the back so kids are less likely to trip themselves on the wheels! (800) 321-0183. Two

past winners: The **Stride-to-Ride Walker** (Fisher-Price $29.99 ●●●●●) starts out as a push toy and converts to a ride-on. It has lights, music, and "wacky" sounds, and a hoop for a ball drop. PLATINUM AWARD '03. (800) 432-5437.

■ **Baby Walker** BLUE CHIP

(Galt $99 ●●●●●) This classic wooden cart is pricier than any of its plastic counterparts, but it is very stable for early walkers and a perfect first wagon for carting treasures. (800) 899-4258.

■ **Classic Walker Wagon**

(Radio Flyer $70 ●●●●) This updated version is heavier and slower moving than the original, better suited for new walkers to hold on to. Makes a quiet clicking sound as it moves about. (800) 621-7613.

First Ride-Ons

Unfortunately, most ride-ons no longer have working steering ability, so kids need to move the whole vehicle with their bodies to change direction. Also, be sure to test-drive with your child before you buy. We found that kids with shorter legs had trouble getting on and off many models.

■ **Push Around Buggy** *2005*

(Step 2 $ 40 ●●●●) Little toddlers can get into this vehicle without climbing. It is not a toy for them to run with foot power, it is more like a stroller for giving your tot a ride. It has a seat belt, push bar, and a storage compartment up front for treasures. Tested far better than Step 2's other ride-ons such as the **Basket Ride-On** ($21.99 ●●●), a low-to-the-ground red three-wheeler with a big yellow basket for treasures. Testers found its lack of steering a drawback. Step 2's red **Motorcycle** ($21.99 ●●) was not balanced enough for toddlers and the small red **Classy Cruiser** ($34.99 ●●) was too difficult for young riders to get in and out of—and too small for older riders. None have steering. (800) 347-8372.

■ Cozy Coupe II Blue Chip

(Little Tikes $44.99 ●●●●●) The classic ride-in toy that a generation of kids has grown up with is still basic gear and will be used into the next age group. They say 1½, we say more like 2 & up. ($69.99 ●●●●●). (800) 321-0183.

■ Musical Rocking Pony 2005

(Fisher-Price $25 ●●●½) While this is a not-too-attractive piece of plastic, it is one of the few pieces of equipment low enough for our 15-month-old testers to get on and off of independently. It works and they loved it—although their moms said they wouldn't buy it! "Too plasticky!"

It plays four rocking tunes and makes three pony sounds (you can eliminate all by not putting in the batteries, but your child will most likely enjoy the noise!). (800) 432-5437. See Preschool Chapter, pp. 95–96, for more rocking horses.

SMART PARENT TRICK: Ask your toddler what she's bringing as she rides by. Fuel her imagination by "opening" pretend packages she delivers. Modeling pretend games helps tots take the leap into fantasy play.

■ Retro Rocket 2005 Platinum Award

(Radio Flyer $69.95 ●●●●●) Our fifteen-month-old testers loved the push-button sound effects, lights, and vibrating motion on this low-to-the-ground ride-on. This vehicle is less wide and lighter than Radio Flyer's Red Roadster, and easier for tots to get on and off of. (800) 621-7613.

Push and Pull Toys

Push comes before pull. Instead of holding someone's hand, young toddlers often find sheer joy in the independence of walking while holding on to a push toy. You probably started walking with Fisher-Price's Blue Chip **Corn Popper** ($8 ooooo) or **Melody Push Chime** ($8 ooooo). They are still great choices! (800) 432-5437. Pull toys are for older tots who are surefooted and can look over a shoulder without tripping. Ambi's **Max** (Brio $17.50 ooooo) is a BLUE CHIP classic pull-along pooch. (888) 274-6869.

■ Eden Bear Musical Pull Toy

(Learning Curve $24.99 ooooo) A friendly 7" tan bear with colorful paws sits on top of a wooden frame with wheels. Pull him along and he plays "Teddy Bear's Picnic." A good choice for toddlers who are truly walking and can now enjoy the pleasure of pulling toys behind them. 18 mos. & up. PLATINUM AWARD '03. (800) 704-8697.

■ Dudley Musical Pull-Along Duck
2005 PLATINUM AWARD

(Mamas & Papas $25 ooooo) Dudley is one of the cutest pull toys to come along in years. Yellow with wings that flap as you pull him along and, to make the whole experience even better, if you squeeze his beak, he quacks a tune! Extremely lovable! 1 & up. (310) 631-2222.

■ Pull Along Pal *2005*

(Tiny Love $24.95) The pal is a snail with three compartmentalized parts that provide lots of interesting sounds and textures for tots to explore. Looked promising but was not ready for testing. 1 & up. (800) 843-6292.

■ Lil' Wagster Dragster

(Fisher-Price $12.99 oooo) A good choice for walking tots. Push it along and it rocks from side to side as its "pistons" light up. Makes less noise and provides a young walker with something to hold onto while letting go. Too bad they added so much sound to **Lil' Snoopy.** ($7.99 oo) This little black-and-white pup now barks and sort of sings the melody of B-I-N-G-O with incessant barking as his "leash" is pulled. This is an example of how less was more. Sorry, Snoopy! 1 & up. (800) 432-5437.

■ Ryan's Room Follow-Along Frog

(Small World Toys $15 **oooo**) Here's a really old-fashioned-styled wooden frog that moves up and down as he's pulled. No sound here, just a pleasing motion. 18 mos. & up. (800) 421-4153.

☞ SAFETY TIP: Avoid pull toys with springs and beads that many toddlers will mouth. Old wooden pull toys from the attic may have dangerous levels of lead paint.

Balls

Big, lightweight balls for tossing, kicking, and chasing, or for social back-and-forth, roly-poly games are favorite pieces of basic gear. Twos are ready to play bounce and catch. Be sure the ball is lightweight so it won't hurt. Soft fabric balls or slightly deflated beach balls are the best choice for now. Avoid foam- and balloon-filled balls that are a choking hazard if nibbled.

■ Little 3-in-1 Sports Set

(Little Tikes $24.99 **oooo**) Toddlers often long to shoot hoops and swing at baseballs like their big siblings. Scaled for little players, this satisfies their love of repetition. Basketballs drop into chutes and there are baseball and golf balls to swing at. 9 mos. & up. (800) 321-0183.

COMPARISON SHOPPER:
Basketball Sets

Baby Play Zone Basketball (Fisher-Price $19.99 **oooo**): small basketball hoop comes with a breakaway net, lights, and music to encourage your toddler to keep going for more baskets! Comes with three small balls. Our tester enjoyed making baskets, but not running after the balls! 9 mos. & up. (800)

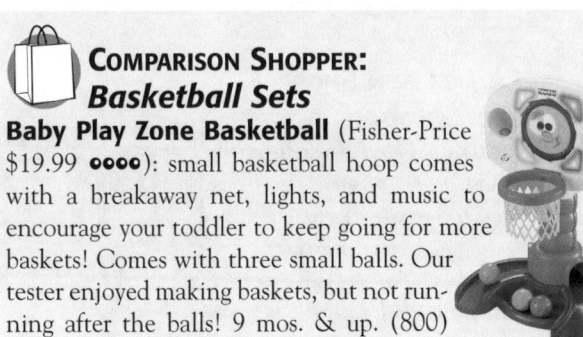

432-5437. Testers also liked the similar game play of the LeapFrog's **Learning Hoops Basketball** ($24.95 ❍❍❍) but not the intrusive alphabet lesson. Making something happen is a big enough deal at this stage! (800) 701-5327.

COMPARISON SHOPPER:
Bowling Sets

Old toddlers and preschoolers like the repetitive action of this game. Two great choices: **Huggy Sport Duck Pins** (Hooray $24.99 ❍❍❍❍) Comes with six squat duck pins and a single ball for knocking them down. (866) 278-7785. For a more realistic set, **TotSport Bowling Set** (Little Tikes $14.99 ❍❍❍❍): six see-through bowling pins with balls inside make a clattering sound when the lightweight bowling ball knocks them down. 2 & up. (800) 321-0183.

Strictly Outdoors

First Climbers and More

Climbers are great for big-muscle play for toddlers who are steady on their feet. We saw a number of low-to-the-ground climbers with open platforms and some that did not have secure enough sides once tots reached the top. Many looked like an accident waiting to happen. If you are shopping for a young or especially small toddler, stick to the lowest climbers. This is not a product to grow into.

COMPARISON SHOPPER
Big Climbers

Step 2's **Naturally Playful Woodland Climber** ($179.99 ❍❍❍❍), done in muted tones, comes with a small ladder up to the 27" high platform with a slide on the other side. 2 & up. Step 2's **Naturally Playful Clubhouse Climber** ($500 ❍❍❍❍❍) is newly re-colored for '05 but still a great combo gym and playhouse for older toddlers and preschoolers with two towers, a slide, and a connecting bridge. One tower is outfitted with table, chairs, and props. PLATINUM AWARD '01. Little Tikes' **8-in-1 Adjustable Playground** ($350 ●●●●), with tunnels and two slides, is packed with places to explore, but without the clubhouse features of Step 2's. Either is ideal for developing coordination, and both are big enough for several kids to share without quarrels! Step 2's towers and bridge were a big hit with our 2- and 3-year-old testers (tall 4s had to bend over to fit). Little Tikes' open-top design extends the age range of their set. Both are hard to assemble. Step 2 (800) 347-8372/Little Tikes (800) 321-0183.

■ Climb and Slide Castle *2005*

(Little Tikes $60 ●●●●) Designed for toddlers, this mini-castle-style climber has a low slide and steering wheel on top for dramatic play. It's 43" high. They say one and up; we'd say more like steady-on-their-feet toddlers—who are rarely younger than 18–24 mos. Requires supervision. (800) 321-0183.

■ Five Alarm Fun Center

(Step 2 $159.99 ●●●●●) This big red fire truck doesn't move, but will provide lots of pretend play opportunities. Comes with two steering wheels (a plus), two firefighters' hats, a pretend CB radio and emergency light and siren! Take the white roof off to accommodate older kids. 18 mos. & up. PLATINUM AWARD '04. (800) 347-8372.

SMART PARENT TRICK: Give 'em a Hand! Toddlers love an appreciative audience—don't we all?

When they finish a puzzle, dance a jig, or go down a slide, clap your hands together—give them a hand! Keep in mind that little children see themselves as you see them. During this often negative time, try to accentuate the positive.

Wading Pools

Our testers preferred inexpensive hard-vinyl wading pools to those that had to be blown up or filled with water to hold a shape (most of these had sides that were too high for younger toddlers to climb over by themselves). Prefab wading pools are also easier to lift, dump, and clean. You'll find an adequate no-frills pool for under $20.

FREEBIE: Toddlers love playing with soap and water and covering things with a sudsy lather. Washing kiddie cars, tabletops, and other surfaces is a favorite sport and a good way to cool off on a hot day. A small pail with soapy water and a sponge will provide endless hours of entertainment! As with all water play, supervision is a must.

Sandboxes

While small boxes are good choices when space is a concern, keep in mind that a bigger box will give more than one child enough room to maneuver. We looked for smooth edges and strong sides that will support a child's weight. The motif is really a personal preference.

Our BLUE CHIP favorites: On the small side, **Frog Sandbox** (Step 2 $30) or **Turtle Sandbox** (Little Tikes $35). 1 & up. Bigger choices: **Crabbie Sandbox** (Step 2 $59.99) or **Dinosaur Sandbox** (Little Tikes $59.99). Step 2 (800) 347-8372 / Little Tikes (800) 321-0183.

Sandbox Props: A basic bucket from any toy store will do—just be sure to check for smooth edges. To toddlers, sand is another opportunity for spilling and dumping. Many of the best props for the sandbox are in your kitchen: a plastic colander, empty margarine containers, strainers, squeeze bottles, etc.

Sprinklers 🟊**2005**

For toddlers ready to get wet, we'd recommend Little Tikes' new **Playful Paws Sprinkler** or **Hook, Line & Sprinkler** ($10 each ●●●●). Both are designed to provide a smaller spray (in one position it's stationary; in the other position it will spin). A better choice than most bigger sprinklers that are often overwhelming. 18 mos. & up. (800) 321-0183.

■ No-Spill Bubble Tumbler Blue Chip

(Little Kids $6.95 ●●●●●) Toddlers love chasing bubbles, even though most are not able to blow their own. When they start, buy one of these no-spill containers that prevent the tears that used to come when the solution would spill! Our testers did not love the new battery-operated **My First Bubble Blower** ($14.95 ●●●). "Didn't hold their attention"; "we prefer the original." 18 mos. & up. (800) 545-5437.

The Youngest Gardener

■ Little Landscaper Garden Tools

(Little Tikes $5 set ●●●●) Just as toddlers enjoy imitating adult indoor chores, they like working like Mommy or Daddy in the garden. A rake for leaves, a shovel for snow, or a garden hoe—all work for active pretend fun. We prefer these lightweight plastic tools to the metal sets (Alex, Brio) since toddlers tend to toss and swing tools. (800) 321-0183. Bring home a pretend mower such as Little Tikes' **Mulching Mower** ($19.99 ●●●●). Our all-time favorite Fisher-Price **Bubble Mower** is now replaced with the **Double Blaster Mower** ($20)—which works, but not as easily as the original. Little Tikes (800) 321-0183 / Fisher-Price (800) 432-5437.

Sit-Down Play

First Puzzles and Manipulatives

Toddlers enjoy toys that invite investigation but don't demand too much dexterity. Toys with lids to lift, buttons to push, and dials to turn give them satisfying feedback along with playful ways to develop fine-motor skills and eye-hand coordination. Once they understand how to use them, toddlers will enjoy many of the toys in this section independently, and that is very satisfying to the "me do it myself!" toddler.

First Puzzles

Start with whole-piece puzzles. Take the time to introduce a new puzzle or toy. Let your child take the lead, giving time to explore the pieces and experiment with them.

■ Puzzibilities Sounds on the Go 𝟮𝟬𝟬𝟱

(Small World Toys $15.95 ●●●●½) Four big puzzle pieces with easy-to-grasp wooden pegs—each vehicle makes a distinctive sound when placed in the frame. Also, **Sounds on the Farm**—this one moos, neighs, oinks, and baas. New for 𝟮𝟬𝟬𝟱, silent, giant peg-handled three-piece **Shapes** or **Numbers** with bold patterns, or **Vehicles** and **Wild Animals** ($9 each four). 18 mos. & up. (800) 421-4153.

■ Puzzle Totes 𝟮𝟬𝟬𝟱

(Lauri $8.99 ●●●●) Our testers enjoyed playing with this collection of puzzles from Lauri, well known for their textured crepe rubber puzzles. Rather than having the traditional tray, these double-thick seven- or eight-piece puzzles have a handle just right for travel and

carrying about. Two-toned pieces are able to stand up for dramatic play. Four versions: **Marine Life, Earthmovers, Dinosaurs,** and, new for 𝟮𝟬𝟬𝟱, **Big Shapes.** Older 2s will be able to manipulate these whole-piece puzzles that 3s and 4s will continue to enjoy. (800) 451-0520.

Manipulatives

■ Musical Pop-tivity Table
2005 PLATINUM AWARD

(Fisher-Price $19.99 ●●●●○) Our testers kept going back to this very classic activity table with lots of buttons to push, dials to turn, and big beads to spin. If tots push the big red button, they activate music and the popping beads in the center dome covered compartment. Will be enjoyed by 1s & up. (800) 432-5437.

■ Pop 'n' Twirl Building Table **2005 PLATINUM AWARD**

(Fisher-Price $29.99 ●●●●○) A new activity table for the 18-month-and-older crowd that is exactly on target. The pop-ons are big chunky pieces that can be stacked easily on the plastic pegs. Great clear lesson in cause and effect: push the red button, and two parts of the table spin with a little music (volume control—a plus!); also interesting, **Peek a Blocks IncrediBlocks** ($19.99 ●●●○), which works with the small see-through peek a blocks. Lots to explore. (800) 432-5437.

■ Pound-A-Ball

(Small World Toys $15 ●●●○) Most toddlers get to a stage when pounding is just the best! Here's a fun plastic variation with four balls that, once pounded, travel through a small see-through ball run. In the beginning you may need to hold the toy for over-eager pounders! (800) 421-4153.

■ Musical Stack & Play
2005 PLATINUM AWARD

(Tiny Love $19.95 ●●●●○) This cleverly designed elephant stacking toy has a place for dropping balls in its top. The balls come out at the base with some fanfare (lights/sound) but nothing over the top. Our testers also liked the soft fabric rings for stacking but really spent most of the time playing with the plastic balls. Marked 6 mos. & up, but will be most enjoyed by 1s and up. (800) 843-6292.

■ Rip Rolling Fun

(Small World Toys $25 ●●●●○) Winner! Five wooden triangles travel down the wooden track on this very handsome retro-looking toy. Designs on triangles create optical illusions as they move. Fun for making something happen and tracking. 18 mos. & up. PLATINUM AWARD '04. (800) 421-4153.

■ Rollipop Toddler Starter and Advanced Sets

(Edushape $19.95 & $24.95 ●●●●○) These are among our favorite toddler toys. Toddlers love to drop the oversized colorful plastic balls into the starter set (a tower) and track them as they go down. The balls also travel slowly down the advanced set (a bridge), making it an ideal toy for developing visual tracking. 18 mos. & up. PLATINUM AWARD '04. (800) 404-4744.

First Construction Toys

Few toys have more long-term use and learning value than construction toys. Blocks give children a hands-on under-standing of words such as *longer, taller, the same, more, less, bigger, and smaller.* These are basic math concepts built into the play. You can help your toddler connect words to these con-cepts by using language to describe the pieces or what he is doing. These hands-on experiences have much more educa-tional value than electronic toys that try to teach symbolic numerals. Toddlers need to experience "two-ness" again and again before they make the leap to symbolic representation. Without taking over, get your child started by modeling ways to make an enclosure, or span two blocks with a third. By adding vehicles and small animals and people figures, you pro-vide the ingredients for imaginative play.

■ Lego Quatro *2005* PLATINUM AWARD

(Lego Systems $9.99 & up ●●●●○) For ones, we still recommend the rounded **Lego Baby** (see p. 18). Twos used to graduate to **Lego Duplo** bricks, but this year there's a bigger brick (twice the size Duplo and four times the size of stan-dard Legos. The bricks are made of a softer, easier-to-grasp material. Here, "more is better," so we suggest starting with the **Large Quatro Bucket** ($19.99/75 pieces; $14.99/50 pieces ●●●●●). 1 & up. Tots who are fond of Dora the Explorer will enjoy the 41-piece **Animal Adventure Set** ($29.99 ●●●●) with play figures, blocks, and a sound effects box with 8 different sounds—not that kids can't make their own sounds. 2 & up. For other Duplo sets, look at the Preschool chapter, p. 83. (800) 233-8756.

How High? Use blocks to see how high a tower you can build together before it goes kaboom! Take turns adding one more piece—and keep a running count as you go. You can play variations of this game with empty frozen juice cans, wooden thread spools, or other collections.

■ Giant Constructive Blocks Bʟᴜᴇ Cʜɪᴘ

(Constructive Playthings $17.99 ●●●●) These big sturdy blocks (printed like red bricks) are lightweight but satisfyingly hefty for lugging about. Perfect for making tall towers and wide roadways for beginning builders. Strong enough to stand on, these are perennial classics that endure years of creative play. Bricks are 12" x 6" x 4". #CP-626. (800) 832-0572.

■ Mega Blok Lil' Cement Truck and Lil' Dump Truck *2005*

(Mega Bloks $9.99 ●●●●) These plastic vehicles are just right for 2s and up. They both come with a truckload of Mega Bloks. Just right for pretend construction sites. Still top rated, the larger **Mega Bloks Wagon** ($30 ●●●●). A tot-sized red wagon loaded with 50 oversized plastic pegged blocks is fun for making big, fast constructions. Pegs on side of wagon can be used for building up and over. (800) 465-6342.

Wooden Blocks

Older twos will begin to enjoy a beginner set of
wooden blocks. We'd recommend
**Ryan's Room Push-Along Block
Cart** PLATINUM AWARD '03 (Small
World Toys $40 ●●●●○) with 36 pieces,
which older tots will enjoy lugging about. (800) 421-4153. For
larger top-rated sets, see Preschool chapter, pp. 81–83.

Wooden Train Sets

It's a great temptation to buy wooden train sets for older
twos—but be forewarned, most have small figures and other
small parts that make them dangerous for kids under three
who still mouth their toys. See Preschool chapter for reviews
of top-rated sets. To address this issue, Brio has introduced a
new line of trains for toddlers.

First Stacking, Nesting, and Shape-Sorter Toys

What You Should Know. Classic stacking toys require the
ability to see and arrange objects in size order—a skill that nei-
ther babies nor toddlers have. Such toys are often labeled 6
months & up, but there's nothing wrong if your child can't do
it—the problem is with the label! Happily, there are more for-
giving choices that introduce stacking without the need for
size order. Toddlers will use them to taste, toss, and explore—
just don't expect them to be expert stackers. As you play with
your toddler, use color or size words to describe the
pieces. Such concepts are learned with greater ease
when they are part of everyday experiences.

For beginners: **Lamaze Stacking
Rings** (Learning Curve $19.99
●●●○) are fabric rings that stack in
any order. (800) 704-8697; or for
high tech, the **Classical Stacker** (Fisher-Price
$19.99 ●●●●○) has a post with twinkling lights and
sounds as each ring is put on. (800) 432-5437.

Nesting and Stacking Toys

Toddlers like the multiple pieces for pulling apart, banging, and stacking long before they can nest them. Stacking and nesting toys develop eye-hand coordination, size order concepts, and even counting skills. They provide hands-on experience with concepts such as *bigger, smaller, taller, inside, under, top,* and *bottom*—to name but a few. You can make the language connection as you play together.

Here are our top-rated choices:

■ Stacking Cups BLUE CHIP

(Sassy $7.99 ●●●●●) Four boldly patterned cups with interesting textures on the rims. Fun for nesting and stacking and hiding Cheerios under! 1 & up. (800) 323-6336.

■ Read to Me Tot Tower

(eeBoo $19 ●●●●●) The latest in a handsome line of sturdy cardboard blocks with storybook quality illustrations of images to know and name. 1 & up. PLATINUM AWARD '04. (212) 222-0823.

☞SAFETY NOTE: Plastic stacking cups should have air holes so they don't form a suction over baby's face. Most toymakers have updated cups, but some old-style products may still be on shelves. Check before you buy!

Shape-Sorters

■ Plan Toys Shape-n-Sort

(Brio $15 ●●●●½) A handsome wooden three-shape sorter. Drop the pieces in place, hit the tray, and pieces drop out. (888) 274-6869.

■ Ryan's Room Pound Around 2005

(Small World Toys $14.95 ●●●●½) A six-sided pounding board with hammer and colorful pegs that don't come out. Just turn the board and start hammering again and again. Big toddlers love the powerful pounding action. 18 mos. & up. Still top rated,

Ryan's Room Get-a-Grip Sorter ($14.95 ●●●●) A triangular sorter that has a handle and a forgiving opening. Beautifully crafted, and a good parent-child toy. (800) 421-4153.

FREEBIE: Many sorters and nesting toys are too hard for young toddlers. You can make your own. Cut holes in the lid of a shoe box for blocks to fall through. Or use a see-through plastic container so tots can see where their pop-beads or blocks have gone.

Pretend Play

As language develops, older toddlers begin their early games of pretend. So much of the real equipment tots see adults using is off-limits to them. Child-sized versions can (sometimes) offer a satisfying alternative and fuel the imagination of little ones, who love to mimic what they see you doing. Never again will sweeping and cleaning be more fun than to a toddler!

Dolls and Huggables

Both boys and girls enjoy playing with dolls and soft animals. For one-year-olds, velour and short-haired plush animals will hold some interest. Twos are ready for both oversized but lightweight huggables to lug about, and small dolls that fit in their fists. Toddlers often get attached to one huggable that becomes an inseparable "lovie." Having a tubbable vinyl doll may also do the trick for a reluctant bather. Since toddlers are still likely to chew on their toys, select uncomplicated dolls without doodads (buttons, long hair). If potty training is on the agenda, see the potty dolls in Preschool, page 71.

SAFETY NOTE: Do not leave large plush dolls or toys in crib, as they can be stepped on and accidentally give tots a boost over the side. Toddlers should not have pillowlike dolls or toys to sleep with, or dolls with chewable doodads and features that pose a choking hazard.

■ **Babicorolle** *2005*

(Corolle $11 & up ●●●○) Corolle has beautiful dolls for
every age group. For ones, we recommend soft huggables
that feel big but are lightweight. New for *2005* , **Miss
Grenadine** (●●●●●) done in deliciously soft hot pink,
red, and orange velour. Still top rated, **Babipouce
Red** or **Pink Stripe** ($25 ●●●○) have painted vinyl
faces and soft bodies. 1 & up. Twos and up will enjoy
Corolle's **Tidoo** collection ($40–$50 ●●●○), sweet
12" tubbable/floatable bald-headed dolls with beanbag
bodies. Come dressed in knit outfits with Velcro. *Safety note:* Some
Tidoo sets have small bottles or fabric balls which we do not recommend for this age group. (800) 668-4846.

■ **Groovy Girls and Groovy Boys** *2005*

(Manhattan Toy $10 & up ●●●●●) This is one
of the few collections of both boy and girl dolls
available in multiethnic variations. All are 13"
and soft, with stitched features, yarn hair, and
groovy clothes. PLATINUM AWARD '99. New for
2005 , **Ailene, Angelique,** and **Ayanna.** 2
& up. (800) 541-1345.

■ **My First Madeline**
2005 PLATINUM AWARD

(RC2/Learning Curve $12.99 ●●●●●) Move over,
Raggedy Ann, this yarn-haired Madeline is just right
for the two-and-up crowd. She comes with a soft, non-
removable blue velour dress, matching shoes, and of
course, a yellow bow in her hair. (800) 704-8697.

■ **Tutti Frutti 11"** *2005*

(Gund $20 ●●●○) Whether you bring home the ele-
phant, monkey, cat, or bear, these soft, 11" ultra-
plush velour dolls have the potential to become a
favorite lovey. With stitched features, they are
done in cheerful bright colors; "they're hard to put
down," noted one parent tester. (We prefer the velour
to the low-pile version.) (800) 448-4846.

■ **Pastel Pancake Bears with Blankets**

(North American Bear Co. $20 ●●●○) These
scrumptious flat bears now come with built-in

blankies! (800) 682-3427.

■ **Snuffles** BLUE CHIP

(Gund $12 & $20 ●●●●●) With his round tummy, this
short, lovable armful of a bear is likely to become a constant companion. He returns this year with his original
fur. 2 & up. (732) 448-4863.

A few words about talking dolls for toddlers

Although soft huggable bears and dolls have long-
term play value, interactive dolls that talk, dance,
and sing are novelty items that may appeal.
Don't be surprised, however, if your toddler is
put off by a popular character that comes to life.
Toddlers are still sorting out what is real and make-
believe—so these "magical" dolls may have more
appeal to adults than the very young.

■ **Sing & Boogie Blue** *2005*

(Fisher-Price $24.99 ●●●●) Now that Blue speaks,
she also dances and sings! Squeeze her
hand and she'll do her new signature
dance. For Blue fans, this will be a hit.
18 mos. & up. **So Much to Say
Blue** ($14.99 ●●●●)—after so many years of not
talking, she now has 80 phrases to share with your
toddler. 18 mos. & up. (800) 432-5437.

Doll Accessories

Most toddlers will try to get into doll furniture you buy. Most
plastic doll furniture is very tippable. Better to wait until the
preschool years for typical baby beds, highchairs, and strollers.
Older 2s may enjoy a shopping cart they can push about and
use for their dolls. We recommend: **Wooden Doll Cradle**
BLUE CHIP (Community Playthings $90 ●●●●), a 29" solid
maple cradle built to last and big enough for kids to climb in
to play baby, or put a family of dolls to sleep in. 2 & up. Item
#C140. (800) 777-4244. **Shopping Cart** BLUE CHIP (Little
Tikes $25 ●●●●): this bright yellow cart with baby seat is more
gender free than most doll carriers. (800) 321-0183.

Vehicles

What to look for: Vehicles with clicky wheels, friction "motors," and passengers to load and unload provide sensory feedback. They are also great props for developing fine-motor skills and pretend play.

What to avoid: A fleet of vehicles with lots of electronic lights, sounds, and voices that will drive you crazy—and, worse, will do nothing to help tots develop language or imagination. Also, avoid small Matchbox or Hot Wheels cars; their small parts can be a choking hazard for kids under 3.

■ Little Driver

(Small World Toys $32 ❍❍❍❍½) This classic steering wheel with lights and sounds comes with a phone, just right for pretend road trips. 18 mos. & up. (800) 421-4153. Vtech's updated version is much louder than last year's. Try it before you bring it home.

■ Little People Cement Mixer Truck

(Fisher-Price $19.95 ❍❍❍❍) Push on the driver's head and the cement mixer tips as the vehicle beeps (not too loudly) with a back-up sound. We also note that the driver is not just female, but she's blond! What next? They say 1 & up. We found this was most enjoyed by 18 mos. & up. (800) 432-5437.

Yum, Yum, Teddy! Pretend Game
Modeling games of pretend can spark toddlers to make up their own games. Stick to familiar actions—for example, pretend to feed Teddy Bear, play patty-cake with Teddy's paws, give Teddy a kiss at bedtime, or cover Teddy with a little "blanket."

Housekeeping Props
Older toddlers, both boys and girls, adore imitating the real work they see grown-ups doing around the house. Sweeping the floor, vacuuming

cooking, caring for the baby—these are thrilling roles to play. Many of the props for this sort of pretend play will be used for several years. They are what we call "bridge toys," which span the years. Unfortunately the handle of the **2 in 1 Vacuum Set** (Little Tikes $19.99 ●●), with colorful balls that "pop" when the upright is pushed, is very hard for toddlers to release, and an adult is needed to release the minivac attachment. (800) 321-0183. Fisher-Price took their classic vac out of the line, so your best bet is to sweep up with Schylling's red and yellow **Broom Set** ($7.99 ●●●●). 2 & up. (800) 541-2929.

SAFETY TIP: Buckets! Beware of buckets used in the house for cleaning. Ever-curious toddlers have been known to fall into them and drown. Old buckets from building bricks also pose a problem. Most new play buckets have a safety bar halfway down to prevent tots from putting their heads all the way in.

Phones 2005

Before you buy a play phone with sound, put the receiver to your ear. Many are alarmingly loud. The quietest of the bunch are **Ambi City Phone** (Brio $10 ●●●●), which has spinning faces, a mirror, a good clicking sound, and lots of buttons to push (888) 274-6869, and **Tolo Mobile Phone** (Small World Toys $12 ●●●●). (800) 421-4153.

For more bells and whistles: **Talk-to-Me Telephone** 2005 (Sassy $17.99 ●●●●). With an old-fashioned rotary dial on one side and push-button pads on the other, this yellow phone has lots of features for your toddler to explore. The phone counts from 1–9, and says hello and goodbye in English, Spanish, and French. 1 & up. (800) 323-6336.

SAFETY TIP: An old real phone may seem like lots of fun, but the cord and small parts pose a choking hazard to toddlers.

It's for You! Game. Older toddlers love talking on the phone. Use the power of pretend to "call" them when lunch is ready or it's time to go out. "Brrringggg! Brrringggg! Telephone! It's for you!" Transitions are often easier if you turn them into a game.

Toy Dishes and Pots

Finding a sturdy, gender-free set of dishes isn't easy! Many sets we tested cracked, were too small for little hands, or were very, very pink! Stay away from sets with small parts and sharp cutlery, and of course, save the pottery and china for later.

Dishes and Tea and Cooking Sets:

There are more elaborate sets in the next chapter. For toddlers you want to keep it simple. Model pouring them a pretend cup of something delicious. Don't be afraid to ham it up: "It's too hot!" "This cake is yummy!" For this stage we recommend: **Little Helper's Dining Room & Pots and Pans** (Step 2 $12 ●●●●) White, magenta, and yellow 22-piece set comes with dishes, pots, and utensils. (800) 347-8372. 2 & up.

Toy Kitchens

Choosing which kitchen center to bring home is really a matter of style preference and space. There are sizes ranging from small single units to elaborate large units that need their own wall, if not room! Few of the sinks hold water, which is too bad. There is also a trend back to pink kitchens—we have noted our gender-free choices because we believe strongly that both boys and girls need to know their way around the kitchen.

■ MagiCook Kitchen *2005*

(Little Tikes $80) Promising to be very high-tech, this new kitchen will say 100 phrases in three different languages. Wonder if it says, "Let's order in," in all three? There will be lots of buttons to push; we believe, however, that less would be more. Was not ready for testing. 2–5. (800) 321-0183.

■ Life Style Dream Kitchen

(Step 2 $139.99 ●●●○) This combo kitchen with stove, oven, microwave, fridge, and phone (electronic) is 35½" long and is designed for the toddler who needs the dream kitchen (in plastic, of course). This one comes with wainscoting, crown molding, and simulated granite! For an even bigger version, there's the **Lifestyle Deluxe Kitchen** (●●●○ $220 / 49" wide)! (800) 347-8372.

■ Wooden Kitchen Appliances

(Small World Toys $101 each ●●●●●) Wooden sets usually cost a lot more. That's why we were thrilled to find these sturdy handsome individual pieces (a sink, a stove/oven, and a washing machine). Best of all, the sink is removable so that you can use "real" water. Most sinks no longer have this feature. PLATINUM AWARD '02. (800) 421-4153.

Miniature Pretend Settings

■ Little People Sweet Sounds Home

(Fisher-Price $29.99 ●●●○) This fully furnished take-along dollhouse that opens up for lots of pretend play has unfortunately been redesigned with lots of pink trim. In the past, we had applauded the gender-free paint job. Still remains a good choice for older toddlers. 2 & up. (800) 432-5437.

■ Little People Discovery Village 2005

(Fisher-Price $39.99 ●●●½) We had great hopes for this mini-setting with roadway and stores and Little People to move about. Problem is that every time you activate the roadway or any other locale, the annoying music comes on. It's intrusive to a child's imaginative play, not to mention how adults are going to feel about it. We still highly recommend the **Little People Ramps Around Garage** ($29.99 ●●●●●) with a cleverly designed garage that opens up, as well as a car wash, elevator, gas station, two ramps, repair shop with two cars and drivers. PLATINUM AWARD '04. We find the classic **Little People Farm** (**oo**), with updated built-in electronic sounds, confusing for young children. Put the horse in the hen's "spot," and the horse will cluck! It's what we call a dumb cluck toy! (800) 432-5437.

FREEBIE: Empty, staple-free boxes are among the best toys known to toddlers. Great for sitting in, climbing out of, coloring on, lugging around, crawling through, or loading up.

Art and Music

Art Supplies

Give your toddler opportunities to explore colors and textures. This is not the time for coloring books and drawing within the lines. Scribbling comes before drawing, just as crawling comes before walking! Twos may give names to their drawings and creations after they are done. Finished products are not as important as getting their hands into the doing.

Even one-year-olds get a sense of "can do" power scribbling with big, easy-to-grasp crayons on blank paper. Older tots love the fluid lines they get with fat washable markers, but keep in mind, you'll need to replace the covers or markers will dry out. Twos also enjoy bright tempera paint with thick brushes, or playdough and finger paints for lively hands-on fun!

You'll need to supervise and establish a place where art materials can be used. You don't really need an easel for now. A low table that children can stand at is fine. In fact, they have less trouble with paint rolling and dripping when they work on a flat surface. If your toddler persists in eating supplies or spreading them on floors or walls, put them away for a while and try again in a month or two.

■ Crayola Kid's First Washable Crayons BLUE CHIP

(Binney & Smith $3 & up **ooooo**) These washable crayons are very big to match toddler's way of grasping with a whole fist. Save the smaller crayons, which snap in tots' hands, for their school days. 1½ & up. (800) 272-9652.

■ Crayola Color Wonder Paper & Markers

(Binney & Smith $8.99 ●●●●●) We thought this product should be called color magic! The marker has no color on the tip and will not "color" on normal paper, sofas, Grandma's wall (you get the idea!). But when you color on the special Color Wonder paper... voilà! Magically your design appears. We prefer the open-ended paper to the coloring books. Drawing at this age should be more about exploring the materials than worrying about lines or premade art. PLATINUM AWARD '02. We don't recommend **Color Wonder Finger Paints,** which require more finger pressure than most kids have at this age. (800) 272-9652.

Play Dough

Playing with premade or homemade dough is marvelous for twos who love pounding, poking, rolling, crumbling, and hands-on exploring. At this stage, the finished product is unimportant. The focus is on smashing a lump flat or pulling it apart into small pieces or mixing blue and yellow to get green. Dough should be used with supervision in a placed established for messy play.

Making Dough Game: Save money by making your own dough with this homemade play-dough recipe. Kids will enjoy getting their hands into the bowl and helping to mix up dough, which can be stored in a covered container. Mix together 1 cup of flour, ½ cup salt, a few drops of vegetable oil, and enough water to form a ball. Food coloring or a splash of bright tempera paint can be added.

■ Play-Doh Case of Colors BLUE CHIP

(Hasbro $7 ●●●●●) Imagine a 10-pack with two-ounce lumps of 10 different colors. Don't let them see all the tubs; open one or two at a time at most. Add plastic dishes for added pretend! 2 & up. (800) 327-8264.

Paints and Easels

Older toddlers will enjoy painting either at a table where the colors won't run or at a standing easel. Start with three colors at most. Thick brushes and washable tempera paint are good choices available at most toy and art supply stores. Try to have the art supplies ready to go for whenever the creative mood strikes.

See Preschool chapter for easels.

Musical Toys

Once they are steady on their feet, toddlers love to move to music. Play a variety of music for them to dance to or accompany with their "instruments." Aside from the usual music for kids, try some marches, ballet scores, or music from other cultures. Better yet, put on your dancing feet and shake, rattle, and roll along.

■ Bug Tunes Music Set 🏅*2005*

(Little Tikes $13 ❍❍❍❍) Get ready to shake, rattle, and boogie with this 6-piece set of bug-shaped maracas, tamborine, and jingler. Designed for younger players than the Remo set below—this is more like a set of rattles shaped like instruments. Also fun, **Chimes the Caterpillar** ($13 ❍❍❍❍).
Two classic musical toys—a xylophone and a keyboard—are combined in one buggy version. Forget the music on the box, the toy is more about exploration than playing a tune. Skip the **Jungle** sets with mallets that are more like traditional drumsticks. Our testers tasted all the mallets—so you're better off with the bigger rounder heads. 18 mos. & up. (800) 321-0183.

■ Lynn Kleiner Babies Make Music Set

(Remo $24.95 ❍❍❍❍½) Many musical instruments for young kids make noise, not music, and many are basically unsafe. Strike up the rhythm band with these instruments that are well crafted with both sound and safety in mind. This set includes a jingle shaker, wrist jingle, small drum, and scarf (all safe enough for toddlers who still mouth their toys). 2 & up. (800) 397-9378.

■ Musical Hands Mat

(International Playthings $29.99 ❍❍❍❍) Following the flashing lights

above each handprint on the 45" mat allows children
to play a tune. This calls for visual attention and
sequencing. Marked for 2s, but this will be
hard for most toddlers under 2½. A much
better choice for preschoolers and beyond!
(800) 445-8347.

■ Sit & Stand Danceband *2005*

(Fisher-Price $39.99 ○○) Great idea, poorly executed. When tod-
dlers activate sounds by stepping on the play mat or by hitting the
keys on the console, too much music plays—so the lessons in cause
and effect are lost. Marked 6 mos. & up.

■ Tolo Baby Concerto *2005*

(Small World Toys $25 ○○○○½) Toddlers will like lifting
the little yellow bear off his sleek red platform or putting
him back and watching as he spins to the music.
Tots can use the five big key pads to make single notes, or activate one of five melodies by
Mozart, Handel, Bach, and Vivaldi. An
empowering toy for making things happen. 1 &
up. (800) 421-4153.

Follow the Leader Toddler Game. Use a full-length
mirror to play a "can-you-do-what-I-do?" game. Use
big and little motions from faces to
toes. Getting kids to copy what
you are doing is more than fun. It
helps kids begin to focus on
details and translate what they
see into actions. Demonstrate a
sequence of two motions—pat
your head and then your tummy.
Can your toddler remember two
motions? How about three?

Bath Toys

For young bathers, the tub is just another locale for learning and
play. Working up a lather, trying to keep a slippery soap from
slipping away, discovering how water spills from a cup, drips
from a washcloth, and splashes when you hit it—these are a

child's way of finding out how things like soap and water work.

■ Sassy Car Wash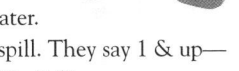

(Sassy $15.99 ●●●○) An innovative tub toy for car play afloat. Three little cars can ride down ramps and get "cleaned" with a big yellow shower head nozzle that squirts tub water. Two vehicles squirt, and another scoops and pours. All three can be transported by a little yellow "ferry" with lot of potential pretend play. A mesh holder works as a "parking lot" when bath time is done. They say 9 months, we'd say this is a better toddler toy for 14 months and up. (800) 323-6336.

> **▷☞ SAFETY TIP: Bath toys need to be completely drained and dried between baths to prevent harmful bacteria and/or mold collecting in them. Squeeze toys, although a lot of fun, are particularly susceptible to this problem.**

■ Tolo Animal Water Slide

(Small World Toys $22 ●●●●) Part shape sorter, part pour and spill, this fun bath toy attaches to tub with big suction cups. Pull a lever and shapes slide down chutes and splash into the water. Comes with three shaped pourers to fill and spill. They say 1 & up— we'd say more like 18 months & up. (800) 421-4153.

■ Tub-A-Duck

(International Playthings $12.99 ●●●●) Attach this big yellow duck to the wall of your tub and use the scoops to pour water and make its head bob, wings tip, wheel spin, and beak squirt. Talk about making things happen! 1 & up. (800) 445-8347.

Basic Furniture

Table and Chairs

These are basic pieces of gear that will be used for years of snacks, art projects, and tea parties. Best bets are going to have steady legs and a washable surface. After that, it's a matter of budget and style to fit your home. Check the underside of tables and chairs for smooth finishes that won't snag little fingers. Twos also enjoy a rocking chair or armchair scaled to their size. 2 & up.

Some basic safety and design questions you may want to ask:

Can your child get on and off chairs/bench easily?

Is this a set that will work when your child gets a little bigger?

If you're looking at a wooden set, are there exposed screws or nuts (check the underside) that can cut your child?

Is the table surface washable and ready for abuse? (A beautiful painted piece will be destroyed by paint, playdough, crayons, etc.)

Best Travel Toys For Toddlers

We ask almost the impossible from toddlers when we travel by car. Sitting still for long stretches is physically stressful for this age group. Having a plan before you get in the car may help make the transition a little bit easier. The most obvious tip would be to try to plan your car travel to happen at nap time. Of course, that's not always possible. While some kids find the movement of the car soothing and fall asleep easily, others seem to feel the need to co-drive the car— staying alert the entire way!

It's at this age that kids do that straightening-of-the-back trick when being put into their car seats. It will help if you:

- Give your child a heads-up about getting ready to go into the car.

- Leave a special toy in the car that she can look forward to playing with only in the car.

- Bring along favorite tapes to listen to in the car.

- Bring snacks and drinks—especially good if you get caught in traffic!

- Bring along a favorite huggable and/or blanket.

- Bring big washable crayons and pad of paper in a travel sack small enough to fit into a diaper bag or glove compartment.

- Bring an inflatable ball for out-of-the-car breaks and when-you-get-there fun.

- Bring small cardboard books he can handle himself when in his car seat.

- Bring a small set of big plastic blocks or the "favorite toy of the week" for extended stays, one you know she'll be happy to play with while you're unpacking!

Our favorites:

■ Fire Truck and My Little Puppy Playsets 2005

(Gund $19.95 ●●●●½) If you're in the back seat with your toddler and you need to go five more exits, these playsets make great choices! The all-fabric fire truck zips open to reveal a firefighter, Dalmatian, hydrant, and water bucket. **My Little Puppy** comes in his own dog house, with a ball, bone, and bowl, and barks quietly when squeezed. Also top rated: **My First Sports Bag** with three fabric balls. (800) 448-4863.

■ Lamaze Snack Cup Stroller Toy

(Learning Curve $24.99 ●●●●½) Here's a stroller toy with lots of interesting features. There are a "puppy" snack cup that can detach for washing—ideal for Cheerios on the go, a mini fishbowl with a pull-out fish on tether that won't get away, a squeaky kitten, and a little mouse that pulls forward and wiggles as it vibrates (without music) back to where it started. (800) 704-8697.

■ The Eensie Weensie Spider Activity Book 2005

(North American Bear Co. $40 each ●●●●½) The all-fabric accordion book tells the story of the familiar song. Can be used as a crib

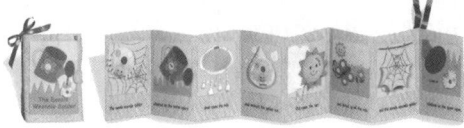

bumper or a just a book to share while you're on the go. Also recommended, **Flatso Farm** (with "e-i-e-i-o"). (800) 682-3427.

A Present for Me! Game One of the best tips we have for toddlers is to wrap small items for them to unwrap. They don't need to be new—little books, a tape, a box of cereal, or a small toy. Don't show your bag of tricks all at once. Dole them out as you go! Toddlers love surprises, and the unwrapping process is part of the fun and a real time burner.

Best Second-Birthday Gifts For Every Budget

Over $100   **Wooden Blocks** (various makers) or **Playhouse / Large Climber** (Little Tikes / Step 2) or **Toy Kitchen** (Step 2 / Small World Toys)

Under $75   **Retro Rocket** (Radio Flyer) or **Sandbox** (Little Tikes / Step 2)

Under $50   **Cozy Coupe** (Little Tikes) or **Little People Ramps Around Garage** (Fisher-Price) or **Ryan's Room Push-Along Block Cart** (Small World Toys) or **Tidoo** (Corolle)

Under $30   **Rollipop Advanced Set** (EduShape) or **Giant Cardboard Blocks** (Constructive Playthings) or **Rip Rolling Fun** (Small World Toys)

Under $20   **Lego Quatro** (Lego Systems) or **Toy Dishes** (various makers) or **My First Madeline** (RC2/Learning Curve) or **Puzzibilities Sounds on the Go Puzzle** (Small World Toys)

Under $15   **Tolo Mobile Phone** (Small World) or **Groovy Girls/Boys** (Manhattan Toy)

Under $10	**Crayola Color Wonder Paper & Markers** (Binney and Smith) or **Mega Bloks Lil' Cement Truck** (Mega Bloks)
Under $5	**Play-Doh** (Hasbro)

A Word about Balloons. Despite the fact that latex balloons are considered unsafe for children under 6, people continue to give them to kids in stores and parks, and at parties. The problem is that kids can suffocate on pieces of latex if they bite and/or inhale a balloon that they break or try to blow up. Yes, they are an old tradition—but a dangerous one. Why take the risk? Stick to Mylar!

3 • Preschool
Three to Four Years

What to Expect Developmentally

Learning Through Pretend. Preschoolers are amazing learning machines! Watch and listen to them at play and you can hear the wheels of their busy minds working full tilt. From sunup to sundown, preschoolers love playing pretend games. Playing all sorts of roles gives kids a chance to become big and powerful people. Providing props for such play gives kids the learning tools to develop language, imagination, and a better understanding of themselves and others.

Social Play. Your once-happy-to-be-only-with-you toddler has blossomed into a much more social being. He enjoys playing with other kids. Sharing is still an issue, but there's a budding understanding of give and take.

Solo Play. Unlike the toddler who moved from one thing to another, preschoolers become able to really focus their attention on building a bridge of blocks, working on a puzzle, or painting pictures.

Toys and Development. Although preschoolers love to play at counting and singing, or even at trying to write the alphabet, informal play is still the best path to learning. Building a tower with blocks, they discover some very basic math concepts. Digging in the sand or floating leaves in puddles, they make early science discoveries.

Big Muscles. Threes and fours also need time and space to run and climb and use their big muscles to develop coordination and a sense of themselves as able doers.

Your Role in Play. A child who has shelves full of stuffed animals or every piece of the hottest licensed character may seem to have tons of toys, but the truth is, no matter how many trucks or dolls a kid has, such collections offer just one kind of play. Take an inventory of your child's toy clutter to see what's really being played with and what needs to be packed away or donated.

BASIC GEAR CHECKLIST
FOR PRESCHOOLERS

✓Set of blocks and props (small vehicles, animals, people)

✓Trike   ✓Dolls and/or soft animals
✓Dress-up clothes   ✓Housekeeping toys
✓Transportation toys   ✓Matching games
✓Picture books   ✓Sand and water toys
✓Art materials—crayons, paints, clay
✓Simple puzzles (eight pieces and up)
✓Tape player and music and story tapes

 Toys to Avoid

These toys pose a safety hazard:

✓Electric toys or those that heat up with lightbulbs, which can burn
✓Toys with projectile parts that can injure eyes
✓Toys without volume control, which can damage ears
✓Two-wheelers with training wheels
✓Latex balloons

These toys are developmentally inappropriate:

✓Complex building sets that adults must build while children watch
✓Teaching machines that reduce learning to a series of right or wrong answers
✓Coloring books that limit creativity

Pretend Play

This is the age when pretend play blossoms. Some kids pretend with blocks, trains, and miniatures they move around as they act out little dramas. Others prefer dressing up and playing roles with their whole being. Either way, such games are more than fun. They help children learn to stretch their imaginations, try on powerful new roles, cope with feelings and fears, and develop language and social skills.

Dress-Up Play and Let's-Pretend Props

Old pocketbooks, briefcases, jewelry, hats, or a homemade badge are often all that's needed to transform young players. Below are a few specialty items you may want to buy:

■ Get Real Gear   *2005* PLATINUM AWARD

(Aeromax Toys $49.95 & up ●●●●●) We were most taken with this company's themed jumpsuits: an orange **Jr. Astronaut** uniform with tons of official looking patches; the **Jr. Air Force Pilot;** and the **Jr. Championship Racer.** Come in sizes for kids 3–12. (877) 776-2291.

■ Let's Pretend Careers

(Small Miracles $29.99 & up ●●●●●) Handsome enough to wear as real clothes, this collection includes: **Doctor** kit with white coat & stethoscope; **Pilot** outfit with hat, headset & shirt; and for the junior horsey set, a red **Equestrian** jacket, with traditional hat & blue ribbon. PLATINUM AWARD '04. Still recommended: **Firefighter, Construction Worker, Police, Chef,** and **Capes** and **Tutus.** PLATINUM AWARD '02. 3–8. (888) 281-1798.

Doctor's Gear

COMPARISON SHOPPER
Doctor's & Vet's Kits

Doctors no longer make house calls, and even the traditional black bag from Fisher-Price is gone. Most of the medical kits do not come with cases large enough for easy re-packing. The roomiest is **Pretend & Play Doctor Set** (Learning Resources $24.95 ○○○○○). Comes in a large plastic case with 19 pieces including a stethoscope with heartbeat and cough, a beeper, a cellphone, a blood pressure cuff, and other chunky tools. PLATINUM AWARD '04. (888) 800-7893. **Fisher-Price's Medical Kit** (Fisher-Price $15.99 ○○○○) comes in a smaller plastic case with almost the same basic gear as the original "black bag." (800) 432-5437. For playing Veterinarian, **Small Miracles' Let's Pretend** (Small Miracles $29.99 ○○○○½) has a child-sized jacket, puppy, and stethoscope and other medical tools. (888) 281-1798.

■ Get-Up Roaring Dinosaur & Clippity Clop Horse *2005*

(big Boing Toys $24.99 ○○○○½) Clever plush dino- or horse-head hat that roars or whinnies, and feet/shoes that stomp or clop. Heads have volume control, and make sound as child moves. For kids who like to use their whole beings to pretend. Also top rated, a charming **Get-up Fairy** set with musical wand. 3–6. (415) 331-7557.

Housekeeping Tools

Both girls and boys use props for cleaning, cooking, and child-care. Few toys will get more use by both boys and girls than a minibroom or -mop. This is an inexpensive favorite that you'll find in most toy supermarkets. Kitchen toys are used for playing house and running restaurants. As children's experiences broaden, so does the scope of their games of make-believe. For more kitchens and toy dishes, see Toddlers chapter.

COMPARISON SHOPPER
Dishes *2005*

There are three high quality dish sets: **Kitchen Wear** (Alex $14.99 & up ○○○○) testers loved the colored translucent kitchenware that comes in see-through backpacks. They are gender specific, however, with licks of pink. (800) 666-2539. For gender-free sets, we recommend either: **Earlyplay Sets** (Brio $14.99 & up ●●●○), which also come in a variety of backpacks with dishes and cutlery all done in primary colors (888) 274-6869; or **Pretend & Play Dishes** (Learning Resources $12.95 ●●●○)—service for four includes sturdy plastic cups and saucers, octagonal plates, and cutlery in gender-free primary colors. 3 & up. (888) 800-7893.

■ Pretend & Play Teaching Telephone   Blue Chip

(Learning Resources $29.95 ●●●●●) You can program in any phone number and leave a message. When your child calls that number they hear your message. A great way to teach important phone numbers and the concept of 911. Even the concept of taking messages is built into the pretend. 4 & up. Platinum Award '00. (888) 800-7893.

Dolls and Huggables

Preschoolers love soft animals and dolls as huggable companions for bedtime and playtime. At this age, playing with dolls gives both boys and girls a chance to try out new roles and language.

■ Lila   2005   Platinum Award

(Corolle $55 ●●●●●) If you're looking for a big, beautiful, soft, sweet-smelling bald baby doll, look no further. This 17" baby cries, laughs, and babbles. A perfect armful for pretend play. 3 & up. (800) 668-4846.

■ Madeline   2005

(RC2/Learning Curve $14.99–$80) If you have a Madeline fan at home, there's lots of good news! A new **Talking Madeline Ragdoll** ($24.99 ●●●○) says five phrases in English and French. Still top-rated, the **16" Dressable Madeline** ($19.99 ●●●○) who seems to step right out of the storybook (complete with appendix scar). The very special **Huggable Madeline** ($80 ●●●●●), child size and 36" tall, was our '03 Platinum Award winner. Preschoolers also love the **Poseable 8" Madeline** ($14.99

oooo). New for **2005**, **Schoolgirls Madeline, Nona,** and **Danielle.** Still top rated, her **dollhouse** (see p. 109). Our testers also loved the new **La Petite Madeline Old House in Paris** setting and mini-doll ($34.99 **oooo**). Because it's scaled like Polly Pockets, preschoolers needed help with many of the smaller pieces but it kept them very engaged. (800) 704-8697.

■ Topsy Turvy Dolls **2005**

(North American Bear Co. $25 each **oooo**) These very old-fashioned fabric dolls retain their charm. **Cinderella** in rags flips into her ball gown. Also special: **Little Red Riding Hood; Dorothy** flips to **Toto** on the Yellow Brick Road; and **Snow White** flips into the evil **Stepmother.** (800) 682-3427.

Multicultural Dolls

Just a few years ago, there were few options that reflected our diversity. Now, there are so many more great choices.

■ Baby Cakes

(Zapf Creation $40 & up) For a 19" doll with eyes that open and close, we recommend the multi-ethnic **Baby Cakes Birthday** line that comes with a knitted sweater and cap. A scrumptious armful. PLATINUM AWARD '03. **My First Baby Annabell** ($19.99 **oooo**) is a sweet and very affordable 14" bald baby doll in terry cloth romper. New for **2005**, **Love Me Chou Chou** ($49.99 **oo**) who babbles, cries, says mama, and moves her feet, was disappointing to our testers who thought she was "too heavy… it had a seam on her head—looked like she had a brain surgery… and you had to put a pacifier in to make her stop crying." (877) 629-9273.

■ Bébé Do, My Real Baby **2005**

(Corolle $50 **oooo**½) Sweet vinyl-faced doll with fabric body comes in two ethnic skin tones. Still top rated, **Les Minis Calins BLUE CHIP** ($16 & up **ooooo**), sweet 8" soft-bodied dolls that also come in Asian and African American versions. (800) 668-4846.

■ Groovy Girls Bombastic Bunk Beds & Supernova Sofa 2005 PLATINUM AWARDS

(Manhattan Toy $10 & $50 ooooo) If these all-fabric 13" multi-ethnic dolls are big in your house, these new furniture pieces are must-have props. The **beds** ($24.99) stack or can be used side-by-side. Testers loved the **sofa** and **Cheeky Chair** ($14.99 each). For a superlative gift, consider **Supersize Groovy Girl** ($50 ooooo), a 40" child-sized fabric doll that's like a pretend play pal. 3 & up. PLATINUM AWARD '01. (800) 541-1345.

■ Language Littles 2005

(Language Littles $35 oooo) Each of these 16" fabric dolls with yarn hair speaks in English and another language (each says 25 words and phrases). Will they make your child bilingual? Of course not, but they are a place to start. Choose Italian, Greek, French, Chinese, Hebrew, Russian, German, Spanish, or Japanese. 3 & up. (212) 535-8122.

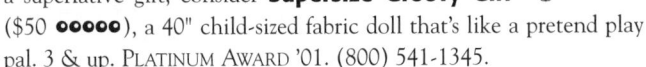

COMPARISON SHOPPER
Drink-and-Wet Dolls 2005

We had a lot of inquiries this year about the best drink-and-wet doll. Our testers gave thumbs up to **Bébé Do Emma** or **Paul Fait Pipi** 2005 (Corolle $40 each oooo½), anatomically correct girl or boy 14" doll with all-vinyl tubbable body. Comes with potty, bottle, and diaper for pretend play. (800) 668-4846. Not nearly as pretty as Corolle's, but really innovative, is the **Little Mommy Potty Training Baby** (Fisher-Price $25 oooo) who drinks but does not tinkle until she's on her special potty seat. It's magic (really creative use of magnets that releases the water)! Unfortunately, she is not tub-able! In the novelty doll category, **Potty Elmo** 2005 PLATINUM AWARD (Fisher-Price $19 ooooo) is amazing. Give Elmo his sippy cup and you'll hear him drink; if you don't get him to the potty, he says, "Oops, Elmo didn't get to the potty. Accidents happen," and if he makes it, "Elmo can do it and so can you!" One of the best and most polite interactive dolls we've ever tested. (800) 524-8697. We pass on Zapf Creations' **Baby Born** ($39.99 ●●) who got low marks from our testers because they had difficulty getting the pretend poop out (no joke). (800) 432-5437.

Bears of the Year 2005

As always, we find selecting one winner totally unbearable! Here are our top picks: **Timber** (Gund $20 ●●●●), with a full tummy and slightly sad expression, looks like he needs a hug—which is easy to do because his shiny mocha fur is extremely soft. (800) 448-4863. **Little Brewster** (Mary Meyer $9–$130 ●●●●) is a lovable, small, silky chocolate brown bear. He's part of the Brewster Bear family, from 9" to 36". (800) 451-4387.

Best of Show: Dogs of the Year 2005

Puppies 4 Sale (North American Bear Co. $12 each ●●●●) Sooo cute! If your preschooler wants a dog but you're not ready, try one of these (8" tall) miniature puppies—a **Golden Retriever** or **Fox Terrier.** (800) 682-3427. For bigger pooches, we suggest **Bernie, Super Flop** (Mary Meyer $45 ●●●●), an incredibly silky huggable black dog with white muzzle and licks of cocoa. Somewhat smaller but equally endearing, a honey-toned **Fancy Flop Rutherford Retriever** ($20 ●●●●). For just a handful of pup, bring home **Pudgies** ($9 each ●●●●): Wag-Wag or Bow Wow, lovable little labs. (800) 451-4387.

Miscellaneous Stuffed Critters

■ Lil' Milo Monkey

(Mary Meyer $15 ●●●●½) A happy looking brown monkey with tan face, fists, and feet. (800) 451-4387.

■ Mamatot Bunny 2005

(Manhattan Toy $20 ●●●●) A big yellowish mama rabbit holds a smaller white bunny in her magnetized paws. Looks like they stepped out of a picture book. We also suggest you take a look at **Tiptoes Touche**

Madge & **Starlet Shimmerella** ($19.95 oooo)—Miss Piggy, move over! Both with fluffy boas, glittery trims, and inspiration for stories to tell. 4 & up. (800) 541-1345. For other talking dolls, see Potty Elmo (p. 71), and Toddler chapter, p. 50.

Interactive Dolls *2005*

The big talking dolls of the season are: **E-L-M-O** (Fisher-Price $29.99 oooo) Elmo does a dance (with body movements) to the tune of "YMCA"; and **Happy Ears Eeyore** (Fisher-Price $19.99 oooo). (800) 432-5437.

Notable Doll Accessories *2005*

Budget and taste will go into making the choices here. Just like real equipment, there are doll carriers for the silver-spoon set and more practical models for your average doll. Still top rated: American Girl's yellow and blue **Collapsible Stroller** ($34 oooo), designed for their 15" Bitty Baby Dolls. Also special, **Bitty Twins Double Stroller** ($48 oooo). (800) 845-0005. Community Playthings' BLUE CHIP **Wooden Doll Cradle** ($95 ooooo) is made of solid maple and built to last. The large 29" model is big enough so kids can climb in and play baby or put a family of dolls to sleep. 2 & up. #C140. (800) 777-4244.

Puppets and Puppet Stages

Through the mouths of puppets, kids say things that they might not otherwise speak about; so puppets provide a way of venting feelings and developing imagination and language skills. Young puppeteers replay stories, create original tales, and develop skills that link to reading and writing. See Early School Years chapter for more puppets and stages.

■ Animal Puppets *2005*

(Gund $16 each oooo) Good news! Gund has re-introduced their beautifully made hand puppets. Choose from some of their favorite bears (**Manni**) or other animals, such as **Luke the Lion** or

Bamboo Panda. (800) 448-4863.

■ **Happy Hands Puppets**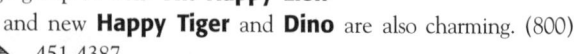

(Mary Meyer $15 each ●●●●) Just right for a lively telling of the Three Pigs, bring home these 13" full-body hand puppets. The pig is very cheerful and the wolf is not too scary! Made with a nubby finish, these are pleasing to use and will be enjoyed by the next age group as well. The **Happy Lion** and new **Happy Tiger** and **Dino** are also charming. (800) 451-4387.

■ **Puppet Theater**

(Alex $79.99 ●●●●½) This has a clock for show time and eye-appealing graphics! This stable floor model is 48" high, with painted trim on one side and a chalk surface for messages. Their tabletop model looks like a fairytale castle and comes with two felt puppets. ($50 ●●●● ½). 3 & up. (800) 666-2539. For more stages and puppets, see Early School Years chapter.

FREEBIE: Do it yourself. A large appliance box can be turned into an excellent puppet stage, and so can a cloth-covered card table that kids can hide behind. Another great option is a spring curtain rod and length of fabric that can be used in any doorway.

Pretend Settings:
Doll Houses, Garages, & Workshop

Some of the mini-settings listed in the Toddlers chapter will be used in more elaborate ways now. Here are descriptions of recommended settings that are more complex:

COMPARISON SHOPPER
Doll Houses

Dollhouses should be kept simple for little hands. Plastic or wood, really comes down to personal preference. Here are our top picks:

Special Edition Townhouse (Fisher Price $100 ●●●●½)
Plastic house comes fully furnished and has sound effects
that our testers loved: crackling fireplace, ringing phone,
running water, chiming doorbell, and lights! 4 & up. (800)
432-5437.

In wooden dollhouses, there are three great collections.
You can't go wrong with any of them.

Plan Toys Dollhouses (Brio $90–$125
●●●●●) Choose either their modern-
looking **A-frame** with open roofs for
easy access, or their **Classic
Dollhouse**. PLATINUM AWARD '01.
(888) 274-6869.

Ryan's Room Dollhouses (Small World
Toys $100 ●●●●●): **Home Is Where the
Heart Is Dollhouse** is their deluxe,
three-stories-high house. PLATINUM
AWARD '03. Or consider the smaller
**Home Again, Home Again A-
Frame** ($130), which can be enlarged
with an add-on basement and stairs
($70). New for **2005**, a two-story
Backyard Clubhouse with "cable car" that connects
dollhouse to clubhouse. Multicultural families available
and interesting furniture collections; new for **2005**,
Multimedia Mania ($15 ●●●●) with a flatscreen TV, of
course. (800) 421-4153.

My Dollhouse (Alex $169 ●●●●●)
Done in a bright-colored, patterned
palette, this house has three floors with
22 pieces of furniture. PLATINUM
AWARD '01. (800) 666-2539.

■ **Plan Toys Stable Set** **2005**

(Brio $30 ●●●●) Charming small
stable with a red roof, two wooden
horses (with movable heads), hay
box, broom, and bucket. Designed to
go with a larger and handsome **Farm
House** ($84.99 ●●●●). A dandy

play setting sans farm animals (sold separately). Has hinged side that opens for dramatic play and working pulley. 3 & up. Still top rated, PLATINUM AWARD-winning **Airport** ($75) or **Garage** ($75). (888) 274-6869.

■ ActionPower Workshop

(Little Tikes $60 ●●●½) The latest in pretend workshops that comes with ActionPower tools (a whirring circular saw, a wrench, and a hammer), and a built-in saw—all with sound effects. The "instructions were a bit confusing," wrote our tester. (800) 321-0183.

■ Ryan's Room Adventures Ahoy
2005 PLATINUM AWARD

(Small World Toys $99.99 ●●●●●) Yahoo! Get ready for imagination to set sail with Captain Hook and two of his mates aboard this magnificent wooden ship with working sails, rigging, hatches, anchor, crow's nest, and even a plank to walk! A stunning gift for years of dramatic play. 34" W x 24" H. Add-on sets with more figures available. 4–8. (800) 421-4153.

■ Ryan's Room Firehouse *2005*

(Small World Toys $75 ●●●●) This wooden two-story firehouse has pole for firefighters to use along with furniture, a fire engine ($25) comes with a revolving ladder. Best of all, a working door and ramp allow fire truck with revolving ladder to go in and out. A great setting for dramatic play— child provides all sound effects! 4 & up. (800) 421-4153.

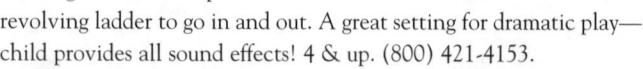

■ Ryan's Room Majestic Castle

(Small World Toys $100 ●●●●●) A truly majestic wooden castle, 20" x 20", with working drawbridge, movable staircases, four towers, and walls that can be arranged in different configurations. Comes with four knights and a horse. Additional figures such as king, queen, jester, wizard, jousting knights, and dragon are available. Easy to assemble, this play setting might become an heirloom. 4 & up. PLATINUM AWARD '04. (800) 421-4153.

■ **Folding Castle Play Set** 🏰*2005*

(Melissa & Doug $70 ●○●●) An all-wood castle that measures 16" x 16" x 12" when closed; 31" x 16" x 12" when open. Comes with three human figures and a horse. (800) 284-3948.

■ **Sir Roderick's Fortress** *2005*

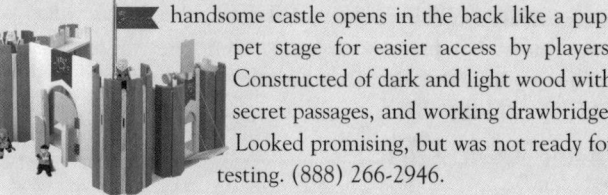

(Maxim Enterprises $139.99) The largest of the three castles, this handsome castle opens in the back like a puppet stage for easier access by players. Constructed of dark and light wood with secret passages, and working drawbridge. Looked promising, but was not ready for testing. (888) 266-2946.

■ **Deluxe Tumble Treehouse & Skycoaster**
    2005 **PLATINUM AWARD**

(Maxim Enterprises $99 ●●●●●) With pulleys and stairways, this furnished treehouse has lots of pretend power and action. A Sky Coaster can be added for vehicles ($30). A gender-free setting that will mix well with block structures. An outstanding value! 4–8. (888) 266-2946.

Trucks and Other Vehicles

Preschoolers are fascinated with all forms of transportation. The real things are out of reach and on the move, but toy trucks, cars, boats, jets, and trains are ideal for make-believe departures, both indoors and out. Choose vehicles with working parts to use with blocks, in the sandbox, or at the beach. BLUE CHIP choices such as Funrise's **Tonka Trucks** or Little Tikes' **Construction Trucks** are perfect gifts for now. So are **Matchbox** or **Hot Wheels** cars, which are now appropriate and often the first "collectible."

■ **Rugged Riggz** *2005*

(Little Tikes $9.99 & 14.99 ●○●●) We're big fans of this updated collection of basic trucks. There are haulers (our favorite hauls two motorcycles); classics (cement, dump, and hauler), and rescue sets (these have sound, which you might not like in a small space). All are just right for the 3 & up crowd. Also new and more complex, several sturdy yellow construction trucks with action parts and sounds: a dumptruck with plow, backhoe, paver, and earthmover. (800) 321-0183.

■ Bendos Old Tyme R/C Bumper Cars

(Kid Galaxy $49.99 oooo½) Two kids can set up an obstacle course or race track and run their two bumper cars with Bendo drivers. Marked 5 & up, we think older 4s and their older siblings will enjoy these together. Less pricey, with just one controller but plenty of action, **My First R/C Dumptruck** ($19.99 oooo½). 3 & up. (800) 816-1135.

■ Ramp Racer *2005*

(Maxim Enterprises $24.99 oooo½) A five-storey-high wooden raceway with double tracks so that you can race two cars at once. It will combine well with blocks. (888) 266-2946.

First Trains and Track Toys

What They Learn

A nonelectric train is a classic toy that will keep growing in complexity as you add working bridges, roundhouses, and other extras. Note: Preschoolers are not ready for electric trains, except to watch!

Trains are really open-ended puzzles with no right or wrong answers. Making the track work often becomes more important to many kids than actually playing with the trains.

Many stores display their trains on tabletops with the track glued down, but much of the open-ended play value is lost when you do that at home. Making ever-changing settings is half the fun. Skip the table and invest in more tracks and bridges.

Good Train Sets

■ Wooden Zoo Set *2005*

(Brio $50 oooo) Here's a good 35-piece starter set with plenty of pretend play built in. Comes with an assortment of animals, special transport cars, and a zoo building. Be forewarned, the pieces in this set are small and not for kids under 3 or for kids who like to mouth their toys. (888) 274-6869.

■ Sky Train Set 2005

(Brio $70 ●●●●●) 24-piece set comes with two trains that run on elevated track with gondola-like wagons suspended beneath. PLATINUM AWARD '04. New for 2005, a **Remote Control Sky Train** ($15 ●●●●) and a deluxe **Sky Train Transporter Set** ($300 ●●●●) with 100 pieces packed in a green storage box. Shouldn't replace a basic set, but the movement and height will impress train aficionados big time. 3 & up. (888) 274-6869.

■ Thomas & Friends Water Tower Figure 8 Set 2005

(RC2/Learning Curve $39.99 ●●●●½) This 25-piece set is a great buy and gives beginners a great place to start. Includes Thomas, a cargo car, water tower, and stone bridge for a figure 8. For a larger set, consider **Down by the Docks** ($149.99/45 pieces ●●●●●) with **Sodor Bay Bridge, Lighthouse,** and **Crane.** PLATINUM AWARD '03. (800) 704-8697.

■ Thomas & Friends Interactive Railway 2005

(RC2/Learing Curve $29.99 & up ●●●●½) Purists may not like this talking plastic railway system—we had some doubts ourselves. The good news is, the mechanisms work well and all are compatible with wooden trains and tracks. Each set has an interactive mechanical prop that directs kids to find a specific color or to count out actions to load trains. True, the train directs some of the play; it does work well, however, and allows for open-ended play, as well. **Deluxe Roundhouse** ($79.99 ●●●●) set has a suspension bridge, three electronic destinations, and plenty of track. Our testers liked the **Lift'n'Load Crane Set** ($49.99 ●●●●) as well as the smaller **Barrel Loader** set ($29.99 ●●●●). 3 & up. (800) 704-8697.

Best New Wooden Train Props

New accessories can inspire fresh layouts and keep interest chugging along.

■ **Thomas & Friend Sodor Scrub & Shine** 🟊*2005*

(RC2/Learning Curve $46.99 ●●●●½) Vehicles
trigger the sounds, lights, and action of this
wash for vehicles. Also fun, a small **Toll
Booth Bridge** $26.99 ●●●●) with push
button that lowers toll arm. Add
multi-level track for over
and under track bed action.
Also outstanding, **Waterfall Tunnel**
($27.99 ●●●●) with knob on top that makes water
appear to "flow"; and a **Deluxe Roundhouse**
with sounds ($120 ●●●●). You may also want to
add the new **Sodor Blocks** ($50 ●●●●), a set
of 49 wooden blocks with a stone façade for
making bridges and tunnels. (800) 704-8697.

■ **Collapsing Bridge** 🟊*2005* Pʟᴀᴛɪɴᴜᴍ Aᴡᴀʀᴅ

(Brio $20 ●●●●●) Oh, no! The
bridge has given way! Most
likely your kids
already play this
game but now, with a press of a button, the bridge really does collapse. Great for suspenseful train rides. (888) 274-6869.

■ **Remote Control Bridge** 🟊*2005*

(Brio $40 ●●●●) Loaded with dramatic play potential, this 25" yellow
and green A-frame bridge can be raised or lowered
thanks to a remote control infrared light.
Activating the bridge sets the
lights and warning bells off, as
well. Our tester loved it, but par-
ents warn that it eats batteries! 3 & up. Also new but not ready for testing, **Smart Track** (Brio $10–$35), which promises to direct the train
to move in certain ways (stop, slow down, or reverse). (888) 274-6869.

Construction Toys

If there's one toy no child should be without, blocks are it!
Few toys are more basic. Stacking a tower, balancing a bridge,
setting up a zoo—all call for imagination, dexterity, decision
making, and problem solving. Built into the play are early
math and language concepts that give concrete meaning to

abstract words such as *higher, lower, same,* and *different.* Best of all, blocks are wonderfully versatile—they build a space city today, a farm tomorrow.

Kids will enjoy both wood and plastic types of blocks, which encourage different kinds of valuable play experiences. Choosing blocks depends largely on your budget and space. Although many of these sets are pricey, they are a solid investment that will be used for years to come.

Wooden Blocks

Unit blocks come in many shapes and lengths and should be carefully proportioned to each other. Many catalogs offer unit blocks in sets of different sizes. Parents are sometimes disappointed when kids don't use the small starter sets they buy. Keep in mind that kids really can't do much with a set of 20 blocks and no props. This is one of those items where the more they have, the more they can do.

COMPARISON SHOPPER
Unit Blocks

No two catalogs have the same number of blocks or shapes in any set, so there are small differences among all the sets listed. The cost of shipping will vary depending upon where you live and the weight and price of the item. Our best suggestion is that you call around and compare. Here's a sampling of what a good basic set will run:

Back to Basics set of 82 blocks in 21 shapes. #2728. $172.99 (800) 356-5360.

Constructive Playthings set of 82 pieces in 12 shapes. #KRP-U312L. $79.99 (800) 832-0572.

Small World Toys' Ryan's Room (120 pieces $104.99); for a set of 50 small-scale blocks that come in a fabric storage bag, **Buncha Blocks** ($14.99). (800) 421-4153.

Props for Blocks

Providing a variety of props such as small-scale vehicles, animals, and people enhances building and imaginative play. Here are some props designed to inspire young builders. Our favorites:

■ Bendos *2005*

(Kid Galaxy $5 & up ●●●●●) These bendable action figures are perfect for pretend play. Available as multi-iethnic athletes, community workers, and animals, they stand up with blocks, fit into vehicles, and satisfy young collectors. PLATINUM AWARD '01. 3 & up. New for *2005*, **Bendos Vehicles** (see p. 78). (800) 816-1135.

■ Rescue Heroes

(Fisher-Price $7.99 each ●●●) As a concept we like this multicultural collection of firefighter, construction worker, and police officer. We thought the new **Hydro Team** (that shoot water) looked like great fun but they all "leaked," which frustrated our testers. Stay clear of the ones that have projectile parts, which pose a safety hazard to preschoolers. 3 & up. (800) 432-5437.

■ Space Heroes, Safety Squad & Pirate Adventures Action Figures *2005*

(Odyssey Toys $17.95 ●●●●½) Sets of three highly detailed action figures with tiny props. These are harder to stand and balance, but they will appeal to block builders as props for dramatic play. (866) 869-7639.

■ Windows and Door Blocks BLUE CHIP

(Constructive Playthings $16.95 ●●●●●) Scaled to standard unit blocks: a five-piece set of four windows and one door. #PCR-62L. (800) 832-0572.

SMART PARENT TRICK: Playful Cleanup. Preschoolers often need help cleaning up. You can get some learning in by saying, "I'll find the trucks, you pick up all the cars," or "Let's find all the smallest blocks first." Set up open shelves for blocks and baskets for props to avoid having a constant jumbled mess!

Cardboard Blocks

See Toddler chapter.

Plastic Blocks

Plastic building sets call for a different kind of dexterity. Here's what you should look for:

Beginners are better off with larger pieces that make bigger and quicker constructions.

Encourage beginning builders to experiment rather than copy or watch you build.

■ Mega Bloks BLUE CHIP

(Mega Bloks $10 & up ●●●●) These oversized plastic pegged blocks are easy for preschoolers to take apart, fit together, and assemble into B-I-G constructions with a minimum of pieces. Select a set with wheels and angled pieces for more flexibility. (800) 465-6342.

■ Kid K'nex *2005*

(K'nex $14.95 ●●●½) Our testers wanted to try these up-sized K'nex that look related to Tinkertoys. There are **Stretchin' Monsters, Footed Friends, Lid Kids,** and the big **Rovin' Rollers** with wheels for building moving vehicles. Our three-year-old testers found them too complicated, but our four-year-old testers loved them. Fitting the pieces together can be challenging and requires finger strength as well as visual discrimination. 4 & up. (800) 543-5639.

■ Lego Duplo Block-o-Dile *2005* PLATINUM AWARD

(Lego Systems $14.99 ●●●●●) Hard to know who will love this most—parents or kids! A chunky sized crocodile on wheels comes loaded with 26 Duplo building bricks which the croc "swallows" when rolled. Works better than earlier versions of this very "neat" toy. Duplos are BLUE CHIP basic gear. (800) 233-8756.

Early Games

Preschoolers are not ready for complex games with lots of rules or those that require strategy, math, or reading skills. Best bets are games of chance such as lotto and picture dominoes, and classics such as Candy Land, where players depend on the luck of the draw rather than skill. Taking turns is often hard, and so is the concept of winning or losing. We've selected games that can be played cooperatively and those that are quick and short so there can be lots of winners.

Active Games

■ Cranium Hullabaloo

(Cranium $24.95 ooooo) Players have to listen carefully to the electronic ringmaster that directs play among the 16 playmats. The player on the "lucky" mat when the ringmaster says, "Freeze!" is the winner. Will also be enjoyed by the next age group. PLATINUM AWARD '04. 4 & up. (877) 272-6486.

■ Pin the Tail on the Donkey

(Eeboo $14 oooo) This classic game is printed on a sturdy reusable poster and comes with a bandanna blindfold and two sets of 16 self-adhesive tails—no tacks needed! A good party prop for several years of play. 4–8 (212) 222-0823.

Color, Counting, & Other Concepts

■ Cookin' Cookies *2005* PLATINUM AWARD

(Fundex $9.99 ooooo) One of a series of fun games that come in their own small metal "lunchbox." Players get recipe cards and use their suction-cupped spoons to be the first to pick up all ingredients. But don't pick up a rotten egg or you have to start from scratch! Also fun, **Wormy Apples** (oooo), a color game, and **Storybook** (oooo), a language memory game. 4–7. (800) 486-9787.

■ Cranium CariBoo

(Cranium $16.95 **●●●●●**) Totally on the mark for preschoolers, this "treasure hunt" game introduces early color, letter, and number concepts. Drop the six balls into the secret tunnels and then go on a "treasure hunt" to find where they are hiding behind one of the 15 doors. Players open the magic doors with a special key, and win if they find the last ball, which opens the Treasure Chest! PLATINUM AWARD '03. (877) 272-6486.

■ Crocodile Dentist 2005

(Milton Bradley $15.99 **●●●●**) An updated classic, now comes with smoother teeth. Players take turns playing dentist by pushing down on his teeth, but beware—you never know when he'll decide to chomp down his jaw! If he does, you're out! Appeals to kids who like the safe scare; others may find it too much like a jack-in-the-box. 4 & up. (888) 836-7025.

■ Letter Factory Game 2005 PLATINUM AWARD

(LeapFrog $24.99 **●●●●●**) The first level of play is really a color matching game. Once you pick the color card the electronic voice asks for, it then identifies the letter on the card. The electronic voice then asks you to move your game piece a certain number of spaces. Once you move along, it magically tells you what color space you're on. (We're grown ups and this got us every time.) Level 2 asks

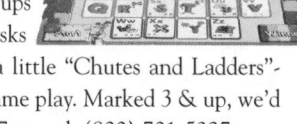

kids to find specific letters. There is a little "Chutes and Ladders"-style going backwards built in to the game play. Marked 3 & up, we'd say more like a great choice for the 4–7 crowd. (800) 701-5327.

■ Duck Duck Goose 2005 PLATINUM AWARD

(Milton Bradley $19.99 **●●●●●**) Thirteen little ducklings sit in a circle. Move the big Goose around the circle, press her head, and she says, "Duck," "Duck," "Duck." Keep moving her until she says, "Goose!" and then pick up the duckling to check the color dot hidden on the bottom of the duckling's shell. Players must collect three different colors to match their "nest" to win. Easy to learn, while reinforcing color concepts for beginners. Preschoolers will love the sound and action of this board version of a favorite childhood game. (888) 836-7025.

A Word About Electronic Quiz Toys for Preschoolers

For the past few years, we have objected (loudly) to many of these platforms because they did not use real books as a foundation and because the games were really nothing more than drill and practice. We are happy to report that things are changing—you'll find that well known storybooks are now being used, and that the games are more open-ended. These toys are attractive to preschoolers, who generally love pressing buttons, making things happen, and working on learning their numbers and letters. That said, preschoolers still learn best through concrete experiences and should have a rich diet of playing games, working on puzzles, and listening to great stories. Here are our top picks:

■ Fridge Phonics Magnetic Letter Set

(Leap Frog $17.99 ●●●●½) For the 21st-century child, magnetic letters that talk! Put the "magnetic phonics reader" onto the fridge and play one capital letter at a time. They say and sing each letter's name and sing the sound they say. Letters are raised to give kids the feel for their shapes. New for **2005**, **Fridge Farm Magnetic Animal Set** ($14.95 ●●●●½), five animals each in two pieces; match front and back, and they say their names. (800) 701-5327.

■ My First Leap Pad **2005**

(LeapFrog $39.99 ●●●●) New for **2005**, two Dr. Seuss books have been adapted for this platform. You can either listen to the story and/or play the games that extend the experience. Each page has items to find with a sensor pen. Many basic preschool counting and language skills, not just the usual alphabet drill. Happily, there's a volume control, so it won't blast their ears. (800) 701-5327.

Matching and Memory

Prereaders match pictures before they match words. These games provide playful ways to develop vocabulary, memory, and visual skills. While there are lots of choices, many sets either have too many images or are not sufficiently distinct for young players. We found the following to be graphically clearer for kids to follow. Here are our top picks:

■ Color Dominoes 2005

(eeBoo $12.95 **oooo**) Handsomely designed sturdy cardboard set of dominoes that focuses on colors and matching shapes (stars, moon, train, heart, blueberries) rather than traditional numbers or dots. Our twin three-year-old toy testers enjoyed playing their "own game" with the dominoes. 3 & up. (212) 222-0823.

■ I Never Forget A Face Memory Game 2005

(eeBoo $12.95 **oooo**) Our almost-five-year-old tester proclaimed this the best memory and matching game ever (after resoundingly beating his grandma in several rounds). Features illustrated faces of kids from around the world. A classic concentration game for a new generation. 3 & up. (212) 222-0823.

■ Ryan's Room Around the Blocks 2005

(Small World Toys $25 **oooo**½) A high-quality set of 26 blocks with upper- and lowercase letters, plus images to match the letters. All store in a big cloth bag. (800) 421-4153.

■ Surprise

(Gamewright $10 **oooo**) The idea is to find all the gifts on your game card by turning over the individual present cards on the table. No reading required, and will appeal to those 4 & up with great short-term memory! For 2–4 players. Playtime will run 10–15 minutes. Also top rated, **Hisss** ($10 **oooo**)—a fun, fast-paced, interactive game to reinforce color concepts. 4–7. (800) 638-7568.

Puzzles

A word about puzzles: Preschoolers gradually move from whole-piece puzzles, to simple puzzles that challenge them to see how two or more parts make a whole. For kids with no previous experience, start with five to seven pieces in a frame. Children's skills vary, so take your cue from the child. Some 4s can handle 20 to 30 pieces, while others are still working on 10 to 15 pieces. Large pieces are easier for little hands. A word of warning: with some notable exceptions listed below, many of the wooden puzzles that came our way continued to be badly finished and were rife with splinters.

■ Alphabet Boat Puzzle *2005*

(Infantino $12.99 ●●●●) Each boat being pulled by the Coast Guard boat has a letter in upper- and lowercase painted on the side and an object that starts with the sound of the letter. Also new, **I Spy My House Puzzle** ($12.99 ●●●●) with objects in the frame to "spy" in the puzzle, and **Town Heroes Puzzle** ($12.99 ●●●●). (800) 840-4916.

■ Beginner Pattern Blocks *2005*

(Melissa & Doug $19.99 ●●●●½) Ten wooden scenes are ready to fill with triangles, circles, squares, rectangles and ovals. Part puzzle/part shape sorter, all beautifully crafted with wooden storage box. 2½ & up. This company also does handsome **Sound Puzzles** with small red peg handles and eight pieces to match. Choose vehicles, animals, or farm creatures. (800) 284-3948.

■ Richard Scarry's Busy House
2005 PLATINUM AWARD

(Mudpuppy Press $15 ●●●●●) This company continues to make marvelous puzzles from picture-book art. This is a big (2' x 3') 24-piece floor puzzle from one of our favorites. The company also makes smaller 36-piece puzzles that are more appropriate for the next age group. Top rated: **Olivia, Curious George,** and **Where the Wild Things Are.** 4 & up. (212) 354-8840.

■ Puzzibilities Sound Puzzles
2005 PLATINUM AWARDS

(Small World Toys $15 each ●●●●●) Six raised pieces are easy to lift,

and when they are put back in the puzzle board, each makes a rip-roaring sound. Choose **Wild Animals, Dinosaurs,** or **Under Construction.** 2½ & up. Also noteworthy, **Counting Out Loud Talking Puzzles** ($25 each ●●●●), with either numbers or the alphabet. Still top rated, **Puzzibilities** nine-piece puzzles with small red knobs (themes: transportation, snapshot wild animals, or community vehicles). (800) 421-4153.

■ Ryan's Room It Takes All Sorts

(Small World Toys $15 ●●●●) Each shape has one, two, three, or four holes to fit on the wooden dowels of the puzzle board. For beginners, this is not as simple as it looks. There are two attributes here: shape and number. This calls for dexterity and counting. They say 2, we'd say late 2s and 3s. Also top rated, **Make-A-Shape Puzzle Board** ($14 ●●●●) introduces fractions with a circle cut in thirds, a square in quarters, a triangle in halves, and a whole rectangle. Obviously, using these terms with sandwiches, fruit, and other everyday objects will teach the same concepts. 2½ & up. (800) 421-4153.

■ Lauri Puzzles *2005*

(Lauri $7.99 ●●●●) Lauri's puzzles come with rubber pieces and a pattern printed in the container/tray for beginners to follow. For building confidence, these are the perfect place to start. New for *2005*, a 16-piece **Dinosaur Apatosaurus** and a 22-piece **Dragonfly.** Past favorites include **Triceratops, Car, Cement Truck, Birthday Cake,** and **Airplane.** 3–7. (800) 451-0520.

■ Super Sized Floor Puzzle (Construction Duty) *2005*

(Ravensburger $7.99 ●●●●) Kids fascinated with all things construction will love working on this oversized (2' x 3') puzzle with 24 pieces. One of our adult reviewers noted that the crew was not multicultural and that the only woman on the site seemed to be the architect, but it's still a handsomely designed puzzle. Zoo animals and dinosaur themes also available. 3 & up. (800) 886-1236.

Lacing Games

Kids dive right into lacing activities without knowing they're a great way to develop the fine-motor skills they'll need for writing. While stringing beads, they can also sort by color and make patterns, learning to see likenesses and differences. Our favorites:

Musical Friends *2005* and **Fairies of the Field** (eeBoo $14.00 each ○○○○), beautifully illustrated sturdy cards that kids will love to work on. Marked 3 & up, but will be most enjoyed by 4s. (212) 222-0823. **Lacing & Tracing Tools** (Lauri $6.99 ○○○○) is made of sturdy chipboard punched with holes that kids "sew" with colorful laces. Also recommended, **Lace & Link Numbers** ($14.99 ○○○○), crepe 4" rubber numerals that reinforce shapes in a tactile way. 4 & up. (800) 451-0520.

Science Toys and Activities

Floating a leaf in a puddle, collecting pebbles in the park, making mud pies in the sandbox, watching worms wiggle— these are a few of the active ways children learn about the natural world.

■ Mighty Magnet *2005*

(Learning Resources $6.50 ○○○○½) A jumbo 8" horseshoe-shaped magnet that can hold up to four pounds! They also have a set of **Six Mighty Magnets,** 5" horseshoes that can be used for hunting up how many places kids can make them stick ($17.95 ○○○○). 4 & up. (888) 800-7893.

■ Live Butterfly Pavilion *2005*

(Insect Lore $29.95 ○○○○) An updated kit includes a 3'-long, wind-sock-like habitat where ten Painted Lady caterpillars (which they mail to you) are transformed. A coil allows the habitat to pop up, stand on a table, and fold away for future use. Take pictures of the metamorphosis, or encourage your child to draw the changes and keep a log. Great for preschoolers as well as early school years. Company also makes a **Ladybug Land** where you hatch ladybugs! (800) 548-3284.

SMART PARENT TRICK: Give your preschooler a magnet and a sheet of peel-off stickers to put on anything they find that the magnet sticks to. Or give kids a bag full of household items to sort into two baskets. Have them put all the things that are attracted to the magnet in one basket and all the rest in another.

Garden Work

Preschoolers love the magic of seeing things grow. If you're looking to get a young gardener started, we recommend plastic **Garden Tools** (Little Tikes $2 each for small tools/$13 for a set of three larger tools. (800) 321-0183). **WHAT TO AVOID:** For preschoolers, stay clear of metal tools. An accidental swing in the wrong direction with plastic will not mean a trip to the ER. They also don't have splintery handles as some metal tools do, and won't rust when they are inevitably left outside.

Sand, Water, & Bubble Toys

Sand and water are basic materials for exploring liquids and solids, floating and sinking, sifting and pouring. An inexpensive pail and shovel are basic gear along with a sand mill for sandbox or beach. Older preschoolers will be delighted with a set of turrets and tower molds for building beautiful sand castles—kids will add moat, imagination, and who knows what else! Some other sand tools are also worth considering.

■ **Naturally Playful Sand & Water Table** *2005*

(Step2 $59.99 ●●●●½) This oversized table is half for sand and half for water, with waterways for boats to travel. A terrific patio toy for stand-up digging and splashing. Comes with several boats, tools, and an umbrella for shade. As with all water toys, adult supervision is a must. 2½ & up. (800) 347-8372.

■ Castle and Bucket Set

(International Playthings $12.99 **oooo**) A castle-shaped bucket doubles as a mold and comes with a watering can, three stout digging tools, and sand/water mill. Everything but the sunblock for an afternoon at the beach! 3 & up. (800) 445-8347.

■ Hook, Line & Sprinkler 2005

(Little Tikes $13 **oooo**) Nemo-esque fish spin around a little starfish. Can be used in a stationary position for younger children. Turn the starfish, and now the sprinkler will spin and shoot water in different directions. Also new but disappointing, the **Ultimate Beach Ball Sprinkler** ($13 **oo**). Once you hook the ball up to the hose, you can't really kick it around. Testers gave this a thumbs down. (800) 321-0183.

Bubbles

Blowing bubbles has come a long way since the small plastic containers of pink liquid with the small, sticky wand. We recommend: **Little Kids' Super Size Bubble Wand** ($7.99 **oooo**) for super duper bubbles. (800) 545-5437. For a large group: The 12-piece **Bubble Party** (Battat $17 **oooo**) includes wands, trumpets, giant rings, and a waffle wand (enough pieces for nine kids!). (800) 247-6144 x280. 3 & up.

> **FREEBIE:** For superlarge bubbles, mix 1 cup of Dawn liquid detergent with 3 tablespoons of Karo syrup in 2½ quarts of cold water. Stir gently. Leftovers (if you have any) need to be refrigerated. Ideal for large groups.

Portable Pools and Sandboxes

See Toddlers chapter.

Active Physical Play

Active play builds preschoolers' big muscles, coordination, and confidence in themselves as able doers. It also establishes healthy active patterns for fitness, relieves stress, and provides a legitimate reason to run and shout. Agreeing on the rules of the game and taking turns promote important social and cooperative skills.

■ 2 in 1 Hitting Trainer Hit-a-Way Jr. *2005*

(Coop Kids $29.99 ●●●●) Our baseball players-in-training can work on their swing with the well-designed low-tech hitting machine. The ball is tethered so that you don't have to run after every hit. Be sure to load the base with water for added stability. (760) 931-5733. For a T-ball that also converts into a battery-operated hitting machine, our testers gave high marks to the new **Triple Hit Baseball** (Fisher-Price $25 ●●●●½). (800) 432-5437.

■ Crawl N Fun Blue Chip

(Playhut $25 ●●●●●) Testers giggled their way through this 6'-long tunnel as they crawled along! Also top rated: longer and more spacious **Yellow School Bus, Red Fire Engine,** and a blue **Deluxe Train** engine. These each easily accommodate two kids for pretend fun. 3 & up. (888) 752-9488.

■ Easy Score Basketball Set

(Little Tikes $29.99 & up ●●●●) Adjustable to six heights from 2½ to 4 feet, folds for storage, and has wheels for portability. Must be filled with sand to avoid tipping. 2½ & up. For big preschoolers consider the **Adjust & Jam** ($35 ●●●●), a hoop that starts at 4' and grows to 6'. (800) 321-0183.

■ Gertie Balls Blue Chip

(Small World $4 & up ●●●●●) Preschoolers need soft, lightweight, easy-to-catch balls that will not bend back a finger or hurt when they hit. Gertie Balls are gummy and soft enough for kids who may be scared of big heavy balls coming toward them. 3 & up. (800) 421-4153.

■ Hopping Sport Balls

(Franklin $14.99 each **oooo**) Our testers liked the sports theme of these classic 18" ball hoppers. Comes either as a basketball, baseball, or soccer ball. Comes with its own air pump. (800) 225-8647.

■ Learn 2 Inline Skates

(Fisher-Price $23.99 **oooo**) Older preschoolers are likely to want skates like their big sibs. These cleverly designed skates start as four-wheeled rollers that convert to inlines. There's a forward-only option for beginners. Worn over shoes, these grow from shoe sizes 8–13½ to 1–2. Our 4- and 7-year-old testers gave these a thumbs-up. Skaters should always wear helmets and knee, wrist, and elbow pads. They say 3, we'd say 4 & up. (800) 432-5437.

■ Mini Golf 2005

(Alex $19.99 **oooo**) Our four-year old testers thought this circus-themed miniature golf set was loads of fun. Comes with two clubs (with foam heads); two balls; and 6 illustrated targets. 3 & up. (800) 666-2539. For a basic plastic set of clubs, **TotSports Golf Set** (Little Tikes $20 **oooo**) comes with a pull cart, two clubs, and three balls. Says 2 & up; we'd say 4 & up. (800) 321-0183.

■ Super Sounds Soccer 2005

(Fisher-Price $29.99 **oooo**) Young soccer players will enjoy hitting the inflatable ball into the goal (approximately 2' tall x 3½' wide). You can adjust the target that yells "goal" when hit! Our experienced builder parent said this was a little tricky to put together. (800) 432-5437.

☞ **SAFETY TIP: Do little kids really need helmets? More than 500,000 people are treated annually in U.S. emergency rooms for bicycle-related injuries. Data shows very young riders incur a higher proportion of head injuries. A hel-**

met can reduce risk of head injury by up to 85%!

Wheel Toys: Trikes and Other Vehicles

Preschoolers will still use many of the vehicles featured in the Toddlers chapter. Vehicles with no pedals remain solid favorites. Older preschoolers are also ready for tricycles and kiddie cars with pedals. The battery-operated vehicles that go 5 mph look tempting, but they won't do anything for big-muscle action. Here's what to look for in a three-wheel drive with pedal action:

- Bigger is not better. Don't look for a trike to grow into. Take your child to the store to test-drive and find the right-size trike. Kids should be able to get on and off without assistance.
- Preschoolers need the security of a three-wheeler, which is more stable than a two-wheeler.
- A primary-colored bike can be reused by younger sibs regardless of their gender.
- See Safety Guidelines section for safety standards for helmets.

COMPARISON SHOPPER
Rocking Horses
2005 PLATINUM AWARD
(Mamas and Papas $99 & up ●●●●●)
Talk about classics, this is the year of the rocking horse! Whatever the size of your preschooler, there's a rocking horse that will fit. These are plush ponies with furry manes, tails, and leather saddles. For younger preschoolers, there's **Topaz** ($99/seat height 16") or **Acorn** ($169.99/seat height 19"). For the biggest rider, consider the gliding **Patches** ($299/seat height 26"). (310) 631-2222. Less pricey, but also very special, **Liberty** (Radio Flyer $120), a classic style spring rocker

with plastic horse, yarn mane, easy step up for mounting, and adjustable heights that grow as your child does. Was not ready for testing. (800) 621-7613.

■ Ultimate Family Trike

(Radio Flyer $99 & up ❍❍❍❍❍) While you can still buy an old-fashioned red trike from Radio Flyer, we recommend their new trike that looks more like Kettler's. Comes with a seatbelt and a rear "co-pilot" parent pushing bar that looks more like the back of a stroller (with a place for your drink!). PLATINUM AWARD '04. Testers thought it was easier to put together (and more maneuverable) than Huffy's **Canopy Trike** (❍❍❍). (800) 621-7613.

■ Scream Machine Jr.

(Razor $99 ❍❍❍❍❍) Remember your classic Big Wheels? Here's the updated version of that low-to-the-ground pedal toy. This year's new junior model is smaller, but just as much fun as last year's gleaming chrome version. We'd add a flag so vehicles can see riders low to the ground! PLATINUM AWARD '04. 4–8. (866) 467-2967.

■ Scrambler Pedal Coupe *2005*

(Step 2 $70 ❍❍❍❍½) Instead of a steering wheel, this innovative little front-wheel-drive pedal car has "center-pivot" steering in the handles on either side of the gender-free red vehicle. Kids use both arm and leg power. Designed with high seat back for support. 2½ and up. (800) 347-8372.

■ Kiddo Supertrike

(Kettler $80 ❍❍❍❍) This gender-proof primary-colored trike has a stroller bar and high back bucket seat (seat belt available), storage bin, and air-filled tires. Well built, this has an adjustable four-position frame for growth. Kettler trikes tend to run small and fit younger preschoolers only. (757) 427-2400.

■ Tikes Patrol Police Car

(Little Tikes $44.99 ❍❍❍❍❍) Kids will get great pretend mileage from this blue squad car with an electronic microphone that has seven different emergency siren sounds (which are mercifully quiet). PLATINUM AWARD '01. 2–5. (800) 321-0183.

Stand-Alone Climbers

■ Little Tikes Playground BLUE CHIP

(Little Tikes $480 ●●●●●) This top-of-the-line climber is part playhouse, part climber. It does not provide the kind of big-muscle climbing, dangling, and jumping that classic monkey bars do, but kids had no complaints. They loved the multiple play areas with mini-tunnel, slides, and platforms for imaginative play. Expensive, but a solid investment. 3 & up. (800) 321-0183. For other climbers, see Toddler chapter.

> **SHOPPING TIP:** Little Tikes suggests using a little liquid detergent or cooking oil on the connecting pieces of their toys if you are having difficulty putting them together.

Playhouses 2005

A playhouse is the ultimate toy for pretend that will be used for years of solo and social play. Kids as young as two love the magic of entering their own domain—being the owner of a space that's scaled to size. Children love opening and closing the door, looking out the windows, or playing with the toy kitchen (in some models). You'll find houses to fit a variety of tastes and budgets. We recommend Step 2's **Naturally Playful StoryBook Cottage** ($349.99 ●●●●) 64" high and done in simulated "stone and sandstone" colors to supposedly blend better with the backyard. There's plenty of space inside for several kids to play with the interior kitchenette. Step 2's 66" high **Welcome Home Playhouse** ($399.99 ●●●●) with skylight is designed for kids as old as 10. New for 2005, Little Tikes'

Pirate Ship ($115 ●○○○) just 49" high, is not ship-shape, but has porthole windows, steering wheel, and telescope. Or consider the **Magic Doorbell Playhouse,** just 46" high ($155.99 ●○○○) which has mail slot, working door, shutters, kitchen, and working doorbell, but will be outgrown. For grander housing, consider the **Playcenter Playhouse** ($450 ●○○○), a big 78" high with kitchen, bay window, deck, slide, and optional ($99.99) add-on swing set. We do not suggest Little Tikes' **ImagineSounds Interactive Playhouse** (●○) with motion sensors that trigger random messages such as "Open the windows!" or "Dinner's ready!" We think kids can do their own imagining! Little Tikes (800) 321-0183 / Step 2 (800) 347-8372.

■ **Megahouse**

(Playhut $39.99 ●○○○) This is one big fabric pop-up playhouse with a roll-up window and a doorway. Five feet tall and almost as wide, this is a big enough play setting for several kids to enjoy. Best suited for indoor use. A good gust of wind would send it flying! We couldn't put it back into its case. (888) 752-9488.

■ **My Playhouse/Theatre**

(Alex $200 ●○○○○) Here is imagination central! A giant 60" high combo playhouse, puppet stage, and store. Sure to be the focal point of any playroom, this sturdy wood-and-laminated play center is done in Maisy-like primary stripes and dots. It has a shelf for a puppet stage, side-window "ticket" office, front and back curtains, and a working door. The new version is now slightly larger, with fabric sides, but is still very sturdy. 3 & up. PLATINUM AWARD '00. (800) 666-2539.

> **FREEBIE:** For temporary indoor housing, don't overlook the charm of a big cardboard box with cutout windows and door or a tablecloth draped over a table for little campers

to use as a tent. A great way to overcome rainy-day cabin fever.

Art Supplies

Markers, crayons, chalk, clay, and paint provide different experiences, all of which invite kids to express ideas and feelings, explore color and shapes, and develop the muscles and control needed for writing and imagination. A supply of basics should include

Big crayons	**Washable markers**
Glue stick	**Safety scissors**
Finger-paint	**Colored construction paper**
Tempera paint	**Plain paper**
Molding material such as Play-Doh or plasticine	

Paints and Brushes

Tempera paint is ideal for young children because of its thick, opaque quality. Watercolors are more appropriate for school-aged children. Young children will have more success with thick brushes than skinny ones, which are harder to control. To reduce the number of spills, invest in paint containers sold with lids and openings just wide enough for a thick paintbrush. Buying paint in pint-sized squeeze bottles is more economical than buying small jars of paint that will dry out. Look for both nontoxic and washable labels on any art supplies you buy.

■ Crayola Color Wonder Paper & Markers

(Binney & Smith $8.99 **oooo**) Our 3-year-old tester couldn't get enough of making pictures "appear"! These are washable markers sans color to stain wallpaper and clothing! We prefer the open-ended paper to the coloring book so kids can make their own designs. Forget the new "magic" finger paints, they don't work well because they require more pressure than kids can exert. 2 & up. (800) 272-9652.

■ Colossal Barrel of Crafts

(Creativity Street $39.99 ooooo) Like a giant jar of treats in an old-fashioned candy store, this huge plastic jar has a mammoth supply of pom-poms, craft sticks, beads and string, foam shapes, pipe cleaners, googly eyes, glitter, metallic spangles, cutters, and plasticine. Add glue, scissors, and imagination for many crafty sessions! 4–8. PLATINUM AWARD '02. (800) 621-1261.

■ Finger Painting Party *2005*

(Alex $20 oooo½) Roll up those sleeves and get ready to make squiggles, swirls, and other delicious patterns with the tools that come in this bucket with six jars of fingerpaint. Assorted tools with chunky handles add new dimensions to the messy whole-hand fun of finger-paints! Also fun, **Collage Party** (oooo). 3 & up. (800) 666-2539.

> **SMART PARENT TRICK:** Painting with straws is a great outdoor game. Take a large piece of construction paper and pour puddles of tempera paint on the paper. Preschoolers love blowing the paint with a straw to create their own designs. Or take an easel outside for painting the great outdoors!

■ Sir Steps-A-Lot *2005*

(imadethat $39.99 oooo) These carpentry kits are just right for parents that aren't particularly handy! The step-by-step instructions are clear and the small wooden hammer is just right for kids to use. Maybe they'll even brush their teeth longer if they stand on a step stool that they make. Also, **Mr. Feet Table** ($49.99 oooo) will be just right for snacks and artwork, and you won't mind having it in your house. Paints sold separately. (877) 804-8004.

> **SMART PARENT TRICK: Magic Painting** is great fun. Have child draw on paper with a piece of wax

or a white crayon. Then water down a bit of tempera and have child paint over invisible drawing. Abracadabra! The drawing appears!

Easels

A flat table may still be easier for young preschoolers, since the colors won't run. Older preschoolers are better able to adjust the amount of paint they load on brushes, and many enjoy painting at an easel. Avoid watering down paint; thicker paint is easier to control. Having an easel set up makes art materials accessible whenever the mood moves young artists.

Plastic Easels

Depending on your space and needs, the following are top-rated choices: **Double Easel** (Little Tikes $50 ●●●○) This bright red easel has a chalkboard on one side and a large clip that holds a pad of 17" x 20" paper on the other. (800) 321-0183. **Easel for 2** (Step 2 $35 ●●●●○) has a chalkboard on one side and a dry-erase board on the other. (800) 347-8372.

Wooden Easels BLUE CHIP

Tabletop Easel (Alex $40 ●●●●●) If floor space is tight, consider a sturdy dual-sided tabletop hardwood easel with four-place paint-cup holder, 16" x 18" magnetic erase-board and painting surface, and a chalkboard on reverse side. Folds flat for convenient storage. PLATINUM AWARD '98. (800) 666-2539.

Modeling Materials

These totally pliable, unstructured materials invite kids to use their hands and imagination to shape something from nothing. Fun for pounding, stretching, kneading, and rolling—three-dimensional experiences that preschoolers love. Older preschoolers may name what they make after the event. Few set out to design something. The focus here is on the process, and not on making something realistic. Some of our favorite materials:

■ Dough Party

(Alex $17 ●●●●) Comes in a see-through canister with six bright colors, a roller, cutters, plus a mat to work on. If you prefer clay, consider their **Clay & Play Party** ($17). 4–7. (800) 666-2539.

■ Crayola Model Magic Bucket

(Binney and Smith $16.99 ●●●●) Our toy testers love working with model magic for school projects and just playing around. We recommend the bucket that comes with four 8-oz. packages. Our testers were not impressed with this year's flower making and jewelry Model Magic sets. 2 & up. (800) 272-9652.

■ Play-Doh Fuzzy Friends Farm *2005*

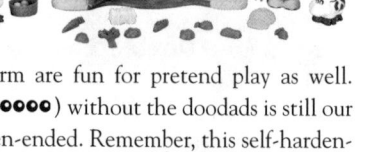

(Hasbro $9.99 ●●●●½) Play-Doh is one of those products you either love or hate as a parent. We are long-time fans—the product can be used to build hand strength, and small pretend settings like this new farm are fun for pretend play as well. **Classic Play-Doh** ($2 & up ●●●●●) without the doodads is still our favorite since it is the most open-ended. Remember, this self-hardening dough dries out if left uncovered. 3 & up. (800) 327-8264.

> **FREEBIE:** Cookie cutters, rolling pins, baby-bottle rings, and other items around your kitchen make great tools for molding clay.

Music and Movement

Many instruments for children have such poor sound quality it's hard to call them musical. Kids at this stage are not ready for reading notation. It's more an exploration of sound and rhythm and movement that makes good sense for preschoolers. You'll find some here and other good choices in the Audio chapter.

■ LP RhythmMix Egghead Family

(International Playthings $5.50 each ●●●●½) Each wooden egghead family member makes a slightly different sound when you clack their mouths open and shut. Great fun for keeping the beat. (888) 576-8742.

■ **Lollipop Drum** Bʟᴜᴇ Cʜɪᴘ

(Woodstock Percussion $25 ❍❍❍❍❍) Preschoolers can easily hold on to the handle of this lollipop-shaped drum. Makes a pleasing sound, according to both kid and parent testers. Still top rated, **Maracas Shakers** ($5.00 ❍❍❍❍), small maracas with great sound and perfect fit for little hands. (800) 422-4463.

■ **RainBoMaker**

(Small World Toys $10 ❍❍❍❍) A see-through plastic "rainstick" with colorful beads that make a soothing sound. Or shake it for a maraca-like sound. 3 & up. (800) 421-4153.

SMART PARENT TRICK: Use drum to beat out someone's first name. For example, Sa-man-tha would get three beats. Take turns guessing whose name is being clanged.

Preschool Furniture Basics

Table and Chairs

These convenient pieces of basic gear will be used for artwork, puzzles, tea parties, and even lunch. You'll find many choices in both plastic and wood. This is a decorating choice as well as a functional one. **Super Art Table** Pʟᴀᴛɪɴᴜᴍ Aᴡᴀʀᴅ '04 (Alex $179.99 ❍❍❍❍❍) is an oval table outfitted with a roll of paper for painting, a chalkboard center, and wells for supplies, and comes with two long stools. For a smaller round table with same style, consider **My First Table** (Alex $100 ❍❍❍❍½). 3 & up. (800) 666-2539.

Best Travel Toys

Preschoolers can entertain themselves for short periods of time with toys and art supplies. A well-loved soft doll or minisetting with multiple pieces make for cozy pretend play. At this stage, a piece of home, whether it's a toy or a blanket, is still important. One of the best ways to make time fly is to bring along a tape player with favorite songs or stories to enjoy. For restaurant stops, pack a plastic baggy filled with simple games, cards, or crayons and paper to fill time before the breadbasket arrives. Bring along a handful of paperbacks to share and for independent "reading." Here are some of our favorites:

■ Travel Toy Tote *2005*

(Alex $24.99 ●●●●) If your child is at the stage where Hot Wheels, Bendos, and crayons are littering the backseat, then this tote will come in handy. Outside pockets are great for cups and paperback books and other must-have take-alongs. (800) 666-2539.

■ Color Pixter *2005* PLATINUM AWARD

(Fisher-Price $84.99 ●●●●●) A hand-held, no-mess art platform that allows kids to create countless combinations of designs with the easy-to-use stylus on the touch-sensitive back-lit screen. Far superior, in terms of graphics, to its black-and-white predecessor. Our testers found the graphics on the new **Pocket Pixters** ($14.99 ●●●) disappointing in comparison. (800) 432-5437.

■ Construction Activity Pack *2005*

(Lauri $14.99 ●●●●) Loaded for dramatic play with lacing and tracing figures; workers and tools; 20 stringing pieces, dump truck, roadway and sawhorses. Plenty of activity here for developing fine motor skills along with pretend play. Also top rated, **Fire & Rescue** or **Space Odyssey Pack.** 4–7. (800) 451-0520.

■ Doodle Pro *2005*

(Fisher-Price $14 ●●●●½) A no-mess magnetic drawing tool that works just like the Magna Doodle. Tied-on "pen" and shapes are perfect for drawing, tic-tac-toe, and even writing letters and numbers. Also available in smaller travel model ($8). 3 & up. (800) 432-5437. (Works much better than the new **Etch A Sketch Draw 'n' Go** (Ohio Art ●●). Stick with the original **Etch A Sketch** for the next age group.)

■ Feltkids 2005

(RC2/Learning Curve $16.99 ●●●●) New for 2005, **Kickin' It,** a multicultural girls soccer team ready for story telling pretend, is Still top rated, **Jumpin' Gymnasts** (with a multicultural team), **Madeline Shopping in Paris,** and **My Pet Vet Feltboards.** A good quiet choice for the car. (800) 704-8697.

■ Groovy Girl Backpack

(Manhattan Toy $50 ●●●●) Designed to carry five dolls and all of their clothes for on-the-go doll play. Our tester thought it was "amazing" and liked the wild groovy-licious colors. We liked the soft straps that won't cut into little shoulders. The cardboard **Groovy Girl Trunk** ($25 ●●) got lower marks because the closure is hard to work. (800) 541-1345.

■ Woodkins 2005

(Pamela Drake $11.95–$25 ●●●●) These wooden "paper" dolls come with fabric choices that stay in place with a "frame" that lifts and closes over the edge of the doll. New for 2005, a charming collection of fairies to dress in gossamer and glittery fabrics plus a necklace for the "designer." Perfect for quiet pretend time. 4 & up. (800) 966-3762.

Best Third and Fourth Birthday Gifts for Every Budget

Big Ticket $100 Plus	**Set of wooden blocks, trains, playhouse,** or **dollhouse** (various makers), **table and chairs**

$100 & under	**Wooden train set or easel** (various makers) or **Huggable Madeline** (RC2/Learning Curve) or **Ultimate Family Trike** (Radio Flyer) or **Color Pixter** (Fisher-Price)
Under $75	**Lila** (Corolle) or **Leapster** (LeapFrog) or **Stroller** (American Girl) or **Supersized Groovy Girl** (Manhattan Toy)
Under $50	**Train Accessories** (various makers) or **Mr. Feet Table** (imadethat)
Under $40	**Colossal Barrel of Crafts** (Creativity Street) or **Pretend & Play Teaching Telephone** (Learning Resources) or **Sir Steps-A-Lot** (imadethat)
Under $25	**Collapsing Bridge** (Brio) or **Pretend & Play Doctor Set** (Learning Resources) or **Letter Factory Game** (LeapFrog) or **Lollipop Drum** (Woodstock Percussion)
Under $20	**Cranium CariBoo** (Cranium) or **Pin the Tail on the Donkey** (eeBoo) or **Richard Scarry's Busy House** (Mudpuppy Press)
Under $15	**Lego Duplo Block-o-Dile** (Lego Systems) or **Rugged Riggz** (Little Tikes) or **Madeline** (RC2/Learning Curve)
Under $10	**Bendos** (Kid Galaxy) or **Birthday Cake Puzzle** (Lauri) or **Model Magic** or **Color Wonder Paper** (Crayola) or **Super Size Bubble Wand** (Little Kids)
Under $5	**Gertie Ball** (Small World Toys) or **Hot Wheels Cars** (Mattel)

4 • Early School Years
Five to Ten Years

What to Expect Developmentally

Learning Through Play. During the early school years, as children begin their formal education, play continues to be an important path to learning. Now more-complex games, puzzles, and toys offer kids satisfying ways to practice and reinforce the new skills they are acquiring in the classroom.

Dexterity and Problem-Solving Ability. School-age kids have the dexterity to handle more-elaborate building toys and art materials. They are curious about how things work and take pride in making things that can be used for play or displayed with pride.

Active Group Play. These early school years are a very social time when kids long for acceptance among their peers. Bikes and sporting equipment take on new importance as the social ticket to being one of the kids. Children try their hand at more-formal team sports where being an able player is a way of belonging.

Independent Discovery. Although these are years when happiness is being with a friend, children also enjoy and benefit from solo time. Many of the products selected here are good tools for such self-sufficient and satisfying skills.

BASIC GEAR CHECKLIST FOR
EARLY SCHOOL AGE

✓ Sports equipment   ✓ Dolls/soft animals
✓ Craft kits   ✓ Board games
✓ Musical instruments   ✓ Tape player and tapes
✓ Water paints, markers, stampers
✓ Two-wheeler with training wheels
✓ Lego and other construction sets
✓ Electronic game/learning machines

🚫 Toys to Avoid

These toys pose safety hazards:

✓ Chemistry sets that can cause serious accidents
✓ Plug-in toys that heat up with lightbulbs and can give
   kids serious burns
✓ Audio equipment with volume controls that cannot be
   locked
✓ Projectile toys such as darts, rockets, B-B guns, or other
   toys with flying parts that can do serious damage
✓ Superpowered water guns that can cause abrasions
✓ Toys with small parts if there are young children in
   the house

The following is developmentally inappropriate:

✓ An abundance of toys that reinforce gender stereotypes;
   for example, hair play for girls and gunplay for boys

Pretend Play

School-age kids have not outgrown the
joys of pretending. They like elaborate
and realistic props for stepping into the
roles of storekeeper, athlete, or racing-
car driver. For some, minisettings
such as puppet theaters, dollhouses, and
castles are a preferable route to make-believe. This is also the
age when collecting miniature vehicles and action figures can
become a passion. Such figures generally reflect the latest car-
toon or movie feature. Nobody needs all the pieces, although

many kids want them all. At this stage, owning a few pieces of the hottest "in" character represents a way of belonging.

Dollhouses, Castles, and Other Pretend Environments and Props

Kids are ready now for finer details in house and furnishings. Specialty dollhouse shops and craft stores sell prefabs and custom houses for all budgets. Some of the settings recommended here require construction skills and adult involvement. For simpler dollhouses, see Preschool chapter.

■ **Zoo** *2005* **PLATINUM AWARD**

(Playmobil $66.99 ●●●●○) Playmobil structures are great parent/child projects with plenty of pretend play down the road, but make no mistake: an adult must do a great deal of the building. Our tester gave high marks to the new **Zoo** that took a long time to build but has plenty of play value. For construction-minded kids, check out the incredible large **Crane** *2005* **PLATINUM AWARD** ($69.99 ●●●●●) that moves up, down, and around! One of the coolest toys of the year. The new **Noah's Ark** ($66.99 ●●●●○) is also special. Previous award-winning **Airport** ($49.99 ●●●●●) and **Fire Station** ($64.99 ●●●●●) have been scaled down in price and size. Add-ons include **Fire Chief's Car** and, as a sign of the times, a **HAZMAT Crew.** 5 & up. (800) 752-9662.

> **PLAY TIP:** Build these large structures on a board or table that they can remain on. Moving them later is an impossible dream!

COMPARISON SHOPPER
Dollhouses

Madeline's Dollhouse (RC2/Learning Curve $99.99 ●●●●○) has been remodeled, with a much more attractive

price tag, too. Scaled for the 8"
poseable doll, comes with working
doorbell and light. The furnishings
are all très jolie! 4 & up. Platinum
Aware '04. (800) 704-8697.
Playmobil's **Family Vacation
House** ($49.99 oooo), smaller
than other houses, relatively easy to
put together. Playmobil's **Modern House** ($119.99 oo) did
not test well; the roof collapses easily! (800) 752-9662. See
Preschool chapter, p. 74 for other dollhouses.

■ Castle of Morcia 2005 PLATINUM AWARD

(Lego Systems $89.99/632 pieces ooooo) If all things medieval
intrigue your builder, bring home this satisfying new
castle from the new Knights' Kingdom series. Each
component fits onto a plastic base, there are
lots of moving pieces, and as our tester com-
mented: "just a lot of pieces—but it wasn't
hard!" There's also a new **Hogwarts
Castle** ($89.99/928 pieces oooo), "smaller
than the original." "Neat, the way you
build several towers that then connect."
Experienced testers found it difficult to
make the wind-up motor for the clock tower
work, but gave overall high marks (they
especially like the moving staircases). Also
a hit, the **Knight Bus** ($29.99/ 242 pieces
oooo), straight out of the pages of Book 3.
8–12. (800) 233-8756.

Props for Pretend
See Preschool chapter for this year's best costumes.

■ My Picnic Basket

(Alex $20 oooo) We liked the sturdiness of this 18-
piece set that comes with blue enamelware including plates, cups, spoons, forks, and tablecloth.
Great for real picnics or pretend tea parties.
Also, **Play Bakeware** (Alex $20 oooo),

now updated with stainless steel pots and pans. (800) 666-2539.

■ Soccer Guys 2005

(Kaskey Kids $14.99 ○○○○) If you're looking for non-violent action figures that your child will love, look no further! Here's a truly satisfying kit that comes with 24 players, one referee, two goals, and a generous green felt 24" x 36" playmat. We like the fact that there are no directions, leaving the play up to your child's imagination. Hooray! (Or should we say, "Goooooal!") Football set also available. (866) 527-5437.

■ Super Saver Teaching Bank 2005 PLATINUM AWARD

(LeapFrog $19.99 ○○○○○) What we loved about this interactive bank is that your child can set a saving goal. The bank helps keep track of how far you've gone in reaching that goal. As you add coins, it identifies them by name and gives a running total. An engaging way of becoming familiar with coins and their value. 4–8. (800) 701-5327.

■ Teaching Cash Register

(Learning Resources $44.95 ○○○○○) A clever way to combine math skills with pretend play! When kids play store with this smart new register they learn to use a calculator, make change, use coupons and charge cards, and even check the customer's credit! It has a pretend scale plus a three-level coin game that asks kids to deposit specific amounts. The screen tallies and kids press enter to self-correct. PLATINUM AWARD '04. (800) 800-7893.

Dolls

Now's the time when girls often get heavily invested in dolls with tons of paraphernalia. Although 5- and 6-year-old boys often find ways to play with a cousin's or sister's doll or dollhouse, they are more likely to choose action figures for this kind of play. Both boys and girls continue to enjoy soft stuffed animals, the zanier the better.

For many years, the only kinds of dolls around were blonde with blue eyes but, happily, more manufacturers today are creating dolls that reflect our cultural diversity. Here are some of the best:

■ American Girl Nellie O'Malley
2005 PLATINUM AWARD

(American Girl $84 ●●●●○) The company alternates each year between historic dolls and current dolls. This year, they introduce Samantha's best friend, Nellie. With a big blue bow in her strawberry blonde hair and a white dress with matching blue sash, she's the image of an Irish girl of 1906. Her story focuses on her promise to care for her younger sisters when her mother dies. Still top rated, **Kaya,** the first Native American doll from the Nez Perce people in the collection. PLATINUM AWARD '03. 7 & up. (800) 845-0005.

■ Hopscotch Hill School Gwen **2005**

(American Girl $48 ●●●●○) Gwen, a soccer player with long braids and dressed for the game, is the newest addition to the Hopscotch collection of dolls (and books) targeted at girls just beginning school. Unlike the American Girl collection, these multicultural dolls are bendable. The books address school-related issue (e.g., sharing, handwriting). The books are not "beginner" readers, but for independent readers (or as read-alouds). PLATINUM AWARD '04. (800) 845-0005.

■ Les Cheries **2005**

(Corolle $36 each ●●●●○) These 14" dolls are marketed as "best friend" dolls and are purposefully not fashion dolls; they are meant to look like girls of today. PLATINUM AWARD '03. New for **2005** , a new **Camille** with locks of hair to style. Think Olson twins before they discovered make-up. Still top rated, **Les Mini Corollines** BLUE CHIP ($22 each ●●●●○), a group of 8" blonde, brunette, Asian, and African American dolls. 4–8. (800) 668-4846.

Puppets and Puppet Stages

Puppets provide an excellent way for kids to develop the language and storytelling skills that are the underpinning of reading and writing. Kids who can tell a story have less trouble writing a story. Many of the puppets and stages in the Preschool chapter will get lots of mileage now. Older kids may also become interested in marionettes or making shadow, stick, or hand puppets of their own.

■ Royal Treatment Theatre Set 📏*2005*

(Manhattan Toy $35 ●●●●) A royal blue brick velour table-top stage has a foldout platform on which finger puppets can perform. New for *2005*, **Puppettos Theatre Stage** (same idea but done in teal with a red curtain—not our favorite color combo, but that's a personal preference). New puppets include **Metropolicity Community** worker types, **Birthday Belles,** and, still wonderful, **Royal Rumpus Finger Puppets.** 4 & up. (800) 541-1345.

■ Puppet Palace

(Reprint Mint $100 ●●●●) Built for hand puppets or marionettes, this wooden 42" x 36" tabletop theater is laminated with graphics and has six backdrops and a curtain that hides stand-up puppeteers. A handsome choice for 7 & up. (888) 440-6468.

Favorite Hand Puppets

■ Emergency Rescue Squad Puppets BLUE CHIP

(Learning Resources $19.95 set of 4 ●●●●●) Multicultural workers—doctor, paramedic, police officer, and firefighter—with vinyl heads and cloth bodies. 4 & up. (888) 800-7893.

■ Border Collie Puppy

(Folkmanis $36 ●●●●½) Black and white with long silky fur on underside, jowls, and tail, this is a huggable full-body puppet with sweet face and mouth that moves. Still charming, a 30" honey-colored **Golden**

Retriever ($60 ❍❍❍❍) or an amazing **Great Horned Owl** ($50 ❍❍❍❍) with moving head and eyes that close. (800) 654-8922.

■ Costumals

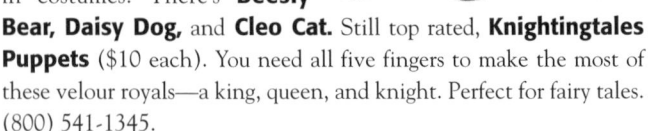

(Manhattan Toy $10 each ❍❍❍❍) It's hard not to play with these animals dressed up in costumes. There's **Beesly Bear, Daisy Dog,** and **Cleo Cat.** Still top rated, **Knightingtales Puppets** ($10 each). You need all five fingers to make the most of these velour royals—a king, queen, and knight. Perfect for fairy tales. (800) 541-1345.

■ Sew & Decorate Lacing Puppets 2005

(Lauri $4.99 & up ❍❍❍❍½) Choose from a variety of precut felt puppets, such as a green witch, bunnies, bugs, or circus animals. New for **2005**, a big **Fairy Fantasy Set** with six precut hand puppets and one finger puppet. Kids lace them up and use them for storytelling. Kits come with yarn and big plastic needle for sewing (which develops fine-motor skills kids need for writing). 5 & up. (800) 451-0520.

Electric Train Sets

Many train buffs will tell you that this is the stage when their romance with trains began. Select HO gauge for beginners. Smaller tracks can be frustrating to put together. Larger-gauge sets take up a tremendous amount of space, so you generally end up with just a boring circle of track. *Safety note:* Since trains are plug-in electrical items, they are labeled for 8 & up. Younger children may enjoy them, but only with adult supervision.

Remote Control Cars and Other Vehicles

■ Mgears Remote Control Racers
2005 PLATINUM AWARD

(Learning Resources $29.95 ❍❍❍❍❍) Our testers liked the speed they got with this 213 piece **Grand Prix Racer.** The base comes with the wheels already on (last year we had trouble getting the wheels on!). "The directions sometimes have too many steps in them—they should be more like Lego's." "It really works, the gears move when you make the car go." "Much better than last year's tethered remote control; it goes much faster too." 7 & up. (888) 800-7893.

■ **Tyco R/C RollCage** *2005* PLATINUM AWARD

(Mattel $49.99 ●●●●○) Our testers gave this RC the highest mark for flip-ability and maneuverability. The body and four chunky wheels are surrounded by a cage that allows the car to do pretty amazing flips. 8 & up. The **Terrain Twister** ($64.99 ●●●) "looks cool with the corkscrew pontoons, but it's hard to make it go forward." The new **Tyco R/C Stuntsters Air Rebound** (Mattel $19.99 ●●●●½) is a really amazing mini-version of the 2003 PLATINUM AWARD-winner. 5 & up. (800) 545-2557. Also in the trend of mini-RCs, **Nascar 1/64 scale** (Jakks Pacific $24 ●●●●), where the "helmet" is the charger. (800) 545-2557.

■ **Erector Vehicles** *2005*

(Brio $25–$200) One tester told us that the starter set was hard but "awesome" while another said it was "way too frustrating." That's how it is with Erector sets—you either love 'em or you don't. That said, your best bet is to try a smaller "starter" set. **Design Set 1** (●●●½) builds three different motorcycles and tested better than last year's small models. New for *2005*, **Design Radio Controlled 4x4 Truck** ($100/618 pieces) is the first remote-controlled Erector vehicle. Builds three models with a 9.6V motor. For advanced builders, **Renault Formula 1 Car** ($200/809 pieces). Both looked promising, but were not ready for testing. 10 & up. (888) 274-6869.

■ **Robosapien** *2005* PLATINUM AWARD

(WowWee $99 ●●●●●) Our eleven-year-old testers were thrilled with this programmable 14"-high black-and-white robot that walks, dances, picks up and tosses objects, and delivers karate chops! Not designed for instantaneous gratification—there's a manual that involves reading and thinking to make things happen. Marked 6 & up, we'd say better for 9 & up. (514) 344-1250.

Construction Toys

What Kids Learn from Construction Toys

Builders learn to follow directions and develop dexterity, problem-solving skills, and stick-to-itiveness. Success is not always instant. Updated classics such as **Lincoln Logs** and **Tinkertoys** are more appropriate for this age even though they are labeled for preschoolers. **Glueless Snap Models** are also a good place to start for beginning model builders.

What You Should Know Before You Buy:

As their dexterity develops, kids can handle smaller pieces and more-complex building sets.

A variety of building sets is better than just one because building with Legos and K'nex, for example, involve different, but equally valuable, skills.

Open-ended sets that can be built in multiple ways are a great place to start. As your child becomes a more confident builder, move on to small models.

Age labels on most building sets are not accurate. If the box says 5 & up and your 5-year-old needs a lot of assistance, the problem is with the label and not your child.

Working on one of these sets together can be rewardinga plus. Be careful not to take over; break the project into doable parts to build confidence.

Less can be more, which is helpful to keep in mind. Start with smaller doable sets that help your child to learn particular building strategies.

Girls as well as boys need to develop spatial/visual skills that are built into construction toys.

■ **Big Air Ball Tower** **2005** **PLATINUM AWARD**

(K'nex $99.99 ○○○○○) The wow-wee set of the season, this ball run is over five feet tall when completed (which will require some adult assistance). Comes with more than 1350 pieces, so not for the meek builders! Four D batteries power the fan that propels the plastic balls through a maze of tubing, and traditional K'nex pieces! A fun parent–child project for those who love to build. 10 & up. (800) 543-5639.

■ B.C. Bones Empire State Building

(Toysmith $19.99 & up ●●●●) Our office is decorated with these stunning wooden structures that include the Eiffel Tower and Golden Gate Bridge. Our complaint with these beautiful sets is that there are no clear directions. The company insists that they make "puzzles," not construction sets. We suggested they put a cheat sheet up on their website. Still recommended, their **Wooden Prehistoric Animal Models** ($30 & up ●●●●). Good parent–child projects. 9 & up. (800) 356-0474.

■ Blocks & Marbles BLUE CHIP

(Tedco $30 & up ●●●●●) There's no right or wrong way to build this open-ended marble run with wooden blocks, ramps, and chutes. (800) 654-6357.

■ Coast Watch HQ *2005*

(Lego Systems $49.99/360 pieces ●●●●) There are a lot of building and pretend possibilities with this coast control base that comes with a landing pad, control tower, boat, helicopter, and two figures. Extensions to the World City line include a police center, cargo lift, airport, and train. The new **NHL Lego sets** (●●●) did not test as well as the previous sports themes—"it's difficult to actually work the players once you're done building." (800) 223-8756.

■ Erector Landmarks of the World Set *2005*

(Brio $130 ●●●) Builds a wow-wee version of either the **Empire State Building, Eiffel Tower,** or **Tower Bridge.** Comes with 1539 pieces. Looked stunning but frustrated our experienced builders. (888) 274-6869.

■ Gears! Gears! Gears! BLUE CHIP

(Learning Resources $20/$40 ●●●●●) These open-ended sets develop problem-solving skills as kids make their own moving machines with plastic gears. Our testers preferred the big set of gears to many of the newer themed sets. 5 & up. (888) 800-7893.

■ Lincoln Logs BLUE CHIP

(K'nex $29.99 & up ●●●●●) Good news! Formerly splintery Lincoln Logs are gone! Keep in mind, building log houses requires visual discrimination and dexterity. Testers loved the **Commemorative Edition** with 115 pieces in a giant tin, PLATINUM AWARD '02. The new themed sets with plenty of plastic roofs and figures are just not the same (●●●). Most 4s can't do these—save for old 5s, 6s, & 7s. (800) 543-5639.

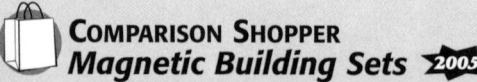

COMPARISON SHOPPER
Magnetic Building Sets **2005**

We love these open-ended magnetic sets. Put one on the coffee table and everyone will take a turn! Shop around because we found prices do vary. There are three main companies vying to attract your magnetic dollars. You won't go wrong with any of them: **Magz-x 106** (Progressive Trading $32.95 ●●●●) Our testers gave high marks to this set because of the plastic Xs that give builders more flexibility. Set comes with 106 pieces (25 Xs, 28 bars, and 53 steel balls). 5 & up.

(800) 903-6249. **Geomag** (Ekos $20 & up ●●●●) comes with straight magnetic rods in different colors and steel balls. New for **2005**, **Geomag Panel** kits were interesting at first, but not as open-ended as the classic sets. (888) 450-9858. **Supermag** (Plastwood $24.99 ●●●●) Testers also liked working with these (the rods are thinner and more tapered at the ends than Geomag). We recommend the colorful 50-piece sets. New model sets sound promising but were not ready for testing. (800) 770-9550.

■ **Prehistoric Creatures** and **Titan XP** *2005*
(Lego Systems $29.99/719 pieces ●●●○)
The large red **T-Rex** that you can build with this set is "amazing looking." Our experienced builders warned: "It's very delicate and could break easily." Set comes with instructions for 10 creatures. Marked 7 & up, we'd say more like 9 & up. About **Titan XP** ($49.99/782 pieces ●●●○) from the same series, our tester wrote "wow, there are a lot of pieces!" Builds a 14"-tall creature that swivels at the waist—but he too is very fragile. (800) 223-8756.

Games

Classic and New Games

Now's the time when kids really begin to enjoy playing games with rules, with both friends and family. Of course, winning is still more fun than losing, and playing by the rules isn't always easy. That's the bad news. The good news is that many of the best board games are both entertaining and educational. Many games can improve math, spelling, memory, and reading skills in a more enjoyable way than with the old flash card/extra workbook routine. Game playing also builds important cooperative social skills.

For 5s and 6s, now's the time for classic Blue Chip games such as:

Parcheesi	**Dominoes**	**Chutes and Ladders**
Checkers	**I Spy Bingo Lotto**	**Pick-up-Sticks**
Uno	**Trouble**	**What's My Name?**
Connect 4	**Lite-Brite**	

For 7s, 8s, and up, try classics such as

Battleship Bingo	**Boggle**	**Chess**
Chinese Checkers	**Clue**	**Life**
Othello	**Mancala**	**Pictionary Jr.**
Monopoly Jr.	**Scrabble**	**Scattergories Junior**
Sorry	**Twister**	**Upwards Quarto!**
Yahtzee		

■ Addictionary

(International Playthings $19.99 ●●●●●) Players add letter cards to the innovative expandable card-holder to create new words. Cards have different point values; the challenge is to use all your letters and score the highest number of points. 2–4 players. 8 & up. PLATINUM AWARD '04. (800) 445-8347.

■ Rumis *2005*

(Educational Insights $29.95 ●●●●½) A three-dimensional strategy game where the object is to place your three-dimensional blocks on the board in such a way as to have the most showing from above. Of course your opponents are there to block you! More challenging to play than last year's award-winning **Blokus** ($29.95 ●●●●●), which is played with flat pieces. While even younger players enjoyed Blokus, Rumis will most likely appeal only to the 10 and up crowd. (800) 995-4436.

■ Balloon Lagoon *2005* PLATINUM AWARD

(Cranium $19.99 ●●●●●) Turn on the musical merry-go-round timer as players take turns fishing for magnetized letters to spell a word, spin wheels to get four parts of an animal lined up, collect matching dice as they fall through the roof of the snack hut, or "tiddly-wink" four frogs into the pond. The first to collect 15 mini balloons is the winner. A lively game that's fun and develops sequencing, dexterity, matching, and simple spelling skills. 5 & up. Still top rated, **Cranium Cadoo for Kids** ($19.99 ●●●●●): in order to win, players must draw, act out, use clay, and retrieve objects from around the house. 7 & up. PLATINUM AWARD '02. (877) 272-6486.

■ 4-Way Spelldown! *2005* PLATINUM AWARD

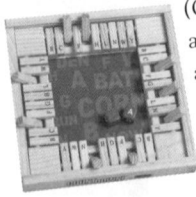

(Cadaco $19.99 ●●●●●) Roll the two "letter" dice and try to make a word with the letters thrown and as many of the 10 letter keys on the playing board. For example, if you roll a "t" and an "o," and you have a "y" and an "s," you can spell "toys." The first to flip all of their keys wins. Marked 6 & up, but we'd say more like 8 and up. (800) 621-5426.

■ Gobblet Junior 2005

(Blue Orange Games $19.95 ●●●●●) This junior edition of PLATINUM AWARD '03 winner is just as much fun. The object is to be the first player to have three gobblets in a row, as in Tic Tac Toe. But beware, you can capture the spot with a larger gobblet! PLATINUM AWARD '04. For an easy color memory game, consider **Maask** ($19.95 ●●●●). (415) 572-3885.

■ Harry Potter Championship Quidditch Game 2005

(Mattel $24.99 ●●●) Our testers wanted to love this two-person electronic version of Harry Potter's favorite sport, Quidditch. Unfortunately, this beautifully designed game does not work very well. The balls often get jammed, it's difficult to hear the voice announcing the score, and the Golden Snitch that pops out into the air freaked out many of our testers! 8 & up. (800) 524-8697.

■ I Spy Word Scramble 2005

(Briarpatch $19.99 ●●●●) This has a big game board with sliding tiles. Players take turns drawing a card, choosing a letter or image on the card, and spelling that word by sliding letters before the timer runs out. Challenging fun for 7 & up. (800) 232-7427.

■ Lego Builder Xtreme 2005

(Rose Art $19.99 ●●●●) An updated version of a game our testers enjoyed very much. Designed for 2–4 players, the object is to be the first to construct your Lego vehicle which you do by collecting pieces as you make your way around the gameboard. 7 & up. Comes with 118 Lego pieces. (800) 447-2151.

■ Operation Shrek 2005

(Milton Bradley $16.99 ●●●●) If you were an "Operation" fan when you were a kid, you won't be disappointed with the Shrek update. Instead of retrieving just your regular body parts, you're after earwax and humongous fungus! As with the original, the player who collects the most money for successful operations, wins. 6 & up. (888) 836-7025.

■ Who? What? Where? 2005 PLATINUM AWARD

(Pazow $29.95 ●●●●●) Each player takes a *who*, *what*, and *where* card, which asks that you draw a certain image—Abraham Lincoln, fishing, in Paris, for example. Players get points for guessing each other's drawings. A fun family game. Marked 12 & up, but our 10-year-old testers had a great time. (650) 341-8256.

■ Word for Word Game

(Learning Resources $29.95 ●●●●) Here's a fun word game for mixed ages. Players take five different letter rods. Start the two-minute timer and combine rods making as many words as you can. Time's up! Write down your words. Now swap play pieces with the person sitting next to you—how many words can you each get? The person with the most words wins! A fun combination of *Boggle* and *Scrabble* with a hands-on experience in phonics. 7 & up. New for 2005, **Take Four** ($24.95 ●●●●), A fast-paced crossword-style game with Scrabble-like tiles. Marked 8 & up, we'd say more like 10 & up! (888) 800-7893.

Top-Rated Card Games

Aside from a deck of cards for a fierce game of Rummy, War, or Old Maid, don't overlook deck-specific classics such as **Uno** or **Mille Bourne.** Here are other card games to play that are fun and quick and even have some learning power built in:

■ MixMatch Game

(NonViolent Toys $14.99 ●●●●) A simple matching game with a twist that develops language (knowing and naming animals), as well as visual matching skills. 50 animal cards are placed on the game board and kids can play solo or with other players to find pairs diagonally, horizontally, or vertically. Once the initial pairs are removed, some strategy is needed to move cards to make further pairs. 5 & up. (866) 688-8697.

■ There's a Moose in the House
2005 PLATINUM AWARD

(Gamewright $9.99 ●●●●●) One of the most innovative card games we've played in years. The cards have pictures of empty rooms, doors, and moose in the same rooms. The object is to place as many moose as possible in your opponents' house of cards. The player with the fewest moose at the end of the game, wins. Easy to learn and a lot of fun to play! 2–5 players. 15 mins. Still top rated, **PDQ,** short for Pretty Darn Quick, a great word game for travel. 8 & up. (800) 638-7568.

■ Zigity 2005

(Cranium $12.95 ●●●●) Our own family played many heated rounds of Zigity! The object is to be the first to get rid of your cards, but watch out—there are different activities that can change the course of the game dramatically. For example, just as you think you're going to win, you may be forced to draw three additional cards. Visual discrimination and word and number play are all part of the fun. 8 & up. (877) 272-6486.

Geography Games

■ Borderline

(Borderline Games $9.95 ●●●●) With the recent African Edition, the European/Middle East edition, or the original US edition, here's a playful, painless way to make maps fun! The object is to get rid of all your cards, but you can only put cards down on a card that "borders" the state, body of water, or country in your hand. If you don't know, flip your card for a map that shows the borderlines. A no-tears-or-fears, entertaining geography game! 8 & up. (973) 761-6260.

■ Great States

(International Playthings $20 ●●●●) This U.S.A. map game includes a board and cards that help young readers learn their state capitals, birds, flowers, and landmarks. What we really liked is that you use the map to find the answers—you're not expected to know them all already. Older players will enjoy playing with the timer, but it's not essential. 7 & up. We'd pass on the Junior edition which doesn't work as well as the original. (800) 445-8347.

■ The Scrambled States of America

(Gamewright $13.99 ⊙⊙⊙⊙) There was disagreement from our testers on this geography game, where the object is to collect as many state cards as possible by matching factoids with the right state. One parent noted that a good part of the game has nothing to do with geography, which is true. But it is a painless way to introduce kids to the U.S. map, states, capitals, and nicknames. 8 & up. (800) 638-7568.

■ This Land Is Your Land USA Map

(eeBoo $16 ⊙⊙⊙⊙) Hang this handsome laminated picture map in your family or child's room. It comes with 50 stickers that kids use to mark places they have visited or locations where friends and family live. (212) 222-0823.

Math Games and Equipment

■ Buy It Right Shopping Game

(Learning Resources $19.95 ⊙⊙⊙⊙½) Making change is not always easy for kids who don't get to handle more than their milk money. This game involves a lot of buying and selling and some flexible thinking. Kids roll three numeral dice and decide if they want to call a 4, 2, 1, $4.21, or $1.24 . . . a choice that depends on whether they are buying or selling. Unlike most shopping games, which are aimed at girls, this is a gender-free game. 6 & up. For working on place-value skills, **Operation Space Chase** ($13.95 ⊙⊙⊙⊙); for help with fractions, **Pie in the Sky** ($12.95 ⊙⊙⊙⊙). 7 & up. (888) 800-7893.

■ Chicken Coop Dominoes *2005*

(Fundex $14.95 ⊙⊙⊙⊙) A new twist on dominoes. An electronic coop is the centerpost of this fun game. Players build "legs" off the coop and when they add a "double," everyone must play matching tiles to form a three-pronged chicken leg. Develops matching, counting, and strategy skills. 8 & up. (800) 486-9787.

■ 4-Way Countdown *2005*

(Cadaco $19.95 ⊙⊙⊙⊙⊙) This PLATINUM AWARD winner just got more interesting. The object is to be the first player to turn over all ten of your pegs by rolling dice. Players may add, subtract, multiply, or divide the numbers they roll in order to get the number they need. 6 & up. (800) 621-5426.

■ Mad Math BLUE CHIP

(Patrix $22.95 **○○○○○**) If math facts are a source of tension in your house, here are two games for working on those skills. Mad Math is a board game that has addition facts on one side and multiplication on the other. The goal is to get three pawns in a row on the board. You collect spaces by rolling the dice and finding the corresponding math fact on the playing board. The board is self-correcting, which is a plus. (888) 834-2380.

■ Maya Madness

(Gamewright $12.99 **○○○○**) A great game for working on negative and positive numbers. To claim their "secret" number token, players must add and subtract numbers on the draw pile to reach their number. So, if your token is a 2 and the card showing is a 6, you could play a 4 card to claim your token. First player to claim five tokens wins. (800) 638-7568.

■ Old Century Shut-the–Box

(Old Century $49.95 **○○○○○**) Here's a handsome wooden chest with numbered tiles that players flip after they roll the big wooden dice. Object is to turn over all the tiles or to have the lowest number of points left when you can no longer make a move. There's room for flexible thinking here since a roll of 7 and 2 means you can flip any combination of 9. Fun for reinforcing addition and place value. Pricey, but the kind of game you'll want to leave out in your living room. 8 & up. PLATINUM AWARD '04. (206) 826-3202.

■ Sum Swamp

(Learning Resources $12.95 **○○○○**) Players toss three dice, one with plus or minus signs, as they move their critter through the swamp where they sometimes have to deal with odds and evens. Right on the mark for late first and early second grade. Also, **Tick, Tac, Tock!** (**○○○○**) (good for reinforcing clock concepts). 7 & up. (888) 800-7893.

Math Manipulatives

Concrete materials give kids a greater understanding of counting and calculating. Don't rush to take these materials away from kids. They help make the transition to abstract thinking easier. A BLUE

CHIP choice is **Unifix Ready for Math Kit** (Didax $12.95 set of 100 ⦿⦿⦿⦿⦿). Beginning math students use these cubes, book, and stickers for understanding early math concepts. We'd recommend pairing them with their activity books. (800) 458-0024.

■ Talking Clever Clock

(Learning Resources $34.95 ⦿⦿⦿⦿½) Hands down, the best electronic clock for teaching kids how to tell time. Our nine-year-old tester had given up on ever learning how to tell time—but within minutes he was having fun using the clock that has self-checking features with both digital and analog clock faces. 5 & up. (888) 800-7893.

Math Electronic Quiz Machines

Most math-quiz machines are like electronic flash cards—good for picking up speed, but if your child doesn't have the basic concepts down, these machines won't help. **What to Avoid:** many machines require that two-digit answers be entered with tens first. This is contrary to the way kids are taught, especially when regrouping is involved, so machines may be confusing. Our best advice: try them before you buy.

■ Talking Math Mat Challenge

(Learning Resources $29.95 ⦿⦿⦿⦿½) Kids step on this talking mat to answer math quizzes programmed at two levels of difficulty. Level One asks kids to find the numeral named and do simple addition and subtraction. More fun than flash cards, but not that different in content. It's for kids who are ready for drill. Labeled 4–7, most fours will do only the numeral game. Far more appropriate for mid-first and second graders. Forget the newer **Factor Frenzy** (⦿⦿⦿) and **Light 'N Strike Math** (⦿⦿⦿). Both require too many steps to enter an answer—totally frustrating. (888) 800-7893.

■ Turbo Extreme 🌟2005🌟

(LeapFrog $34.99 ⦿⦿⦿½) You can work on math, spelling, science, and social studies with this hand-held toy with add-on cartridges ($9.99 each). For drilling this got high marks: "games are fun"; "better than flash cards." When you enter a math answer, however, the machine asks for the tens place. Since kids are taught to add the "ones" first, this can be confusing. 6 & up. (800) 701-5327.

Other Electronic Equipment and Learning Tools

■ Leap Pad Plus Writing Learning System *2005*

(LeapFrog $59.99 ●●●●) We were delighted that many Dr. Seuss classics, such as *Fox in Socks* and *One Fish Two Fish*, have been adapted for this platform or the Leap Pad. In addition, kids who are learning to write their letters and numbers will like this electronic workbook with stylus that really writes. More books and innovative games are slated for this platform but not ready for testing. Although the toy is marked 3 & up, the skills are more appropriate for 5s & up. Also, see **Letter Factory Game,** p. 85. (800) 701-5327.

■ Powertouch Learning System *2005*

(Fisher-Price $49.99 ●●●●) A well designed interactive electronic book format that kids activate with a finger rather than a stylus. New for *2005*, two books feature familiar characters Arthur and Franklin; the latter is told in verse. Extra games on top of pages are targeted at K–second graders. But that's a broad range, and many quizzes will be too hard for younger players and pointless for older ones. (800) 432-5437.

COMPARISON SHOPPER
Talking Globes

Although less expensive than they used to be, they don't work as well. Why ask questions that can't be answered by looking at the globe? Our testers liked pushing the buttons but quickly felt frustrated. The **LeapFrog Explorer Globe** (Leap Frog $99 ●●) comes with a sensor pen and lots of information (the pace is frenetic). (800) 701-5327. We had trouble knowing how to "buzz in" on the quiz-styled **GeoSafari Challenge Globe** (Educational Insights $59.95 ●●)

with 7,500 questions. 8 & up. The **GeoSafari World** ($59.95 ●●●) has 5,000 questions, but again you'd need an atlas to answer many of the questions. (800) 995-4436.

Puzzles

Putting jigsaw puzzles together calls for visual perception, eye-hand coordination, patience, and problem-solving skills. During their early school years, kids should build puzzles from 25 pieces to 50- and 100-plus pieces.

Beginners' Puzzles—Under 50 pieces

■ A–Z Panels BLUE CHIP

(Lauri $9.99 ●●●●●) Not only does fitting the rubbery letters in and out of the puzzle frame help kids learn to know and name the letters, but handling the 3-D letters also gives kids a feel for their shapes. Also, **Kids Perception Puzzle** ($7.99 ●●●●●), figures in slightly different poses that help kids look at small differences, just as they must when reading words that look almost alike, such as *cap* and *cup*. 4–7. (800) 451-0520.

■ Parquetry Blocks Super Set BLUE CHIP

(Learning Resources $26.95 ●●●●●) Thirty-two geometrically shaped tiles are arranged on top of 20 colorful patterns. Advanced players can use tiles without the patterns. Develops skills in matching and sequencing patterns—skills that are needed in putting letters together to make words. 5–8. (888) 800-7893.

Intermediate & Advanced—
50 &100+ Pieces and Shaped Puzzles

■ 3x49 Puzzles *2005*

(Ravensburger $8.50 ●●●●) Comes with 3 forty-nine-piece puzzles (that you sort out first by using the different patterns on the puzzle backs). Choose either the dinosaur or jungle animals motif. Challenging but satisfying. (800) 886-1236.

■ Lite Brite Illumin-Art Easel *2005*

(Hasbro $34.99 ●○○) As huge fans of Lite-Brite, we wanted to love this new oversized easel with the added drawing dimension. However, we were taken aback by the typical black sheet with a huge skull and cross bones and "Get Out" message. Such dark and unpleasant images have no place in the world of young children's playthings. We'd stick with PLATINUM AWARD-winning **Lite Brite Cube** ($21.99 ●●●●●). (800) 327-8264.

COMPARISON SHOPPER
USA & World Map Puzzles

For tabletop we suggest **Puzzibilities USA Puzzles** (Small World Toys $20 ●●●○) A classic wooden version with landmarks, capitals, and a vinyl sheet for arranging pieces out of the frame is a good choice. 6 & up. (800) 421-4153.

Testers also loved the oversized **Wonderfoam Giant USA Puzzle Map** (Chenille Kraft $44 ●●●○) Testers enjoyed putting together this giant-sized (4' w x 2½' h) floor puzzle with 73 thick foam pieces. State names are printed on the map with 16 landmarks (state capitals marked by a star but not named—you might want to add the capitals with a marker on the back of each state). Also, **Wonderfoam Giant World Puzzle Map** ($44 ●●●○). (800) 621-1261. Less pricey, a cardboard 51-piece **USA Floor Puzzle,** 2' x 3' with state names and capitals. (Melissa & Doug $9.99 ●●●○). (800) 284-3948.

Activity Kits and Art Supplies

For school-age kids, art class is seldom long enough. Besides, such classes are usually teacher directed, with little chance for kids to explore their own ideas. Giving kids the tools and space for art projects at home provides more than pure entertainment. Art helps kids develop their ability to communicate ideas and feelings visually, to refine eye-hand skills, and to learn how to stick with a task.

⚙ BASIC GEAR CHECKLIST
FOR EARLY SCHOOL YEARS ARTISTS

✓ Crayons, chalk, colored pencils, and pastels
✓ Watercolor and acrylic paints
✓ Watercolor markers

✓ Paper for origami	✓ Loom (weaving, beads)
✓ Sewing supplies	✓ Sand art supplies
✓ Lanyard kits	✓ Colored wax
✓ Rug hooking supplies	✓ Needlepoint supplies
✓ Woodworking supplies	✓ Cutting/pasting supplies
✓ Flower press	✓ Fabric paints
✓ Stamps	✓ Air-hardening clay

Activity and Craft Kits

Again this year there seemed to be more craft kits than ever before. We had our network of testers get to work—with a mixed bag of results. Some kits that looked fantastic were disappointing; others were surprisingly good. Our testers complained that the packaging was deceiving, making products look bigger than they actually were. Both boys and girls love making things they can play with, wear, or give as gifts. Many require adult assistance. Here's a sampling of our testing. For even more reviews, visit our website.

Drawing, Painting, Coloring, and Gluing
■ Ceramic Allowance Bank *2005*

(Creativity for Kids $14.99 ●●●●) A chubby white ceramic pig ready to paint and hold spare change or allowance. It has an easy-to-pull-out rubber stopper, so they don't need to break the bank when they want to spend some of their savings! Includes a "chores" booklet with star stickers... the idea being that they earn their allowance. We have mixed feelings about paying kids for chores... but we do like the idea of encouraging them to save their pennies, nickels, and dimes!

Also new from the ceramic line, **Le Most Petite Purses** ($15.99 ●○○○) comes with three different small ceramic purses, paint, and rhinestones. Our testers thought these would make great gifts for mom or a decoration for their own vanity. 7 & up. (800) 311-8684.

■ Crayola Window Mega Markers 2005

(Binney & Smith $4.99 ●○○○) Great for a rainy day. Kids can decorate sliding doors and windows with these four extra-thick washable markers. Also a good way to temporarily note a special occasion. For sunny days, **Crayola Sidewalk Paint** ($9.99 ●○○○) Have your own sidewalk art show with this three-color paint kit. "Colors not as vibrant as on the box, but the kids had a great time. I had to fight with the kids to get them to stop and get ready for bed!" New for 2005, comes in a reusable plastic paint tray. 5 & up. (800) 272-9652

■ Make-Your-Own Cards 2005

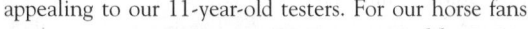

(Made By Hands $17.95 ●○○○) There's no need to cut, and pasting is a snap with the glue stick and precut shapes. There are several sheets of "pop-out" shapes that can be used to decorate pre-folded cards. Kit includes 20 envelopes for mailing finished artwork. Store all the goodies in this kit in a neat box with Velcro closure. This comes two ways, with pastel colors that are no doubt designed to appeal to girls and a primary color kit that is likely to appeal to both boys and girls. We go for the latter! Also top rated from this new line, **Make-Your-Own Puppets** (●○○○) and **Make Your Own Games** (●○○○). (800) 839-7369.

■ My Jewelry Box Kit 2005 PLATINUM AWARD

(Balitono $19 ●●●●●) Our testers gave this 8" wooden jewelry box high marks for the way it was finished inside with velvet finished fittings and little hooks for hanging necklaces. This is a more grown-up jewelry box than most we've tested. While marked 6 & up, it was appealing to our 11-year-old testers. For our horse fans, **My Horse Stable & Corral Kit** ($25 ●○○○½) got rave reviews. Comes with a wooden stable (8" x 6" x 7") with two stalls, one wooden horse, and an 18"-long wooden corral, and paint. (609) 936-8807.

■ Music Box 2005

(Creativity for Kids $15.95 ●●●●½) This charming little 4" x 4" music box, which plays Tchaikovsky's "Waltz of the Flowers," is just large enough for small trinkets. While marked 7 & up, our younger testers enjoyed painting this one. (800) 311-8684.

■ Ribbon Plates 2005

(Alex $17 ●●●●) Our 8-year-old testers thought this set was "very grown up." Comes with two lattice-edged porcelain plates (one heart shaped), paint, and ribbon. Marked 8 & up. (800) 666-2539.

■ Scrapbook and Memory Box Gift Set
2005 PLATINUM AWARD

(Creativity for Kids $28.99 ●●●●●) Scrapbook fans are going to love this commodious box with picture-frame cover, which holds a spiral-bound scrapbook plus 16 sheets of patterned paper, stickers, stencil, scalloped scissors, paper punch, stamper, pens, glue stick and great ideas. This will appeal to older girls ready to memorialize a school year, a trip, or a big event. Marked 7 & up, but was coveted by our 10- and 11-year-old testers. The **Groovy Girls Perfectly Picturific Scrapbook Kit** ($19.99 ●●●●) will appeal to younger girls who play with Groovy Girl dolls. (800) 311-8684. The hardcover scrapbook made these two kits preferable to our testers than the **Alex My Scrapbook** ($19.95 ●●●), which comes with a soft-covered spiral.

■ Scratch & Sparkle Deluxe Kit 2005

(Scratch Art $14.99 ●●●●) For fans of Scratch art products, this is a satisfying kit. Comes with 16 sheets (four each multicolor, glitzy gold, silver, and blue), stencils, drawing tools and frames. Still top rated, **Scratch-Lite Sketcher** ($19.99 ●●●●½) a lightbox on which kids place scratch art paper and draw or write with one of two fancy tipped drawing tools. Comes with stencils and 10 sheets of special paper, so bring home a refill pack. A good quiet-time toy that develops dexterity needed for writing. 5 & up. (800) 377-9003.

■ Wake Up! Alarm Clock 2005

(Creativity for Kids $17.99 ●●●●½) If you have a child who is working on learning to tell time or developing independent wake-up skills, here's a good gift. A working alarm clock that can be painted with a unique design and then used. A good back-to-school gift. 7 & up. (800) 311-8684.

■ Wooden Shoe Wanna Paint These? 2005

(The Bead Shop $24 ●●●●) Hands down one of the favorite kits of the year for our testers. Kids paint their own designs on the wooden base of these Dr. Scholl's-like slides. Comes with paint, brush, and design ideas. Our testers liked the "cherry" motif best! Comes in five sizes, from a kids' 12½ to a ladies' 8½. (800) 492-3237.

Candles, Cooking, and Mixing

■ Beeswax Candles BLUE CHIP

(Creativity for Kids $16 ●●●●●) The best candle making kit—fun to do and makes great presents. Comes with five sheets of colored wax that you can cut to make different-sized candles. 6 & up. (800) 311-8684. We'd skip Alex's **Candle Painting** set, which our testers found disappointing—"my candle doesn't look like the box." 6 & up.

■ Crayola Gadget Headz Car 2005 PLATINUM AWARD

(Binney & Smith $29.99 ●●●●●) Crayola has come up with the perfect solution to all those old crayon stubbies! Put them in the crayon maker and make your own special "designer" crayons. Melts via the light bulb. Comes with wheels and bases for two pull-back racing "crayon" cars—very neat. 8 & up. (800) 272-9652.

■ Wax Works BLUE CHIP

(Chenille Kraft $5.49 ●●●●●) These waxy sticks can be twisted and shaped into free-form sculptures. Great for developing fine motor skills. 5 & up. (800) 621-1261.

Beads, Jewelry, & Accessory Kits

Using beads is more than engaging in a creative craft; it's helping kids develop fine-motor skills.

■ Me Jewelry *2005*

(Creativity for Kids $14.99 oooo) Testers liked being able to personalize the three long clay beads with messages. Kit also includes patterned and metal beads and plenty of cord for necklaces and bracelets. 7 & up. (800) 311-8684.

■ Tutti Frutti Safety Pin Bracelet Kit
2005 PLATINUM AWARD

(The Bead Shop $5 ooooo) Our eleven-year-old testers were thrilled with the results of this small kit that includes colored safety pins, beads, elastic and clear directions for making a very pleasing bracelet. Younger girls will need adult help. Past favorites: last year's PLATINUM AWARD-winning **Alphadot Bracelet Kit** ($19.99 ooooo), with 85 Alphadot beads that slide onto three thin watch-like bands; **Block Party Bracelet Kit** ($19.99 ooooo) comes with metal sliding letters; **Ribbon Raps** ($14 ooooo), has beads to string on gossamer ribbon; and **Mystix** ($16 oooo) includes semi-precious stones. 8 & up. (800) 492-3237.

■ Clikits *2005*

(Lego Systems $11.95 & up ooooo) We found a real age divide with Clikits this year. Younger girls love them but our 9-year-olds felt the kits were "too young looking." That said, Clikits are great for developing fine motor skills along with creativity. Flower-shaped beads snap together with larger cutout flowers and leaves. Top rated for *2005* : **The Ultimate Jewelry Collection** ($29.90 oooo). 7 & up. (800) 223-8756.

■ Paint Ceramic Beads
2005 PLATINUM AWARD

(Alex $16.95 ooooo) Here's a really juicy kit that our testers wanted to do. Comes with two large heart pendants, 16 square beads, 10 shaped beads, seed beads, paints, brushes, and cord. You can choose to paint and also bake them, in which case adult supervision is a must. 7 & up. Also highly rated, **Love Beads** ($5.99 ●●●●) includes two pairs of hoops for earrings, metal beads with heart, peace sign, and stars, plus enough glass beads for ten bracelets. Testers felt the instructions could have been clearer. 8 & up. (800) 666-2539.

Sewing and Designing Kits

Learning to sew and/or design makes kids feel very grown-up—something they find especially satisfying. They're also ideal ways to develop fine-motor skills. This category has exploded with great choices. Here are our testers' favorites:

■ Beginning Stitcher Deluxe Set

(Quincrafts $12.99 & up ●●●●) Try your hand at needlepoint, cross stitch, and sewing with this set. Comes with safe plastic needle, a needlepoint keychain and picture frame, and two square grids (one for cross stitch, one for needlepoint). New for **2005**, **Make Your Own Teddy Bear with Scarf** ($8.99 ●●●●) now comes with yarn, needles, and instructions for making a scarf for the bear. 9 & up. (800) 342-8458.

■ Crunch Art

(Hands On Toys $7–$11.95 ●●●●●) Kids simply place a small piece of fabric on the foam board and push down with the "cruncher/puncher" tool (which is not sharp), and the fabric is in place. They can make designs or draw pictures to fill with colorful fabric, mylar squares, or chenille stems. PLATINUM AWARD '03. We prefer the open-ended kits, but some kids find the themed kits comforting. (888) 442-6376.

COMPARISON SHOPPER
No-Sew Design Kits **2005**

Our 9- and 11-year-old testers worked seriously to make original costumes for the set of four super-sized **Fashion Angels** (The Bead Shop $24.99 ●●●●) which come in a kit with fabric, patterns, glitter, trims, and glue for making very cool outfits. Sturdier than paper dolls, players need dexterity, patience, and the ability to deal with details. 8 & up. (800) 492-3237. Slightly easier and more flexible, **Groovy Girls Design Studio Woodkins** (Pamela Drake $19.99 ●●●●) comes with one "woodkin" style doll with wooden frame

that lifts and closes down to hold the fabric and trims. It comes with scissors, glitter, stickers, and lots of details for designing special outfits that are easy to keep changing. 8 & up. (800) 966-3762.

■ Potholders & Other Loopy Projects

(Klutz $16.95 ●●●●●) Don't look any further, this is the best potholder set on the market. The supplies are vibrant and inviting and the book really does explain what to do. Weaving not only develops eye-hand coordination, it also involves following patterns and problem solving. Marked 6 & up, we'd say more like 7 & up. PLATINUM AWARD '04. (800) 737-4123.

COMPARISON SHOPPER
Knit One, Purl One—Knitting *2005*

Knitting has become trendy again. While we think it's always easier to learn how to knit from another person, here are two kits that will appeal to kids. **Yarn Craft** (Alex $20 ●●●●) The big draw of this kit is the basket it comes in. "I love the red and white checked lining." The yarn colors (six skeins) are very bright (crafty looking) and surprisingly soft. Comes with a nice set of wooden needles, a crochet hook, and some instructions that our teenage knitter said were clear. There's also **Knitting** PLATINUM AWARD *2005* (Klutz $24.95 ●●●●●), which comes with 140 grams of rich variegated yarn (more grown-up looking than Alex's), bamboo knitting needles, crochet hook and a much fuller book with instructions for six projects (done with crisp illustrations). 8 & up. (800) 666-2539.

COMPARISON SHOPPER
Weaving Looms BLUE CHIP

Begin to Weave (Quincrafts $4.99 ●●●●●) has a cardboard loom, a blunt needle, yarn, and some beads for extra finishing touches. A simple way to introduce beginners to weaving. Some kits are simply color patterns, others are more challenging with designs for hearts and butterfly. (800) 342-8458. For the next step up, the wooden **PegLoom** (Harrisville Designs $19.95 ●●●●●), a small over/under loom with large needle, makes a good choice for true beginners. 5 & up. For a larger rigid heddle loom, consider **Harrisville Easy Weaver** ($96.95 ●●●●), which comes prethreaded with enough 100% wool to make two beautiful rainbow plaid scarves. Refill kits ($19.95). 7 & up. (800) 338-9415.

Art with a Scientific Edge

■ Kids' Sundial Kit

(Milestones $18 ●●●●) This is a fun but very parent-intensive project that calls for mixing concrete as the first step to creating a working sundial. Testers suggest mixing your concrete in a disposable bucket—you'll have to throw away whatever pail you use. (800) 289-1637.

■ Tabletop Greenhouse *2005*

(Creativity for Kids $24.99 ●●●●½) A handsome kit that combines science with art. This greenhouse comes in natural wood with plastic windows and it is ready to decorate with paints. Put it in a sunny location and get small plants started that can be moved to your garden. We suggest herbs that can be used in the kitchen. An opportunity for kids to see not just how the plants grow, but how the moisture from the soil and plants recycles itself. Still recommended, **Build a Bird Bath** ($25 ●●●●) 4–9. (800) 311-8684.

Musical Instruments

■ Chimalong & Mini Chimalong BLUE CHIP

(Woodstock Percussion $20 & up ●●●●●)
The tone of this metal-chime xylophone is
lovely, and it can be played by number/color or
musical notation. Reinforces reading from left to
right. Mini version is not as sweet sounding. Marked 3 & up; we'd say
4–8. (800) 422-4463.

■ Hit Clips

(Hasbro $9.99 & up ●●) Great idea but poorly executed. The sound
quality of the music is terrible and you don't even get the whole song.
For the money you're better off buying your child the whole CD!
(800) 327-8264.

■ Kids' Tom Tom

(Remo/Woodstock Percussion $48 ●●●●) If you're lucky,
they'll let you play this colorful drum while they dance!
Comes with mallets, but testers say that tones are better
when played by hand. Also terrific: a **Kids' Konga
Drum** and **Two-Headed Bongo.** Their new line of
less expensive instruments does not have the same
rich sound. (800) 422-4463.

■ Music Maker Harp BLUE CHIP

(European Expressions $32 ●●●●●) No electronic sounds here. This
is a cross between a zither and an autoharp, but much easier to learn
to play. Slip one of 12 follow-the-dot song sheets under the strings
and pluck. Has a soft and lovely tone. Includes folk, Beatles, and classical music sheets. 6 & up. (800) 779-2205.

Active Play

Young school kids are often more eager than able
to play many games with rules. Sometimes the
real equipment is too heavy for them to use. Balls
that are softer don't hurt as much and promote
kids' confidence. The same is true of scaled-
down bats, rackets, and other equipment.

■ Beamo

(Stuff Design $25 ●●●●●) We really wish that we

had had one of these when we were younger! These fabric discs are about two feet wide and have a foam outer core that doesn't hurt as much as a regular frisbee if you miss! Great for multi-generational play. 6 & up. PLATINUM AWARD '04. (888) 946-7464.

■ Critter Leg Stilts

(Critter Leg Stilts $69–89 oooo) We love the look of these wooden stilts that come in three different sizes (48", 64", & 82"). They come in different animal designs and again take some time to get the hang of but are fun for older kids, teens, and even adults. (423) 743-0104.

■ ESPN Game Station *2005*

(Fisher-Price $179 oo) We worry when a toy comes with a warning not to return the toy to the store, but to call the help line. The thick instruction book and three hours of assembly are ridiculous for a $179 toy. Proceed at your own risk with this 6-in-1 play center for soccer, basketball, golf, hockey, football, and baseball games. 5 & up. (800) 432-5437.

■ Jump 'N Splash *2005*

(Wham-O $12.99 oooo) Imagine a jump rope made out of water—that's what you have with this latest water toy. Adjustable to different heights with single and double-dutch play possible. 6 & up. (800) 247-6570. Our testers also loved **Dunk Seat** (Wild Planet $19.99 oooo)—when you hit the target, the person on the seat gets sprayed with water (the actual seat does not dunk). (800) 247-6570.

■ Play Sports Croquet Set

(Small World Toys $50 oooo) This nifty updated croquet game comes with two mallets, six balls, two tees, and nine bendable, weighted foam wickets. Better than the old metal wickets that used to rust, this will survive the elements. (800) 421-4153.

■ **Yoga Play & Learn System**

(YogaYears $39.95 ●●●●) Yoga is catching on as a great activity for kids. Here's a child-sized mat (24" x 50") with many standard yoga positions printed on it. Also comes with a fun game for introducing the concepts and positions. (248) 302-1110.

Wheel Toys
Shopping Checklist

Fives will continue to enjoy many of the wheel toys in the Preschool chapter.

By 6 or 7, most kids are ready and eager for a two-wheeler with training wheels. Steer clear of bikes with gears or hand brakes. Learning to balance is a big enough deal.

Tempting as it may be to surprise your child, your best bet is to take your child to the store.

Buy a bike that fits, rather than one to grow into. When kids straddle a bike they should be able to put a foot on the ground for balance.

Budget and size will dictate the choices. **Schwinn, Huffy,** and **Razor** ($100 & up) offer solidly built 16" bikes with adjustable training wheels and an assortment of accessories.

Helmets do help! According to the Consumer Product Safety Commission, one in seven children suffers head injuries in bike-related accidents. While studies show that wearing helmets reduces the risk of injury by 85 percent, the sad fact is that only 5 percent of bike-riding kids actually wear helmets. See Safety Guidelines for helmet standards.

■ **Green Machine**

(Huffy $100 ●●●●●) You'll want a turn on this truly innovative ride-on. Steer the two chunky rear wheels by moving the two hand levers (one also has a brake). Solidly made for even bigger kids (and small adults!). PLATINUM AWARD '04. (800) 872-2453.

■ Flying Turtle

(Mason Co. $69.95 **oooo**) Low to the ground, this seat on skate wheels zips along on any smooth surface by twisting the handlebars from side to side. No pedals, no batteries, no motor! This is kid powered and fun for kids up to 150 pounds. One test family keeps this indoors and claims that all visiting kids from 4–12 enjoy it! (800) 821-4141.

■ Trikke 5 **2005** PLATINUM AWARD

(Trikke Tech $139 **ooooo**) Our testers wrote: "A HUGE HIT! The kids love this! It works well, and looks super cool, too. It operates much like the flying turtle." Designed for kids 7–11 with a maximum rider weight of 150 lbs., the three-wheeled scooter will go where the rider leans. The company sells bigger models for teens and grown-ups but we did not test them. 8 & up. (877) 487-4553.

Science Toys and Equipment

■ Box of Rocks **2005**

(GeoCentral $21.99 **oooo**) If you have a young rock hound in the family, this box with 16 specimens and an informative booklet will be a hit and may inspire further discoveries. **Activity Rocks** ($5.25 **oooo**) has four specimens—including one that floats! (800) 231-6083.

■ Discovery Awesome Avalanche Kit **2005**

(Discovery Kids $19.95 **oooo**½) At first glance this looks like most of the volcano kits you may have seen—a five-minute wonder. But our 11-year-old tester liked painting the model of Mt. Everest, reading the excellent booklet about avalanches, and the "insta-snow," white polymer that comes with the kit. Add water and, "Watch out below!" It cascades from the mountaintop! Also has a number of other hands-on experiments. Adult supervision suggested. 8 & up. (800) 938-0333.

Science is still best understood with hands-on materials. Favorite equipment: magnifiers, magnets, gyroscopes, kaleidoscopes, prisms, and a compass.

■ Hoberman Switch Kick *2005* PLATINUM AWARD

(Hoberman $14.99 ●●●●●) From the folks that brought us the now-BLUE-CHIP Hoberman spheres, they've come up with a new and improved design for their color-changing spheres. **Switch Kick** is foam-covered, and the smaller **Switch Pitch** ($4.99) are softball-sized plastic spheres that change more easily than the originals. (888) 229-3653.

■ I Dig Treasures: Dinosaurs and Mysteries of Egypt Excavation Adventure

(Action Products $24.99 each ●●●●) Both boy and girl testers enjoyed playing archeologist with these sets that require patience to unearth treasures from pebbly bricks. We rate them higher than other similar kits, since these come with digging goggles. Smaller kits ($10) make affordable birthday gifts. (800) 772-2846.

Nature Houses & Lodges

■ My Birdhouse Kit *2005*

(Balitono $19 ●●●●) One of the best outdoor crafts is to prepare a birdhouse for backyard visitors. This new wooden house is pre-constructed (7½" x 5½" x 6½") with drainage holes, removable roof, and a ventilation slot for added comfort! Kids can enjoy painting the house. We'd recommend pairing this kit with a bird guidebook, a pair of binoculars, and a log. Also for the outdoors, **Spiral Windchime Kit** ($17 ●●●●½). 7 & up. (609) 936-8807.

■ Hanging Bird Feeder and Bird Houses Kits

(TWC of America $16–$20 ●●●●) If you'd like to build your own birdhouse, these beautifully crafted pine kits come with rounded edges and predrilled holes, making them the best kids' kits on the market. Adult assistance required. Also, **Deluxe Clear-View Nature House** ($17.99 ●●●●½), a sturdy hut-shaped wooden house, half see-through, half screened, with sliding door; a perfect temporary habitat for observing bugs and small critters. 6 & up. Also, **Soil Dweller Nature House Kit** ($20 ●●●●) for making a wooden-framed house for earthworms. 8 & up. (800) 301-7592.

■ Garden Pinwheel Activity Kit 2005

(Alex $9.99 ●●●●) Our testers enjoyed painting either the oversized flower or the bug pinwheel. The center pinwheel spins easily, attaches to the larger frame, and makes a cheerful decoration that is fun to watch spin in the wind. While the kit is marked 8 & up, our younger testers also had great fun painting their pinwheels. (800) 666-2539.

The Scoop on Scopes

■ Discovery Kids SL-70 Telescope

(Discovery Kids $149.95 ●●●●●) With many of the same features usually found on expensive adult models, this is a terrific value. Includes precision ground lenses, an erecting prism, and universal 10mm and 25mm Kellner eyepieces. Comes with a tripod that extends to 55" viewing height and a padded shoulder carry bag—the whole kit (tripod, scope, bag) weighs just 16 lbs. Ultra neat are the illuminated night-vision dials. PLATINUM AWARD '04. 7 & up. (800) 938-0333.

■ ETX 90AT Telescope

(Meade $595 ●●●●●) Our reviewers gave high marks to the ETX-90AT because it comes with the Autostar computer controller (usually only found on much more expensive models). The Autostar allows the viewer to find celestial objects by using the hand-held automated controller. The AT model also comes with a tripod. We would recommend this model for tweens and up. A worthy investment for a family of stargazers! 10 & up. PLATINUM AWARD '04. (800) 626-3233.

Best Travel Toys and Games

As kids get older they enjoy traditional games such as I Spy, Twenty Questions, Geography, or Facts of Five. They are also ready for word games and travel books. While we don't recommend plugging your kids into electronics for long stretches of time, there are times when everyone needs some down time! **Leapster, Pixter,** and **Gameboy** are among our testers' favorites. Be sure to bring along some story tapes (see Audio chapter). Here are some neat take-alongs:

■ Disney Classic Portable DVD Player
2005 PLATINUM AWARD

(Memorex $222.99 ❍❍❍❍❍) Sometimes watching a favorite movie gives everyone some needed down-time. This red set comes with a 5"-wides creen, a carry bag and two sets of wraparound head phones. Comes with both a car and AC power adapter that you can also use in your hotel room. (877) 347-6923.

■ 20Q *2005* PLATINUM AWARD

(Radica $9.99 ❍❍❍❍❍) How does it know? Play twenty questions with this handheld machine and it really seems like magic! The programmed answers also have a sense of humor.... Truly one of the innovative products of the year. (800) 803-9611.

■ Jelly Flyer Night Flyer *2005*

(Noodle Head $10 ❍❍❍❍) Bringing along an active toy is important for those long road trips when kids need to get out of the car and stretch their legs. The **Jelly Flyer** is made of a soft material so it won't hurt like a traditional Frisbee. We liked the **Night Flyer,** which glows in the dark. (866) 892-7311.

■ Leapster *2005*

(LeapFrog $79.99 ❍❍❍❍½) If you have been looking for a hand held game machine that's more age appropriate than Gameboy, look no further. Billed as a learning machine, it's a lot more playful than most.

The games and skills are well targeted to older preschoolers and early school age kids. It has a larger screen and games that can be played at three levels of difficulty. There are math, phonics, reading, and spelling games, as well as an art program that takes some help to learn how to use. Software cartridges are available for pre-K, Kindergarten, and 1st Grade. 4–8. (800) 432-5437.

■ Road Trip Activity Journal 2005

(Mudpuppy Press $10 ●●●●) There's lots to keep a tween busy with this clever activity journal that has a place for addresses, bingo, lots of other games, and space to write and draw as they travel. 9 & up. Still top rated, **Totable Journals** ($10 ●●●●) These 144-page journals come with a handle, stickers, and an assortment of lined, graph, and blank pages for kids to keep track of their adventures. 7 & up. (212) 354-8840.

■ Travel Bingo

(eeBoo $10 ●●●●) An old-fashioned game that still helps pass the time while you're on the road with your kids. Comes with four bingo pads and four pencils. Objects to look for include stop signs, bikes, flags, cows, railroad crossing signs, etc. 4 & up. (212) 222-0823.

■ Wig Out 2005

(Gamewright $5.99 ●●●●) The object is to match all of your wig cards to those on the table. Be fast… there are no turns here. Everyone is trying to do the same thing, whether it's matching ponytails, beehives, or Mohawks! First player to get rid of all her cards wins. Still top rated, last year's **Hocus Focus** ($5.99 ●●●●●) where the object was matching wizards (harder than Wig Out), PLATINUM AWARD '04; and **Stampede** ($5.99 ●●●●), where the player with the most complete hippos, rhinos, and elephants before the deck runs out wins. 6 & up. (800) 638-7568.

Best Birthday Gifts for Every Budget

Big Ticket **Telescope** (various makers) or
$100 plus **Trikke5** (Trikke Tech) or **Disney Classic Portable DVD Player** (Memorex)

Under $100 **The American Girls Collection Doll** (American Girl) or **Robosapien** (Wowwee) or **Gameboy Advance SP** (Nintendo)

Under $80 **Leapster** (LeapFrog) or **Color Pixter** (Fisher-Price)

Under $50 **Tyco R/C RollCage** (Mattel) or **Coast Watch HQ** (Lego Systems)

Under $40 **Les Cheries** (Corolle) or **Yoga Play & Learn System** (YogaYears)

Under $30 **Mgears Remote Control Racers** (Learning Resources) or **Crayola Gadget Headz Car** (Binney & Smith) or **Scrapbook and Memory Box Gift Set** (Creativity for Kids)

Under $25 **Magnetic Building Sets** (various makers) or **Wooden Shoe Wanna Paint These?** (The Bead Shop)

Under $20 **Balloon Lagoon** (Cranium) or **Make-Your-Own Cards** (Made By Hands) or **My Jewelry Box Kit** (Balitono)

Under $15 **Puzzles** (various makers) or **Bead Kits** (various makers)

Under $10 **Moose in the House** (Gamewright) or **20Q** (Radica) or **Tutti Frutti Safety Pin Bracelet Kit** (The Bead Shop)

II • Books

Reading to children is more than a great way to entertain them. Studies show that young children who are read to every day learn to read earlier and with greater ease. But quite aside from the academic benefits, sharing books with children is one of the pleasurable ways of being together. With books we can share the thrill of adventure, the excitement of suspense, and the warm satisfaction of happily-ever-afters. Through books we can help children find answers to their questions about real things and how they work. Books give grown-ups and children a ticket that transports them from everyday events to a world of faraway, long ago, and once upon a time.

You'll find useful lists of BLUE CHIP Classics for each age group as well as reviews of the best new and recent award winners. Many classic picture books can also be found in the Audio and Video chapters.

Books are primarily arranged by age groups. "Coping with Life" and holiday-book sections include books for mixed ages. You'll also find recommended reference books and encyclopedias for mixed ages at the end of the section. An "also" after a review indicates other recommended titles by that author, or other related books.

Babies and Young Toddlers

At this stage, books are not merely for looking at. Babies and toddlers tend to taste, toss, and tear their books. Even sturdy cardboard books may not survive this search-and-destroy stage. Cloth and vinyl make good chewable choices. The mechanics of turning pages, pointing to pictures, and even listening make books among baby's favorite playthings and a key to language development.

Ten Blue Chip Books Every Baby and Young Toddler Should Know

✓ **Baby Animal Friends,** by Phoebe Dunn
✓ **Baby's First Words,** by Lars Wik
✓ **I See,** by Rachel Isadora
✓ **Spot's Toys,** by Eric Hill
✓ **This Is Me,** by Lenore Blegvad
✓ **Tom and Pippo series,** by Helen Oxenbury
✓ **Pat-a-Cake,** by Tony Kenyon
✓ **What Do Babies Do?** by Debby Slier
✓ **What Is It?** by Tana Hoban
✓ **My Very First Mother Goose,** edited by Iona Opie

Cloth, Vinyl, and Board Books for Babies and Toddlers

Choose books with round corners and clear pictures of familiar things to know, name, and talk about. For the littlest reader, single images on a page are easier to "read." There may be one word or no words on the page, but you can use many words as you talk about the familiar objects and relate them to baby. Older babies will like pointing and finding the red cup that's full of milk or the sweet yellow banana. Little stories that center on the child's world are most appropriate for young toddlers. Here are some favorites:

■ Baby Animals
2005 PLATINUM AWARD

(DK $7.99 ●●●●●) On one side of each double-page spread is a large picture of a baby animal; on the facing page are three smaller photographs of the baby animal doing different things (napping, washing, hiding). The images of the tiger, kittens, and elephants are so striking, that there's lots to share and talk about with your baby. 6 mos. & up.

■ Hello, Spot!
2005 PLATINUM AWARD

(by Eric Hill, Putnam $8.99 ●●●●●) Spot is looking behind a bush, in a basket, under a flowerpot, and in other places, where he dis-

covers many familiar animals. A charming lift-the-flaps fabric book, which little hands can safely explore. Beyond the peek-a-boo stage, this reinforces animal names and position words.

■ Peekaboo, I Love You

(Lamaze $8.99 ○○○○○) An adorable fabric book with a cast of family members hiding under flaps on each of the bright cotton pages. PLATINUM AWARD '04. Also charming, **I See You, You See Me,** a mirrored book for checking out eyes, nose, ears, etc. 9 mos. & up.

■ Wake Up and **Time for Bed** *2005* PLATINUM AWARD

(by Sue King, Chronicle $5.95 each ○○○○○) Wiggle the pages and the illustrations seem to magically move as they follow a toddler getting washed, dressed, eating and going out to play; or getting ready for bed. Not much story, but plenty of action and things to talk about. 1 & up.

Resources for Parents

■ Head, Shoulders, Knees and Toes

(by Zita Newcome, Candlewick $15.99 ○○○○○) More than fifty hand-clapping, finger-snapping, action games and rhymes wonderfully illustrated with close-up directions for motions and jolly looking toddlers. PLATINUM AWARD '03. 2 & up.

■ A Treasury of Children's Songs

(Metropolitan Museum/Henry Holt $19.95 ○○○○½) A collection of 40 classic children's songs paired with artwork from the Metropolitan Museum. Each song is complete with easy piano arrangements and guitar chords. Still top rated: **Lullabies: An Illustrated Songbook** BLUE CHIP (Metropolitan Museum $23 ○○○○○): words and music for 35 memorable lullabies illustrated with works of art from the Met. PLATINUM AWARD '98.

■ My Mother Goose Library

(edited by Iona Opie/illus. by Rosemary Wells, Candlewick $40 ○○○○○) Both PLATINUM AWARD volumes come in a handsome gift set or in board books for tots to enjoy ($8 each) with the same delicious art.

■ Baby Story BLUE CHIP

(Creations by You $29.95 ●●●●●) Create your own story about your baby with favorite photos and captions. Decorate pages with over 100 stickers and the book will be returned professionally typeset and bound. (800) 706-8697.

Older Toddlers

Toddlers are ready for new kinds of books. Just as they can understand almost anything you say, they can also follow books with small stories that center on their familiar world.

They like playful language with rhythm, rhyme, and repetitive lines they can chime in on. They enjoy stories about children like themselves, and playful animal stories in which a dog or a bear is really a "child in fur." Toddlers also love books about real things, such as colors, caterpillars, and cars. Choose books you really like, because toddlers like to hear their favorites again and again!

TEN BLUE CHIP BOOKS EVERY TODDLER SHOULD KNOW

✓**Goodnight Moon,** by Margaret Wise Brown
✓**Jamberry,** by Bruce Degen
✓**Wheels on the Bus,** adapted by Paul Zelinsky
✓ **Polar Bear, Polar Bear, What Do You Hear?** by Bill Martin Jr.
✓**Sheep in a Jeep,** by Nancy Shaw
✓**Where's Spot?** by Eric Hill
✓**The Little Red Hen,** by Byron Barton
✓**You Go Away,** by Dorothy Corey
✓**When You Were a Baby,** by Ann Jonas
✓**The Very Hungry Caterpillar,** by Eric Carle

First Little Stories, Adventures, and Mysteries

■ A Lovely Day for Amelia Goose 2005

(by Yu Rong, Candlewick $14 ●●●●) Amelia is a happy-go-lucky goose out to spend the day with her friend Frog. They play hide-and-seek and hang out on the log. Rong's illustrations are playfully crisp and pleasing. A good first storybook. 2 & up.

■ Little Owl 2005 PLATINUM AWARD

(by Piers Harper, Scholastic $15.95 ●●●●●) Toddlers will enjoy this oversized picture-book about independence that has soft textures to feel as the story is read. Baby Owl is afraid to leave his mother's side, but as his friends invite him to join them, he discovers that he his ready to fly. 2 & up.

■ Mommy Loves Her Baby

(by Tara J. Morrow/illus. by Tiphanie Beeke, HarperCollins $15.95 ●●●●●) Here's another clever flip book that reverses to **Daddy Loves His Baby.** How much does Mommy love her baby? ". . . like the fishies love the seas . . . and squirrels love the trees." PLATINUM AWARD '04. 18 mos. & up.

■ Peedie 2005

Peedie

Olivier Dunrea

(by Oliver Dunrea, Houghton Mifflin $9.99 ●●●●) Peedie the gosling forgets things, often. Toddlers can follow along as he tries to find his lucky red baseball cap. From the author of last year's PLATINUM AWARD winner, **Ollie.** 2 & up.

■ Under My Hood I Have a Hat

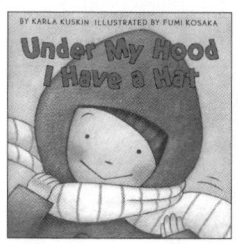

2005 PLATINUM AWARD

(by Karla Kuskin/illus. by Fumi Kosaka, HarperCollins $14.99 ●●●●●) As the story unfolds, we see all of the clothes the little girl has to wear to go outside to play. Kuskin's sense of humor is wonderfully matched by Kosaka's playful illustrations. 2 & up.

Rhythm and Rhyme and Repetitive Lines

■ Big Red Tub 2005

(by Julia Jarman/illus. Adrian Reynolds, Orchard $14.95 ●●●●) As Stan and Stella take their bath they are joined by a tubful of their animal friends. The bath tub then shoots off into space but, not to worry, they are saved by a flock of flamingos. Reynolds' cheerful illustrations match Jarman's bouncy verse. 2 & up.

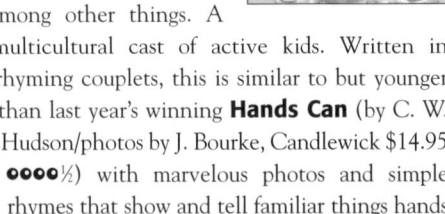

■ Busy Fingers 2005

(by C. W. Bowie/illus. by Fred Willingham, Charlesbridge $6.95 ●●●●½) Fingers count, stroke, squish, and poke… among other things. A multicultural cast of active kids. Written in rhyming couplets, this is similar to but younger than last year's winning **Hands Can** (by C. W. Hudson/photos by J. Bourke, Candlewick $14.95 ●●●●½) with marvelous photos and simple rhymes that show and tell familiar things hands can do. 2–5.

■ Does a Cow Say Boo?

(by Judy Hindley/illus. by Brita Granstrom, Candlewick $15.99 ●●●●●) A repetitive refrain gives this playful story a pattern that toddlers can chime in on. A truly interactive book that toddlers will want to hear again and again. Features charming art and a multicultural cast of kids. PLATINUM AWARD '03. 2 & up.

Slice-of-Life Books

■ Daddies Give You Horsey Rides 2005

(by Abby Levine/illus. by John Bendall-Brunello, Albert Whitman, $14.95 ●●●●) A modern ode to all the things that daddies do, including the typical horsing around. Levine also shows them cooking, and taking care of you when you're sick or have a nightmare. Bendall-Brunello's illustrations are so inviting and charming! 2 & up.

■ Minnie and Her Baby Brother

(by Melanie Walsh, Candlewick $7.99 ●●●●●) Minnie has a baby brother and, like all big brothers and sisters, Minnie can do a lot of things the baby can't do. Lift the flaps on every spread to see all the things baby can't do. A very positive spin on sibling rivalry. PLATINUM AWARD '04. 2–5.

■ Mo's Stinky Sweater 2005

(by David Bedford/illus. by Edward Eaves, Hyperion $14.99 ●●●●) Mo's a little monkey with a truly dirty sweater. His mom wants him to take it off and have it washed. A tug of war ensues between the baby animals and their parents. The babies get the upper hand and all the parents end up in the mud! Everyone gets clean (including the sweater). Both parents and kids will find this a satisfying story! 2 & up.

Coping with Life's Little Ups & Downs

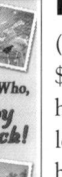

■ Guess Who, Baby Duck! 2005

(by Amy Hest/illus. by Jill Barton, Candlewick $14.99 ●●●●) When Baby Duck is home sick, his Grandpa comes to take care of him. They look at a photo album together. If only every baby duck had a grandpa like this one! 2 & up.

■ On Mother's Lap BLUE CHIP

(by Ann H. Scott/illus. by Glo Coalson, Clarion $4.95 ●●●●●) A small Inuit boy is enjoying some snuggle time on mother's lap when the new baby cries for attention. Mother helps him discover that there's room for both of them. A classic reissued in board-book format. 2 & up.

■ Za-Za's Baby Brother

(by Lucy Cousins, Candlewick $6.99 ●●●●) If there's a new baby in the family, big brothers and sisters will relate to the problems Za-Za is having. Life is not the same for poor Za-Za, who has to share everyone's attention. Using a "zebra" family takes this one step away from reality and may help older sibs talk about their feelings. 2–5.

Potty Corner (Results not Guaranteed!)

■ Going to the Potty BLUE CHIP

(by Fred Rogers/photos by Jim Judkis, Putnam $5.95 ●●●●) In his usual reassuring way, Mr. Rogers talks with children about using the potty. This photo essay reinforces the idea that using a potty is another step toward growing up. Also excellent: **Your New Potty,** by J. Cole, Morrow. 2 & up.

■ My Big Boy/Girl Potty

(by Joanna Cole/illus. by Maxie Chambliss, HarperCollins $5.95 ●●●●) If you're introducing the concept of potty training, you can make a gender-specific choice with either version of this little book that makes the transition from diapers to potty sound "doable"—let's hope! We find this more age-appropriate than the "What to Expect for Kids" book on the same subject. 2 & up.

Sweet Dreams—Bedtime Books

■ Goodnight Moon BLUE CHIP

(by Margaret Wise Brown/illus. by Clement Hurd, HarperCollins $6.95 ●●●●●) Happy news! This bedtime classic is available in a sturdy board book that toddlers can enjoy without ripping. 18 mos. & up.

■ It's Bedtime, Wibbly Pig! 2005 PLATINUM AWARD

(by Mick Inkpen, Viking $15.99 ●●●●●) It's time for bed, but is lovable little Wibbly Pig ready? Not yet. He needs to take a bubbly bath, dry his toes, and so it goes… from one delay to the next. A familiar slice-of-life storybook that tots are sure to recognize. 2 & up.

■ Little Bo-Peep 2005

(by Tracey Campbell Pearson, Farrar Straus Giroux, $8.95 ●●●●) Using the original Mother Goose rhyme, a new story unfolds through the illustrations about an unhappy toddler who has tossed her toy sheep out of the crib and wants them back. Encourages toddlers and parents to interpret the visual storyline. 18 mos. & up.

■ The Noisy Way to Bed 2005

(by Ian Whybrow/illus. by Tiphanie Beeke, Scholastic $15.95 ●●●●) As a little boy heads for home to go to bed, he collects a

noisy duck, horse, pig, rabbit, and duck. Toddlers will love chiming in on the repetitive refrain. 2 & up.

Early Concept Books— Color, Counting, and More

■ Babies On the Go

(by Linda Ashman/illus. by Jane Dyer, Harcourt $16 ❍❍❍❍❍) Some animal babies get up on all fours and run about to play. But this book is about the ones who, like human babies, need to be transported for a while. Charming watercolor paintings and rhythmic rhymes introduce children to a science concept that the "Uppees!"crowd can relate to. PLATINUM AWARD '04. 2–5.

■ My Car 🏷2005 BLUE CHIP

(by Byron Barton, HarperTrophy $6.99 ❍❍❍❍❍) If you have a toddler obsessed with cars, here's the perfect book. Clear illustrations that are all about cars and transportation. A reissue of one of our old favorites in a larger format. 2 & up.

■ Teeth Are Not for Biting

(by Elizabeth Verdick/illus. by Marieka Heinlen, Free Spirit $7.95 ❍❍❍❍) A message book that may be helpful for toddlers who use their teeth when they get angry or frustrated. It's a little off, semantically—we do use our teeth to bite—but the repeated refrain, "Ouch! Biting hurts!" might be useful as a reminder. Also highly recommended: **Hands Are Not for Hitting** (by Martha Agassi/illus. by Marieka Heinlen ❍❍❍❍❍) PLATINUM AWARD '03. 1½–3.

■ Is This Maisy's House ? 🏷2005 PLATINUM AWARD

(by Lucy Cousins, Candlewick $7.99 ❍❍❍❍❍)
A new lift-the-flap book with chances to shout "No!" and to see the right answers confirmed by lifting the flaps. Objects to "know and name" on the left, objects in use are under the flaps. Great companion book to **How Will You Get There, Maisy?** 2 & up.

■ Mama and Me `2005`

(by Julie Aigner-Clark/illus. by Nadeem Zaidi, Hyperion $5.99 ●●●●½)
If you get beyond the cover you'll find handsome photos and a few facts
about each of the parent-child animal pairs that make this an interesting early science book for toddlers.

■ Whose Nose and Toes? `2005`

(by John Butler, Viking $10.99 ●●●●½) First
you see a nose and foot. Turn the page, and discover the whole animal. Handsome art and simple information for young animal lovers. From
the creator of **Whose Baby Am I?,** which
introduces like parent-and-child pairs. For tots
ready to go beyond farm animals.

Books to Sing

■ Fiddle-I-Fee

(illus. by Melissa Sweet, Little, Brown $5.95 ●●●●●) Once you have
a refresher course in this folk song, you will be singing, "Cat goes fid-
dle-I-fee" all day long. Sweet's illustrations are charming, and the
board book edition will hold up to many go-rounds! PLATINUM
AWARD '03. 2 & up.

■ The Itsy Bitsy Spider `2005` PLATINUM AWARD

(Sassy $11.99 ●●●●●) You can play the music
as you look at the pages, or press the
polka-dot button on each vinyl page,
and the book sings the words with you
as you turn the pages. One of three
clever songbooks. Also fun, **Hey Diddle
Diddle** and **Three Little Monkeys.**

■ This Little Light of Mine `2005`

(Adapted by Raffi/illus. by Stacey Schuett, Knopf $15.95 ●●●●½)
Seeing connections between the words we speak and sing to words on
the printed page is a great way to develop pre-reading and early reading skills. This delightful song has plenty of repetition, so the sight
vocabulary grows as you sing this together. 4 & up.

■ Wheels on the Bus BLUE CHIP

(by Paul Zelinsky, Dutton $17.99 ●●●●●) For the traditional song in
a delightful, though very rippable pop-up format, bring home
Zelinsky's version, but save for parent/child together times. 2 & up.

Preschool Books for Threes and Fours

Preschoolers delight in books of all kinds. They enjoy longer stories about real kids like themselves and animal stories that are really about "kids in fur" with whom they can identify. Folktales and fantasy are fine as long as they're not too scary. They like the rhythm and rhyme of verse as well as prose that touches their hearts and funny bones. Eager to learn, they like playful counting and alphabet books. Kids are also interested in true facts about real things that satisfy their curiosity about the world.

**BLUE CHIP BOOKS
EVERY PRESCHOOLER SHOULD KNOW**

✓ **Caps for Sale,** by Esphyr Slobodkina
✓ **Curious George,** by H. A. Rey
✓ **If You Give a Mouse a Cookie,** by Laura J. Numeroff
✓ **The Little Engine That Could,** by Watty Piper
✓ **Make Way for Ducklings,** by Robert McCloskey
✓ **Mama, Do You Love Me?** by Barbara Joosse
✓ **Millions of Cats,** by Wanda Gag
✓ **The Nutshell Library,** by Maurice Sendak
✓ **Olivia,** by Ian Falconer
✓ **The Tale of Peter Rabbit,** by Beatrix Potter
✓ **The Runaway Bunny,** by Margaret Wise Brown
✓ **A Snowy Day,** by Ezra Jack Keats

Great New Read-Alouds for Preschoolers

■ **Four Friends In Autumn**
   2005 PLATINUM AWARD

(by Tomie dePaola, Simon & Schuster $14.95 ●●●●●) Miss Piggy invites everyone for a dinner party to celebrate autumn, but alas, she eats all the food. A slight but funny story, reissued from 1977, that will tickle your preschooler. 3–6.

■ **Gigi and Lulu's Gigantic Fight** **2005**

(by Pamela Duncan Edwards/illus. by Henry Cole, HarperCollins $15.95 ●●●●) One of the joys of life is friendship, but for young children, sorting out what it means to be a friend can be confusing. Gigi and Lulu like all the same things until they have a gigantic fight and stop speaking to each other. They figure out that they don't have to do everything the same to be friends. Reassuring. 4 & up.

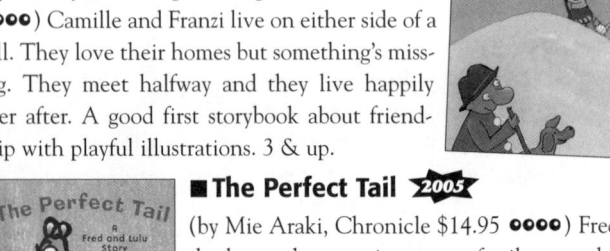

■ Mr. Murry and Thumbkin 2005

(by Karma Wilson/illus. by Ard Hoyt, Little, Brown $15.99 ●●●●) There's a very old-fashioned flavor to this tale of two mice: Mr. Murry, who worries about everything, and Thumbkin, who worries not at all. When Thumbkin loses his home, Mr. Murry comes to his rescue. Think Oscar and Felix. 4 & up.

■ On the Hill 2005

(by Lisa Jahn-Clough, Houghton Mifflin $15 ●●●●) Camille and Franzi live on either side of a hill. They love their homes but something's missing. They meet halfway and they live happily ever after. A good first storybook about friendship with playful illustrations. 3 & up.

■ The Perfect Tail 2005

(by Mie Araki, Chronicle $14.95 ●●●●) Fred the bunny has a serious case of tail envy—he likes everyone's but his own, until his rhino friend Lulu pays him a compliment. A great book for addressing a common issue for kids (and adults). 3 & up.

■ The Pigeon Finds a Hot Dog!
2005 PLATINUM AWARD

(by Mo Willems, Hyperion $12.99 ●●●●●) Sharing is not easy—especially sharing something as delicious as a hot dog! With few words and no preaching, Pigeon works through his reluctance and does the right thing. If only it were that easy! 3–6

■ Sock Monkey Boogie Woogie 2005

(by Cece Bell, Candlewick $14.99 ●●●●) Sock Monkey wants to go to the dance, but all his friends are out of town. But will that stop a clever monkey? A fantasy that celebrates creative thinking and friendship. 4 & up.

All in the Family

■ Angelina, Star of the Show *2005* PLATINUM AWARD

(by Katherine Holabird/illus. by Helen Craig, American Girl $17.95 ●●●●○) Angelina excitedly sets off to the Mouseland Dance Festival with her grandparents on their boat. More interested in practicing her steps, Angelina doesn't help her grandparents on the boat and causes a series of mishaps. Her grandparents are firm but understanding and ultimately save the day. 4–7.

■ April Foolishness *2005* PLATINUM AWARD

(by Teresa Bateman/illus. by Nadine Bernard Westcott, Whitman $15.95 ●●●●●) All the grandkids have come to visit at the farm and try their best to tell Grandpa that the animals are running wild. Clever Grandpa isn't falling for their April Fool's tricks. Grandma steps in to have the last laugh! Good fun. 5 & up.

■ Did I Tell You I Love You Today? *2005*

(by Deloris Jordan & Roslyn M. Jordan/illus. by Shane W. Evans, Simon & Schuster $16.95 ●●●○) A reassuring message to children that grown-ups show their love by taking care of them, and a reminder to grown-ups to say, "I love you." Written by the basketball star's mother and sister. 3 & up.

■ Ruby in Her Own Time *2005*

(by Jonathan Emmett/illus. by Rebecca Harry, Scholastic $15.95 ●●●○½) Ruby, the littlest of five ducklings, is not the first to hatch, swim, or eat. But in her "own good time" she does all this and more. A reassuring picture book for the littlest ducking in any family. 3 & up.

■ Twice as Nice *2005*

(by Nicole Rubel, Farrar Straus $15.95 ●●●○) With so many twins in the world today, this book will appeal to more than a select few! Rubel explains how twins come to be, the difference between fraternal and identical twins, and a host of interesting historical tidbits about twins. 5 & up.

■ Watch Out!
2005 PLATINUM AWARD

(by Jan Fearnley, Candlewick $15.99 ⦿⦿⦿⦿⦿) Exuberant preschoolers will relate to Wilf, a little mouse who means well but is always going "crash, bang, wallop." While his mother pleads with him to slow down, her own exuberance leads to her own messy mishap. 3 & up.

■ You're All My Favorites **2005 PLATINUM AWARD**

(by Sam McBratney/illus. by Anita Jeram, Candlewick $15.99 ⦿⦿⦿⦿⦿) A tender book that addresses sibling rivalry with a sympathetic ear and heart. Although the cubs know they are loved, there comes a moment when each wants to be the favorite one. From the gifted creators of **Guess How Much I Love You.** 3 & up.

Separation

■ Don't Forget I Love You **2005**

(by Miriam Moss/illus. by Anna Currey, Dial $15.99 ⦿⦿⦿⦿) The frantic race to work and school is told through the eyes of a dawdling little bear, Billy. His mom leaves him at preschool without saying, "I love you," and she mistakenly takes his toy rabbit with her. Mama rushes back to the school to make things right. A little too sweet and perfect, but will appeal to preschoolers that are working on morning rituals. 3 & up.

■ When I Miss You **2005**

(by Cornelia Maude Spelman/illus. by Kathy Parkinson, Albert Whitman $15.95 ⦿⦿⦿⦿) Knowing that your parent will come back is a big step to a happier separation. Told through animals, this is a good talking book for reassuring your child that you miss them when you're apart and that you look forward to seeing them too! 3 & up.

Bedtime

■ Good Night Sam

(by Marie-Louise Gay, Groundwood $14.95 ●●●●●) Big sister Stella is having a problem with her little brother Sam. He can't go to sleep because he can't find his cuddly dog Fred. There's humor along with patience in this totally charming bedtime tale. PLATINUM AWARD '04. 3 & up.

■ How Many Kisses Do You Want Tonight? 2005

(by Varsha Bajaj/illus. by Ivan Bates, Little, Brown $15.95 ●●●●) Lyrical images of animal parent and child add much to the soothing lilt of a lullaby-like rhyme. A repetitive refrain, "How many kisses do you want tonight?" grows with each turn of the page and is bound to inspire lots of goodnight hugs and kisses! 3 & up.

■ The Magic Bed

(by John Burningham, Knopf $16.95 ●●●●●) Georgie has outgrown his bed. Instead of buying a new bed he and his father bring home an antique that is said to be magic. It takes some doing, but Georgie figures out the magic word and, abracadabra!, his bed takes him far and wide— until Grannie sells the bed, thinking that new is better. A collection of fearless flights to spark sweet dreams. PLATINUM AWARD '04. 3–8.

Concept Books— Numbers, Letters, Words, and More

■ Alphabet Mystery

(by Audrey Wood/illus. by Bruce Wood, Scholastic $15.95 ●●●●●)

All of the lowercase letters are ready to go to sleep when they discover that "x" is missing! And where can he be? An imaginative mystery for children who are playing with and learning their letters. This is no ordinary ABC. PLATINUM AWARD '04. 4–7.

■ Babar's Book of Color
2005 Platinum Award

(by Laurent de Brunhoff, Abrams $16.95 ●●●●○) When Babar's children come to see him in his art studio they explore colors and what happens when colors are mixed. The children create playful "color" illustrations that are also perfect for knowing and naming animals of the appropriate color. 2–5.

■ Chicka Chicka 1 2 3 **2005**

(by Bill Martin Jr., Michael Sampson/illus. by Lois Ehlert, Simon & Schuster $15.95 ●●●●) Fans of **Chicka Chicka Boom Boom** will enjoy this older concept book. 100 numbers race up the apple tree, but watch out for the bumblebees! It's a brave number zero that saves the day. 3 & up.

■ How Do Dinosaurs Count to Ten? **2005**

(by Jane Yolen/illus. by Mark Teague, Scholastic $6.99 ●●●●) Young preschoolers will enjoy counting the familiar household objects along with the big dinos on each page. Teague's illustrations are humorous and inviting. 2–4.

■ Joey and Jet **2005**

(by James Young, Atheneum $15.95 ●●●●) While Joey and his dog Jet play a game of fetch throughout their neighborhood, the place concepts of *between*, *through*, *over*, *under*, and *around* are playfully explored. 4 & up.

■ Five Little Monkeys Play Hide-and-Seek **2005**

(by Eileen Christelow, Clarion $15 ●●●●) They're back! Mama wants her five little monkeys to go to bed but they convince her that a fast game of hide-and-seek would be in order. While not vastly different from the five previous books, kids love the playfulness of this series and there are plenty of opportunities for counting! 4 & up.

Young Science

■ Bugs Pop-Up 2005

(by Sally Hewitt/illus. by Chris Gilvan-Cartwright, Abrams $14.95 ●●●●) With a playful rhyme about each of the creatures, this is a spectacular pop-up book with giant faces of a wasp, bee, and other creepy crawlers that almost leap off the pages! A memorable novelty book. 3 & up. Also ideal for bug fans, **Big Bugs! Giant Creepy Crawly Pop Ups** (by Keith Faulkner/illus. by Stephen Homes & Jonathan Lambert, Scholastic $10.95 ●●●●) with big fold-outs that answer riddles posed on each page. 3 & up.

■ Hello, Snow! 2005

(by Hope Vestergaard/illus. by Nadine Bernard Westcott, Farrar Straus $16 ●●●●) "Hello pants. Good-bye knees. I don't want you guys to freeze!" All the excitement of a snowy day is captured in this rhythmic celebration of snow! 2–5.

■ Mister Seahorse 2005 PLATINUM AWARD

(by Eric Carle, Philomel $16.95 ●●●●●) Get ready for a Johnny Carson "I did not know that" kind of moment when you share this handsome early science book. Carle visits the important role of fathers in the sea. Male seahorses carry the eggs in their pouch and male tilapia carry their eggs in their mouth. Lift up see-through pages add visual surprises. 3 & up.

■ My First Jumbo Book of Dinosaurs 2005

(by James Diaz, Melanie Gerth & Francesca Diaz, Scholastic $9.95 ●●●●) If you have a young dino-holic in your midst, bring home this introductory knowing and naming book that's done with colorful illustrations, pop-ups, and phonetic pronunciation help. This book will be looked at again and again. 4 & up.

■ **Pie in the Sky** *2005* PLATINUM AWARD

(by Lois Ehlert, Harcourt $16 ●●●●●)
Starting with the somber brown tones of
early spring, a child looks for evidence
that the tree in the yard is what Dad calls
a "Pie Tree." The text invites children to
search for lists of bugs, bark, and other
natural items that are easily found in the
stunning cut-paper collages that are Lois
Ehlert's trademark. No pie is found, but

as the season changes the artist's palette bursts forth with blossoms,
birds, butterflies, and a bright red cherry feast that lights up the
pages! One of Ehlert's very best! 3 & up.

■ **Who Are You,
Baby Kangaroo?** *2005*

(by Stella Blackstone/illus. by Clare
Beaton, Barefoot $14.99 ●●●●) A puppy
wants to know what the baby kangaroo is
called. In his search for an answer he learns
the names of several other baby animals.
Done in Beaton's stunning wish-you-
could-touch-it felt appliqué. 3 & up.

Starting to School

■ **Ella the Elegant Elephant** *2005*

(by Carmela and Steven D'Amico,
Scholastic $16.95 ●●●●½) Ella is about to
start at a brand new school. Her Grandma's
special red hat is her good luck charm—or is
it? A satisfying tale about daring to be yourself. 4 & up.

■ **I am Too Absolutely Small for
School** *2005* PLATINUM AWARD

(by Lauren Child, Candlewick $16.99
●●●●●) With her usual determination,
Lola has decided that she is not ready for
school. After all, she has a lot of things to do
at home! Once again, her big brother
Charlie convinces her that school is not all
bad. Comforting for kids not sure about the
whole growing-up thing! 4 & up.

■ Little Brown Bear Won't Go to School

(by Jane Dyer, Little Brown $15.95 **ooooo**½) After he is dropped off at the school, Little Bear decides he'd rather have a job, like Mama and Papa Bear. But he soon discovers that the only job he's really ready for is waiting for Papa in school. Dyer's drawings are charming and the pace of the book is just right for the kindergartener-to-be. 4½ & up.

Early-School-Age Children

During the early school years, as kids become readers and not just listeners, keeping them "in books" is a challenge. Reading is something they should do for pleasure, not because it's "good for them." By bringing home a rich variety of books—fact and fantasy, science and history, humor and adventure, read-alouds, and read-alones—you will be building a link to a lifetime of pleasure found in books.

 BLUE CHIP BOOKS EVERY EARLY-SCHOOL-AGE KID SHOULD KNOW

✓ **Alexander and the Terrible, Horrible, No Good, Very Bad Day,** by Judith Viorst
✓ **Amazing Grace,** by Mary Hoffman
✓ **Amos and Boris/Sylvester and the Magic Pebble,** by William Steig
✓ **Martha series,** by Susan Meddaugh
✓ **Jolly Postman books,** by Janet and Allan Ahlberg
✓ **Magic Schoolbus series,** by Joanna Cole
✓ **Olivia** and **Olivia Saves the Circus,** by Ian Falconer
✓ **Ramona series,** by Beverly Cleary
✓ **Tar Beach,** by Faith Ringgold
✓ **The True Story of the Three Little Pigs,** by Jon Scieszka
✓ **Where the Wild Things Are,** by Maurice Sendak

Great Read-Alouds for Older Listeners

■ **Baby Brains** **2005** PLATINUM AWARD

(by Simon James, Candlewick $15.99 **ooooo**) Even before Baby

Brains is born, Mrs. Brains is reading to her baby and playing him music. Small wonder that hours after he is born he is reading the newspaper, going to school, and days later going to college and med school. This LOL tall tale is so far-out that Baby Brains ends up in outer space, where he discovers being brainy is not everything! A refreshingly light tale! 4–8.

■ Bad Bears in the Big City 2005

(by Daniel Pinkwater/illus. by Jill Pinkwater, Houghton Mifflin $16 ●●●●½) In an amusing sequel to **Two Bad Bears,** Irving and Muktuk, two polar bears with an appetite for muffins, are exiled from their home in the frozen North to the zoo in Bayonne, New Jersey. Once again these untrustworthy friends break out in a zany adventure. 5 & up.

■ Detective LaRue: Letters from the Investigator
2005 PLATINUM AWARD

(by Mark Teague, Scholastic $15.95 ●●●●●) Once again, the story is told in a series of letters from Ike the dog to his vacationing owner, Mrs. LaRue. Ike is being held in jail for the mysterious disappearance of two cats. Ike breaks out of jail and "rescues" the cats with a nod to the readers that the cats were responsible for a series of bird mishaps! As in the original, **Dear Mrs. LaRue,** Ike is a hero at the end of the day. A fun read-aloud. 5 & up.

■ It's Hard to Be Five 2005

(by Jamie Lee Curtis/illus. by Laura Cornell, HarperCollins ●●●●½) Curtis hits the ambivalence about growing up on the nose. The subtitle, "Learning How to Work My Control Panel," is an apt description of this transition to bigger-kid status. As usual, Cornell's witty illustrations capture the mood. For soon-to-be 5s and 5s.

■ Liberty's Journey 2005

(by Kelly DiPucchio/illus. by Richard Egielski, Hyperion $15.99 ●●●●½) Here's a tribute to a national treasure. Lady Liberty leaves her island and takes her own tour of America. DiPucchio and Egielski bring the great statue to life with both words and striking illustrations that culminate in a joyous celebration of her return to New York Harbor. 5 & up.

■ Perfectly Martha *2005* PLATINUM AWARD

(by Susan Meddaugh, Houghton Mifflin $15 ●●●●●) Martha, the talking dog, is back with another adventure that will remind grown-ups of the Stepford Wives for canines. The Perfect Pup Institute sets out to transform the town's dogs into a perfectly obedient group. Martha figures out how they are getting such results and exposes the plot. 4–8.

■ Pinuli *2005*

(by Janell Cannon, Harcourt $16 ●●●●½) Pinuli, a hyena, thinks all the other animals are better than she is. But when she accidentally changes her appearance, she discovers a way to make the others do her bidding. 5 & up.

■ The Princess Knight *2005*

(by Cornelia Funke/illus. by Kerstin Meyer, Scholastic $15.95 ●●●●) This tale about a princess who wants to be trained to be a knight like her brothers almost seems dated, but does provide the message that girls are as capable as boys. The King decrees that his daughter must marry the finest jouster in the land. The Princess enters the contest and of course is victorious. 6 & up.

■ Toot & Puddle: The New Friend
2005 PLATINUM AWARD

(by Holly Hobbie, Little Brown $15.95 ●●●●●) Toot and Puddle are back; this time Puddle's adorable cousin Opal has come for a visit with her friend Daphne. Opal feels that Daphne is far better than she is at many things, but in the end she discovers all of her own special talents. A well-constructed story that will surely hit a chord with kids, who often feel that they don't measure up. 5 & up.

■ **The Trial of Cardigan Jones**
2005 PLATINUM AWARD

(by Tim Egan, Houghton Mifflin $15.95
●●●●●) The jury jumps to the conclusion that
Moose must have eaten Mrs. Brown's apple pie.
A smart judge sees another possibility. A great
read-aloud with an important message. 6 & up.

Families Then and Now

Kids love stories about families like their own as well as those
that are totally different. We've chosen family stories about kids
today and those who lived in the past. The historic settings and
figures offer kids a glimpse into another time and place. Past or
present, good stories speak to kids about human experiences.

■ **Eddie: Harold's Little Brother**
2005 PLATINUM AWARD

(by Ed Koch & Pat Koch Thaler/illus. by
James Warhola, Putnam $16.99 ●●●●●) A
home run of a book. No matter how hard little Eddie tries, he doesn't have the same ability in baseball that his older brother Harold
displays—a hard lesson for many siblings. In
the end Eddie discovers his own special tal-
ent—public speaking—and of course little Eddie becomes the Mayor
of New York. 5 & up.

■ **A Fire Engine for Ruthie** **2005**

(by Lesléa Newman/illus. by Cyd Moore,
Clarion $16 ●●●●) When Ruthie visits her
Nana she is confronted, much to her dismay,
with dolls and tea sets. Very good naturedly,
Nana gets the idea that Ruthie much prefers
the trucks and trains of her neighbor's child.
For many doll-phobic girls this will be a reassuring tale that should be shared with well-
meaning doll-giving grownups! 5 & up.

■ **Photographer Mole**
2005 PLATINUM AWARD

(by Dennis Haseley/illus. by Juli Kangas,
Dial $16.99 ●●●●●) Although he's an
admired and well loved photographer, Mole

is dissatisfied with his life. Looking at the photos of the many friends and families he has taken, Mole feels he must go off into the world to discover what is missing in his life. A sweet story about love.

Legends, Bible Stories, and Folktales

■ Apples to Oregon
2005 PLATINUM AWARD

(by Deborah Hopkinson & Nancy Carpenter, Atheneum $15.95 ●●●●●) Here's a fun tall tale about a girl named Delicious and how she helps her father bring his precious fruit trees from Iowa to Oregon. They fend off hail, desert heat, and frost before they make it to their destination. A humor-filled tale that makes a great read with a little history thrown into the mix. 6 & up.

■ Clever Beatrice and the Best Little Pony **2005**

(by Margaret Willey/illus. By Heather M. Solomon, Atheneum $15.95 ●●●●) In this French Canadian tall tale, there's a *lutin*, an elf, who is trying to steal Beatrice's pony. Encouraged by her mother to ask the help of Monsieur le Pain, the baker, Beatrice doesn't seem to see that it is her own cleverness that repeatedly saves her pony. 6 & up.

■ Ella's Big Chance **2005** PLATINUM AWARD

(by Shirley Hughes, Simon & Schuster $16.95 ●●●●●) Set during the roaring '20s, this Ella is forced to design and sew dresses for her evil stepmother and stepsisters. While her Fairy Godmother comes and does the usual magic, in a nice twist Ella turns down the Duke's proposal of marriage to be with her beloved co-worker. 5 & up.

■ Jonah and the Whale **2005**

(by Jean Marzollo, Little, Brown $14.95 ●●●●½) Jonah tries to run away rather than deliver God's message to the Ninevites, people Jonah considers his enemies. Marzollo manages to tell this story about forgiveness without turning it into a solemn preachment. In fact, her signature "chorus" (octopi, this time) at the bottom of the page adds a breezy good humor. Also recommended in this fine series, **David and Goliath,** the story of a boy's faith in God, and earlier titles **Daniel in the Lion's Den** and **Miriam and Her Brother Moses.** 4–8.

■ The Giant and the Beanstalk
2005 PLATINUM AWARD

(by Diane Stanley, HarperCollins $15.95 ●●●●●)
Here's a familiar story told from the perspective of the exceedingly polite Giant Otto. Otto must go in search of Jack, who has stolen his pet hen. The author then takes Otto on a wonderful adventure through Nursery Rhyme land to see all the other Jacks that live there! A clever adventure for kids who are storybook-savvy and get the references. 7 & up.

■ The People Could Fly 2005

(by Virginia Hamilton/illus. by Leo and Diane Dillon, Knopf $16.96 ●●●●½) It is said that there was a time in Africa when some people could fly. But when these same people became slaves in America the magic was lost, until one old man whispers the special words that uplift. Originally the title story in a stunning collection of 24 African American folktales, this handsome stand-alone picture book is re-illustrated by the masterful Dillons. 7 & up.

Alphabet Books

■ A is for Abigail:
An Almanac of Amazing American Women

(by Lynne V. Cheney/illus. by Robin P. Glasser, Simon & Schuster $16.99 ●●●●½) A worthy sequel to **America, a Patriotic Primer,** this is no ordinary ABC. It celebrates American women who have led the way in many fields of endeavor—the arts, sciences, sports, and gov-  ernment. Glasser's illustrations are full of details to explore and talk about together. 6–9.

■ The Queen's Progress,
An Elizabethan Alphabet 2005

(by Celeste D. Mannis/illus. by Bagram Ibatoulline, Viking $16.99 ●●●●½) Not an alphabet for those who are learning their letters, but rather an amazing pictorial introduction to Elizabethan England, telling the story of the annual journey Elizabeth took into the coun-tryside to be with her people each summer. Stunning paintings capture the clothing, feasts, and festivities of the "Progress," as her trip was called. 9 & up.

Math Books

■ Math Appeal

(by Greg Tang/illus. by Harry Briggs, Scholastic $16.95 ○○○○½) Like the original **Grapes of Math,** these math riddles deliver new ways of looking at and solving math problems by grouping, subtraction, multiplying, and seeing patterns. The riddles give young readers hints (the answers and solutions are thankfully at the back of the book). Also see **Math for All Seasons.** 7 & up.

■ What Time Is It, Mr. Crocodile? *2005*

(by Judy Sierra/illus. by Doug Cushman, Harcourt $16 ○○○○½) Mr. Crocodile has great plans for every hour of the day, but his schedule is constantly undone by five silly monkeys. Told in breezy rhyme with illustrations that add to the fun, there's a clock on every page that introduces reading the time on the hour. Younger listeners may like the story, but telling time is beyond them. A better choice for 5 & up.

Tales out of School

■ The Blue Ribbon Day *2005*

(by Katie Couric/illus. by Marjorie Priceman, Random House $17.95 ○○○○½) Is there anyone who has not known the disappointment of not being picked for the team? Ellie and Carrie, the same clever pair from **The Brand New Kid,** are back with their winning ways in this sequel that addresses an all-too-familiar childhood problem. 5 & up.

■ The Bully Blockers Club *2005*

(by Teresa Bateman/illus. by Jackie Urbanovic, Whitman $15 ○○○○) Lotty and a lot of others are bothered by a bully in school who knows just when to annoy others—when the teacher is not looking. Lotty cleverly finds a solution. A good choice for a not-so-uncommon problem. 5 & up.

■ Mrs. Watson Wants Your Teeth *2005*

(by Alison McGhee/illus. by Harry Bliss, Harcourt $16 ○○○○) The

first grade teacher is thought to be an alien who steals teeth from her students. Of course, the reality is much more comforting; students who lose a tooth get a piece of candy. Learning not to believe everything people tell you is an important message. 5 & up.

■ **Too Loud Lily** *2005*

(by Sofie Laguna/illus. by Kerry Argent, Scholastic $14.95 ○○○○) Lily, an exuberant hippo, is just too noisy at home and at school. But then one day a new music teacher arrives and Lily's special talents are appreciated! A merry romp that proves there's a time and place for everything! 4–7.

Information, Please: Science, History, Art, and More

School-age kids have an appetite for information about the real world. They want to know where things come from, how they are made, and how they work. Though they live very much in the present, they are curious about the past and how things were. Such information used to be found only in encyclopedias or dull textbooks. Today there are gloriously beautiful and lively nonfiction books for young readers.

Science

■ **Animal Snackers** *2005*

(by Betsy Lewin, Henry Holt $15.95 ○○○○) Junk food snacks may be an issue with kids, but this collection will have young readers crying "gross!" and "yuck!" as they discover what animals eat for snacks. Lewin captures it all in delicious verse and impish images. 4–8.

■ **Forest Explorer, A Life-Size Field Guide** *2005*

(by Nic Bishop, Scholastic $17.95 ○○○○½) Young naturalists will pore over the stunning photographs of seven life-sized habitats searching out the dozens of creatures that live in the forest. A fine sequel to *Backyard Detective: Critters Up Close*. 7 & up.

■ **Squirrel and John Muir** 🏅2005

(by Emily Arnold McCully, Farrar Straus $16 ❍❍❍❍)
While best known today for the Redwood Forest
named in his honor, John Muir founded the Sierra
Club and became respected for his theory of glacial
formation. McCully introduces us to Muir through
the eyes of Floy Hutchings, a real girl who lived in
Yosemite. 7 & up. For the story of John James
Audubon, look at **The Boy Who Drew Birds** (by Jacqueline
Davies/illus. by Melissa Sweet, Harcourt $16 ❍❍❍❍), which explains
how Audubon came to America to avoid Napoleon's army and fol-
lowed his passion for birds. 8 & up.

■ **Tigress** 🏅2005 PLATINUM AWARD

(by Nick Dowson/illus. by Jane Chapman,
Candlewick $15.99 ❍❍❍❍❍) Lyrical prose is coun-
terpointed with interesting facts that together convey the story of the Tigress and her young.
Chapman's illustrations capture the cubs as they
grow from small enough to be carried by their
necks, to big enough to pounce and hunt for food. Imagine—in 18
months, tiger cubs learn all they need to know, and slink off through the
jungle grass to begin their independent lives. 5 & up.

■ **Next Stop Neptune** 🏅2005

(by Alvin Jenkins/illus. by Steve Jenkins,
Houghton Mifflin $16 ❍❍❍❍½) Take a tour of
the solar system with the Jenkins' informative
and visually breathtaking view of what's happening above us. Illustrated with cut paper and
sprinkled with nuggets of information, this can
be read from beginning to end, or browsed to
reveal factoids about specifics in space. 8 & up.

■ **Volcanoes: Journey to the Crater's Edge**

(by Philippe Bourseiller/adapted by Robert Burleigh, Abrams $14.95

❍❍❍❍❍) Stunning photographs give armchair
travellers a sense of the drama that erupts in so
many different ways from volcanoes around the
world. PLATINUM AWARD '04. A worthy sequel to
PLATINUM winner **Earth From Above** (by Yann
Arthus-Bertrand / Robert Burleigh, Abrams,
$12.95). 7 & up.

People and Places in History

AMERICANA

■ **America the Beautiful** **2005** PLATINUM AWARD

(paper engineered by Robert Sabuda, Simon & Schuster $26.95 ●●●●●) Each page of this patriotic song comes to life with Sabuda's breathtaking paper engineering. From the Golden Gate Bridge to the Statue of Liberty, this will be enjoyed by kids and grown-ups alike. 5 & up. For a more traditional but equally patriotic book, **O, Say Can You See?** (by Sheila Keenan/illus. by Ann Boyajian, Scholastic $16.95 ●●●●) takes a look at America's landmarks such as the Liberty Bell, the White House, and the Washington Monument. 7 & up.

■ **The Flag Maker** **2005**

(by Susan Campbell Bartoletti/illus. by Claire A. Nivola, Houghton Mifflin $16 ●●●●) Here's the back story for the flag that inspired Francis Scott Key to write "The Star-Spangled Banner." Told through the eyes of the flag maker's daughter, this story reminds us of the real bravery and courage the flag embodies. 7 & up.

■ **If the Walls Could Talk: Family Life at the White House** **2005** PLATINUM AWARD

(by Jane O'Connor/illus. by Gary Hovland, Simon & Schuster $16.95 ●●●●●) O'Connor gives readers lots of interesting factoids about the presidents and their families—the jumbo-sized bathtub installed for President Taft, for example, or the goat the Lincolns kept in their family quarters. Hovland's cartoons give kids plenty of detail to pore over. 7 & up. See also, **Wackiest White House Pets** (by Gibbs Davis/illus. by David A. Johnson, Scholastic $16.95 ●●●●), interesting facts about Presidents and their pets. 7 & up.

■ **Island of Hope** **2005**

(by Martin W. Sandler, Scholastic $18.95 ●●●●) Ellis Island was more than a landmark to the 12 million immigrants who came to America seeking a new life. After what was often a harrowing voyage, Ellis Island was a series of obstacles that the newly arrived needed to get through. Using first-person accounts, Sandler chronicles the fears and frustrations of the frightening process that could end with being sent back to Europe. 8 & up.

■ Remember: The Journey to School Integration **2005** PLATINUM AWARD

(by Toni Morrison, Houghton Mifflin $18 ○○○○○) Thankfully, today's generation has a hard time comprehending segregated schools and workplaces. Morrison takes readers through this tumultuous period of American history from the perspective of the children that lived it. The historical photos will also spark conversation. 7 & up.

■ The Salem Witch Trials **2005** PLATINUM AWARD

(by Jane Yolen & Heidi Elisabet Yolen Stemple/illus. by Roger Roth, Simon & Schuster $16.95 ○○○○○) In a well designed format, the authors give the history of the Salem Witch Trials of 1692, as well as background information important for understanding this dark period in American history. 8 & up.

■ Twenty-One Elephants **2005** PLATINUM AWARD

(by Phil Bildner/illus. by LeUyen Pham, Simon & Schuster $16.95 ○○○○○) It's hard to believe that there was a time when people were afraid the Brooklyn Bridge was not stable. While Bildner employs some fictitious characters, he also chronicles that P. T. Barnum did walk his 21 elephants across the bridge to assure people it was safe. 5 & up.

■ Walt Whitman, Words For America **2005**

(by Barbara Kerley/illus. by Brian Selznick, Scholastic $16.95 ○○○○½) Despite its picture book format, this is a biography for older readers who may be reading Whitman's poems for the first time or for budding Civil War buffs. Whitman's involvement in caring for wounded soldiers and his fondness for Abe Lincoln give new meaning to his famous "Oh, Captain! my Captain! Our fearful trip is done." Brian Selznick's illustrations are glorious! 9 & up.

■The Greatest Skating Race 2005

(by Louise Borden/illus. by Niki Daly, McElderry Books $18.95 ●●●●½)
It's 1941 and the Germans have occupied the Netherlands. Piet, a
Dutch schoolboy, is given the responsibility of taking two young
neighbors across the Belgian border to their aunt. Their father has
been taken away by Nazi soldiers and their mother fears for the children's safety. There is just one way to get them away and that is by
skating on the frozen canals where German soldiers strand guard. A
story of courage and friendship. 9 & up.

■ Mummies, Pyramids, and Pharaohs 2005

(by Gail Gibbons, Little, Brown $16.95 ●●●●) If you have a younger
child interested in Egypt, Gibbons' book is a good place to start.
Through her inviting illustrations and limited text, Gibbons gives
kids a basic guide to the geography, culture, and pyramids. Unlike
many books on the topic, there are no disturbing pictures or illustrations. 5 & up.

■ Secret of the Sphinx 2005 PLATINUM AWARD

(by James C. Giblin/illus. by Bagram Ibatoulline, Scholastic $17.95
●●●●●) Handsome illustrations inform a masterfully crafted text that
introduces readers to the many strange legends
and theories that surround the ancient wonder,
the Great Sphinx. Giblin manages to spin a
captivating tale that leaves us with a continuing sense of mystery and awe for the massive
statue—part lion and part man—that has
guarded the pyramids of Egypt's Giza Plateau
for 4500 years. 9 & up.

Dinosaurs

■ Dinosaurs Big and Small

(by Kathleen Weidner Zoehfeld/illus. by Lucia Washburn, Harper-
Collins $15.95 ●●●●½) A smart new addition to the excellent *Let's
Read and Find Out* series. Comparing the size of dinosaurs to things
children know in the real world adds to the wonder of their size and
variety. Told in child-friendly language, this is a book that will not
overwhelm a young listener or reader. 4–7.

■ Dinosaur Hunter

(by Elaine M. Alphin/illus. by Don Bolognese, HarperCollins $15.99
●●●●½) Back in the 1880s when bone hunters were searching for

dinosaur fossils, a boy named Ned dreams of finding a dinosaur that will go to a museum. A good adventure story for young history buffs, dinosaur enthusiasts, and beginning readers. 8 & up.

The Human Body and Reproduction

■ Hello Benny!

(by Robie H. Harris/illus. by Michael Emberley, McElderry Books $16.95 ●●●●½) The lively illustrations and narrative tell the story of how it feels to be a baby. Each big idea is further explained with scientific explanations that are easy to understand. For example, Benny is shown smiling at himself in a mirror and enjoying playing peek-a-boo with Grandma. But stranger-anxiety is explained in 50¢ words instead of the $5 variety. 4–8.

■ How Are Babies Made?

(by Alastair Smith/illus. by Maria Wheatley, Usborne $7.95 ●●●●) Simple, clear text and illustrations on flap pages give children an intro to the facts of life. 5 & up. Also top rated, **How You Were Born** (by Joanna Cole/photos by Margaret Miller, Morrow).

Sports

To get reluctant readers to pick up a book, try a topic they have a lively interest in. Reading about sports is a key for some kids. Older readers will enjoy both the *Eyewitness* books on different sports and Matt Christopher's many sports-centered chapter books.

■ By My Brother's Side *2005*

(by Tiki & Ronde Barber/illus. by Barry Root, Simon & Schuster $16.95 ●●●●) Though Tiki and Ronde Barber are not the most compelling story tellers, fans of these twin NFL Superstars will most likely enjoy the story of their childhood, which was marked most importantly by their devotion to each other and the support of their mother. 6 & up.

■ Mia Hamm: Winners Never Quit! *2005*

(by Mia Hamm/illus. by Carol Thompson, HarperCollins $15.95 ●●●●½) Young sports players, no matter what sport they play, should

be required to read this book about learning how to lose gracefully. A young Mia is shown quitting when she begins to lose. When her friends stop wanting to play with her, she is forced to regroup. She realizes that playing the game she loves is more important than the outcome.

■ Mighty Jackie, the Strike-Out Queen

(by Marissa Moss/illus. by C. F. Payne, Simon & Schuster $16.95 ○○○○½) Based on a true event, this entertaining biography tells the story of a mighty pitcher who managed to strike out both Babe Ruth and Lou Gehrig. A member of a minor league team, Jackie Mitchell was just 17 years old on that big day when the Yankees rolled into Chattanooga to play an exhibition game that made history! Little League players are sure to enjoy this story. 7 & up.

Art and Art History

■ Seurat and La Grande Jatte 2005

(by Robert Burleigh, Abrams $17.95 ○○○○½) A guided tour that examines a famous painting, giving young readers an introduction to several big ideas about how one may look at the details and story the painting tells. It also examines how the artist created his masterpiece with dozens of smaller studies. For younger art lovers, see **Babar's Museum of Art** (by Laurent de Brunhoff, $16.95 ○○○○○) PLATINUM AWARD '04. 7 & up.

■ Ish 2005 PLATINUM AWARD

(by Peter Reynolds, Candlewick $14 ○○○○○) Drawing is what Ramon does, until a foolish comment by his big brother makes Ramon doubt his own ability. It's his sister Marisol who rekindles Ramon's joy in creating wonderful-ish drawings. Like last year's PLATINUM winner, **The Dot,** this is another small book with a giant-sized idea. 5 & up.

Easy-to-Read Books

Many of the books in this section are from series designed

especially for young readers and are available in paperback. Keep in mind that many regular trade books listed elsewhere may also be easy to read.

BLUE CHIP BOOKS
EVERY BEGINNING READER SHOULD KNOW

✓ **Amelia Bedelia,** by Peggy Parish
✓ **Are You My Mother?** by P. D. Eastman
✓ **Frog and Toad,** by Arnold Lobel
✓ **Go, Dog, Go!** by P. D. Eastman
✓ **Green Eggs and Ham,** by Dr. Seuss
✓ **Henry and Mudge** and **Poppleton series,**
  by Cynthia Rylant
✓ **Little Bear,** by Else H. Minarik
✓ **My Father's Dragon,** by Ruth S. Gannett
✓ **Polk Street series,** by Patricia R. Giff
✓ **The Stories Julian Tells,** by Ann Cameron
✓ **Fluffy Series,** by Kate McMullan
✓ **Let's Read and Find Out Series** (HarperCollins)

To help your beginner:

📖 Choose books that are not a struggle. Easy does it!

📖 If every other word is too hard, you've got the wrong book for now.

📖 If your child gets stuck on a word, say the word. Some words can't be sounded out.

📖 A bookmark under the line your child is reading can help to keep the place.

Just Beginning Books: Easy to Read

■ Biscuit's Big Friend

(by Alyssa S. Capucilli/illus. by Pat Schories, HarperCollins $14.99 ○○○○) Newest in a series about a little dog and his friends. Lots of repetition and picture cues to help the beginner.

■ Brand New Reader Sets

(Candlewick $12.99 ○○○○) A set of ten small books by various well known authors and artists; no better choice for building the beginner's sense of success. Context clues, simple sentences, repeated phrases—all mixed in with a sense of humor! We recommend both the *Red* and *Blue* sets, which also include a parents' guide, a blank book for creating your own original book, and a chart with stickers for those who need incentives.

■ Daniel's Pet

(by Alma Flor Ada/illus. by G. Brian Karas, Harcourt $3.95 ●●●●½) Newest in the level 1 Green Light Reader series, Daniel gets a pet chick that grows up quickly into a hen that produces more chicks. Also very good, but a bit harder, **The Fox & the Stork** (by Gerald McDermott ●●●●½), the fable of a tricky fox who is outfoxed by a stork.

■ Pearl and Wagner Three Secrets 🏅2005

(by Kate McMullan/illus. by R. W. Alley, Dial $14.99 ●●●●) Children will relate to these engaging three connected stories that have to do with keeping secrets. Pearl the rabbit and Wagner the mouse are good friends who help each other work out their common childhood issues.

■ Puppy Mudge Takes a Bath 🏅2005

(by Cynthia Rylant/illus. by Isidre Mones, Simon & Schuster $3.99 ●●●●½) With few words and plenty of action, Henry gets a reluctant Mudge into the tub not once, but maybe twice. Designed for beginners, one of three new books that introduce Mudge as a pup. It's better than the new **Funny Lunch,** from the regular series.

■ The Red Book 🏅2005

(by Barbara Lehman, Houghton Mifflin $12.95 ●●●●½) A wordless story that begins with a book found in the snow, transporting one child on a journey where she meets another child. This imaginative adventure invites children to tell the story in their own words as they interpret a magical story through illustrations. 5–8.

■ Three Little Bears 🏅2005

(by David Martin/illus. by Akemi Gutierrez, Candlewick $12.99 ●●●●) There's no Goldilocks in this little collection of four repetitive, super easy-to-read stories about Brother, Sister, and Baby Bear. Part of the *Brand New Readers* series, these are funny, short, and designed for the success of the beginning reader.

■ Shanna's Bear Hunt *2005*

(by Jean Marzollo/illus. by Maryn Roos, Hyperion $3.99 ●○○○) Shanna's friends are hunting a strange bear who is heard but not seen until the end of this lively mystery. Young readers can depend on the repeated refrain that makes this super easy to read. **Bear Hunt** is the simplest of three Shanna books designed for true beginners. Also, see **Shanna's Party Surprise,** a birthday book, and **Hip, Hop, Hooray.**

Intermediate Readers

■ Beach Day! *2005*

(by Patricia Lakin/illus. by Scott Nash, Dial $15.99 ●○○○) Sam, Pam, Will, and Jill are a family of crocs planning on going to the beach, but will they get there? With a lot of repetitive lines and illustrations that cue the new words, this is a strong (and humorous) choice for new readers. Don't be put off by the picture book format.

■ Gus and Grandpa Go Fishing

(by Claudia Mills/illus. by Catherine Stock, Farrar Straus $15 ●○○○) Gus has never been fishing before. It's tricky learning how to cast, but Grandpa, as always, encourages Gus to keep trying. This is not as sparkling as usual, but it's a good enough story in a consistently warm and meaningful series. Don't miss **Gus & Grandpa and the Two Wheeled Bike** We found this year's **Piano Lesson,** with a disastrous recital, resistible.

■ Jess and the Stinky Cowboys *2005*

(by Janice Lee Smith/illus. by Lisa Thiesing, Dial $14.99 ●○○○) Jess and her aunt are keeping things in order while her Sheriff Pa is out of town. That's when three stinky cowboys show up. They are so smelly a stink cloud hangs over them! Reluctant bathers may see the humor in this sassy, well paced tale. Plenty of repetition makes it reasonably easy to read.

■ Just In Time for New Year's! *2005*

(by Karen Gray Ruelle, Holiday House $4.95 ●●●●) Kids who have tried to stay up for midnight on New Year's Eve will appreciate Harry and Emily's plan to keep themselves awake!

■ Mr. Putter & Tabby Write the Book
2005 PLATINUM AWARD

(by Cynthia Rylant/illus. by Arthur Howard, Harcourt $14 ●●●●●) During a big snowstorm, Mr. Putter decides that he should write a book with the support of his cat, Tabby. All writers, young and old, will appreciate Mr. Putter's delicious procrastination. 6–9.

■ Oliver the Mighty Pig *2005*

(by Jean Van Leeuwen/illus. by Ann Schweninger, Dial $14.99 ●●●●) Oliver's very best birthday present is a superhero's cape that gives him the power to rescue people and keep the world safe. Children who love pretending will relate to Oliver and enjoy his adventures.

■ Tigers *2005*

(by Sarah L. Thomson, HarperCollins $15.99 ●●●●) From the I Can Read Series, Thomas provides interesting information about tigers such as why they have stripes. The photographs from the Wildlife Conservation Society will also appeal to first and second graders. 6 & up.

■ Worm Gets a Job *2005*

(by Kathy Caple, Candlewick $15.99 ●●●●) Worm is desperate to earn money for art supplies so that he can enter the local art contest. Intermediate readers will enjoy reading the captions. The story has a clichéd ending (he wins, of course), but will be satisfying to new readers. 6 & up.

Transition Chapter Books
for Advanced Beginners and Beyond

Kids at this stage often love reading books in series with continuing characters and familiar settings. Reading every book in a series may seem boring to adults, but satisfies young readers and helps them gain fluidity in their reading. Among our top-rated series to consider are:

Polk Street series, by Patricia R. Giff; **Sports series,** by Matt Christopher; **Boxcar Children,** by Gertrude C. Warner; **Amber Brown** series, by Paula Danziger; **Ramona** and **Henry Huggins** series, by Beverly Cleary; **Arthur** chapter books, by Marc Brown; **Song Lee** and **Horrible Harry** series, by Suzy Kline; **The Zack Files,** by Dan Greenburg; **Junie B.** series, by Barbara Park; **Magic Treehouse** series, by Mary Pope Osborne; and the **Star Wars Jedi** series, by Jude Watson.

True Readers

■ **Blue Jasmine** *2005* PLATINUM AWARD

(by Kashmira Sheth, Hyperion $15.99 ●●●●●) In her debut novel, Sheth pulls from her own experiences of immigrating to America from India. While most readers are familiar with long-ago immigration stories, **Blue Jasmine** captures the culture shock in modern-day Iowa City and the universality of fitting in wherever you call home. 9 & up.

■ **A House of Tailors** *2005* PLATINUM AWARD

(by Patricia Reilly Giff, Random House $15.95 ●●●●●) 13-year-old Dina Kirk quickly finds herself on a ship to America to live with her uncle, his young wife and baby. She finds herself torn between the family she hopes to return to and the new life she makes for herself in America. Giff beautifully captures the heartache of young immigrants. 9 & up.

■ **More Perfect than the Moon** *2005*

(by Patricia MacLachlan, HarperCollins $14.99 ●●●●) In the latest sequel to **Sarah, Plain and Tall,** Caleb's little half sister Cassie isn't thrilled with the news that there is a new baby on the way. Fearful that Sarah, her mother, will die as Caleb's mother did when he was born, Cassie records her wildest thoughts about the "terrible baby" to be. 8 & up.

■ **Peter and the Starcatchers** *2005*

(by Dave Barry and Ridley Pearson, Hyperion $17.99 ●●●●) Ever wonder how Peter Pan knew Captain Hook? Best-selling authors Barry and Pearson join forces to write their own fast-paced prequel to the J. M. Barrie classic. 10 & up.

■ The Sea of Trolls 2005

(by Nancy Farmer, Atheneum $17.99 ●●●●½) For fans of fantasy, Farmer has stirred up another rich broth that teems with adventure, dragons, spiders, a shape-shifting half-troll, and an 11-year-old boy and his younger sister, who have been kidnapped by Olaf One-Brow! 10 & up.

Read-Aloud Chapter Books

Long before school-age kids can tackle big chapter books on their own, they enjoy the more fully drawn characters, richer language, and multilayered plots found in storybooks. These first novels, with more words than pictures, push children to imagine with the mind's eye—something they will need to do as they grow into reading. In time these books may be reread independently. For now, the best way to motivate the next level of readership is to continue reading good books to your child. Among the most beautiful and collectible for the family library are the Books of Wonder editions. After seeing films such as *The Borrowers* and *Charlotte's Web*, try reading the originals and do a little comparative literature with young listeners.

- **The Black Stallion,** by Walter Farley
- **The Borrowers,** by Mary Norton
- **Catwings,** by Ursula LeGuin
- **Charlie and the Chocolate Factory,** by Roald Dahl
- **Charlotte's Web** and **Stuart Little,** by E. B. White
- **Freddy the Pig Series** by Walter R. Brooks
- **Harry Potter series** by J. K. Rowling
- **The House at Pooh Corner,** by A. A. Milne
- **James and the Giant Peach,** by Roald Dahl
- **Lassie Come-Home,** by Eric Knight
- **Little House series,** by Laura Ingalls Wilder
- **The Littles,** by John Peterson
- **Mary Poppins,** by P. L. Travers
- **My Father's Dragon,** by Ruth S. Gannett
- **The Real Thief,** by William Steig
- **Sarah, Plain and Tall; Skylark;** and **Caleb's**

Story by Patricia MacLachlan

 **Wizard of Oz series,** by L. Frank Baum

Resource/Activity Books

■ The Klutz Book of Paper Airplanes *2005*

(by Doug Stillinger, Klutz $16.95 ●●●●)
Here are the instructions for ten different
paper airplanes. Our testers raved about
the interesting patterned paper (40 sheets)
that comes with the kit. If you're a novice,
the instructions are clear, and if you're a
pro, you might pick up some new designs. 7
& up.

■ Spool Knit Jewelry *2005*

(by Anne Akers Johnson, Klutz $16.95 ●●●●) Our 11-year-old tester
gave this book an "A++" and loved making bracelets with the old-fash-
ioned knitting spool and crochet hook. Comes with elastic cord, and
glass and plastic beads. Marked 8 & up, we'd say more like 10 with
parental help. Still top rated from the same author, last year's PLATINUM
AWARD-winning **Origami** (Klutz $16.95 ●●●●●). Our in-house origa-
mi master says this is the best origami book for beginners. 6 & up.

Coping with Life's Ups and Downs: Books for Mixed Ages

Many of the books in this section are what we call *bridge
books*—they span two age groups. Some are on the young side,
others are for older kids, and many will do for both. Included
are books that address problems that families often need to
cope with.

Feelings

■ Courage

(by Bernard Waber, Houghton Mifflin $16 ●●●●●) Waber explores
all the large and small everyday kinds of acts that can be thought of as
courageous: doing tricks on skates, riding a two-wheeler, keeping a
secret, trying new things, saying good-bye. Most important of all,
"courage is what we give each other." A gem! PLATINUM AWARD '03.
4–8.

■ That's What Friends Do ⬥2005

(by Kathryn Cave/illus. by Nick Maland, Hyperion $15.99 ●●●●½)
A celebration of the give and take of friendship. Using familiar emo-
tional events that preschoolers will relate to, this is a reassuring picture book that speaks to the comforts of someone who cares. 2 & up.

■ Words Are Not for Hurting ⬥2005

(by Elizabeth Verdick/illus. by Marieka Heinlen, Free Spirit
Publishing $7.95 ●●●●) If harsh words are a problem your child is
dealing with, this board book may be useful. There is no story here,
just plain talking about being kind with your words. 3 & up.

A New Baby

■ Little Brown Bear and the Bundle of Joy
⬥2005 PLATINUM AWARD

(by Jane Dyer, Little, Brown $15.99
●●●●●) Little Brown Bear wants to
know what the "little bundle of joy" is
that his parents are expecting. The
neighboring animals show him their
own new bundles of joy. When he
returns home, he is introduced to his
baby sister, and is reassured that he
remains their "big" bundle of joy! 2½
& up.

■ The Story About Me ⬥2005

(by Miriam Schlein/illus. Kristina Stephenson, Whitman $15.95
●●●●½) Grandma is full of family stories, but none more satisfying
than the one she tells to her granddaughter about the excitement surrounding her arrival. After sharing this storybook it would be good
fun to share your own family stories about the excitement and antici-
pation surrounding your child's arrival in your own family. 2½ & up.

■ Hi New Baby!

(by Robie Harris/illus. by Michael Emberly, Candlewick $16.99
●●●●) Although many big sibs have warm and positive feelings for
the new baby, some feel genuinely displaced. No book can solve these
feelings, but here's a useful story that helps kids know that other kids
have felt the same way. 3 & up.

Adoption

■ I Love You Like Crazy Cakes

(by Rose Lewis/illus. by Jane Dyer, Little, Brown $14.95 ●○○○)
Heart-melting art blends with prose in this moving celebration of
love and adoption. Although the baby is from China, the feeling
and mood make this a universal story. 4 & up.

■ The Red Blanket *2005*

(by Eliza Thomas/illus. by Joe Cepeda,
Scholastic $15.95 ●○○○) A single woman tells
her adopted child of her journey to get her in
China and their first shaky days together. She
brings a red blanket from home, which gives the
baby comfort. 4 & up.

■ You're Not My Real Mother! *2005*

(by Molly Friedrich/illus. by Christy Hale, Little, Brown $15.99
●○○○) A reassuring answer to an adopted child about what it means
to be someone's mother. Addresses differences in appearance, birth
mothers, and the bonds that truly make us family. 5 & up.

NOTABLE PREVIOUS WINNERS: **Tell Me Again About the Night I
Was Born** BLUE CHIP (by Jamie Lee Curtis/illus. by Laura Cornell,
HarperCollins ●○○○○); **Happy Adoption Day!** (by John
McCutcheon/illus. by Julie Paschkis, Little, Brown ●○○○○)
PLATINUM AWARD '97; **Mommy Far, Mommy Near** (by Carol A.
Peacock/illus. by Shawn C. Brownell, Whitman ●○○○).

Moving

■ Absolutely Positively Alexander BLUE CHIP

(by Judith Viorst/illus. by Robin P. Glasser, Atheneum $20 ●○○○○)
Now in one volume, three well loved stories about Alexander,
including **Alexander, Who's Not (Do you hear me? I mean it!)
Going to Move.** 5 & up.

■ Good-Bye, House

(by Robin Ballard, Greenwillow $14 ●○○○) Room by room, a child
says good-bye to the house she has always lived in. A tender book
with an upbeat ending. 3 & up.

■ I Like Where I Am *2005*

(by Jessica Harper/illus. by G. Brian Karas, Putnam $15.95 ●○○○)

Moving is not what the six-year-old narrator of this sad tale wants to do. But moving day does come and the new home turns out to be not such a bad place, after all. A gentle mix of anger and humor with a reassuring ending. Also see **My Best Friend Moved Away** by Nancy Carlson, Viking) 5 & up.

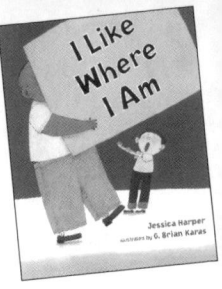

Divorce, Separation, and New Families

■ Mama and Daddy Bear's Divorce

(by Cornelia M. Spelman/illus. by Kathy Parkinson, Whitman $13.95 ●●●●) Dinah Bear is frightened when she learns that the two people she loves best are getting divorced. A reassuring story that says important things stay the same. 3–6.

■ Two Homes

(by Claire Masurel/illus. by Kady M. Denton, Candlewick $14.99 ●●●●½) Alex has different things at Mommy's and Daddy's. But the one thing that is the same in both places is the love that continues between parents and child. A reassuring book for young listeners. 2 & up. For older preschoolers, **A New Room for William** (by Sally Grindley/illus. by Carol Thompson, Candlewick $15.99 ●●●●). Moving is tough, but moving because of a divorce is a double whammy! 4 & up.

NOTABLE PREVIOUS WINNERS: **Amber Brown series** BLUE CHIP (by Paula Danziger, Putnam ●●●●●) 7 & up; **On the Day His Daddy Left** (by Eric & Kathleen Adams, Whitman ●●●●); **I Live with Daddy** (by Judith Vigna, Whitman ●●●●) 7 & up; **Stepfamilies** (by Fred Rogers, Putnam ●●●●). 5–8.

Staying Healthy

■ Froggy Goes to the Doctor

(by Jonathan London/illus. by Frank Remkiewicz, Viking $15.99 ●●●●½) Going to the doctor is not a laughing matter, unless you go along with Froggy! Silly Froggy forgets to wear underpants or brush his teeth. Like some of the earlier books in this series, this has pace and laugh-out-loud fun! 3–7.

Coping with Life's Ups and Downs

■ How Do Dinosaurs Get Well Soon?

(by Jane Yolen/illus. by Mark Teague, Scholastic $15.95 ●●●○) No whining, or tossing tissues on the floor, or refusing to swallow his pills. Kids who might be feeling sorry for themselves will see the humor of this great big dino with the flu who does what he should. A fine sequel to **How Do Dinosaurs Say Good Night?** 4–7.

■ Mabel the Tooth Fairy

(by Katie Davis, Harcourt $16 ●●●○) Aptly subtitled "and How She Got Her Job," there's a lot of tongue-in-cheek humor that also builds on the idea that brushing is important. 4–8.

NOTABLE PREVIOUS WINNERS: **Going to the Doctor** and **Going to the Dentist** (by Fred Rogers, Putnam ●●●●); **Don't You Feel Well, Sam?** (by Amy Hest/illus. by Anita Jeram, Candlewick ●●●○).

Illness

■ What's Happening to Grandpa? ⭐2005⭐

(by Maria Shriver/illus. by Sandra Speidel, Little Brown $15.95 ●●●●) Kate recognizes that something is not right with her beloved Grandpa. Drawing on her own life experiences with her own father, Shriver gives parents the language for speaking intelligently and, most importantly, truthfully with our children about Alzheimer's disease. 7 & up. For two more traditional picture books about Alzheimer's: **Faraway Grandpa** (by Roberta Karim/illus. by Ted Rand, Henry Holt) and **Remember, Grandma?** (by Laura Langston/illus. by Lindsey Gardiner, Viking).

Death

■ Lighthouse, A Story of Remembrance

(by Robert Munsch/illus. by Janet Wilson, Scholastic $13.95 ●●●●½) From the moment you see Sarah with a flower in her hair, waking her dad, you know it's a flower left from her grandfather's funeral. Going to their favorite place, the lighthouse, Sarah and her dad know this was the right night and the right place to share their loss—and love. 5–9.

■ Thank You, Grandpa

(by Lynn Ploude/illus. by Cockcroft, Dutton $15.99 **oooo**) From the time she was old enough to toddle, a granddaughter and her Grandfather have enjoyed their walks together. As she grows up, there are walks with sad moments when a grasshopper no longer hops or a butterfly no longer flies. Grandpa prepares her for the time when he will not be walking with her. A moving book for a child who is dealing with loss. 4–8.

NOTABLE PREVIOUS WINNERS : **Annie and the Old One** BLUE CHIP (by Miska Miles/illus. by Peter Parnall, Little, Brown **ooooo**); **Flamingo Dream** (by Donna Jo Napoli/illus. Cathie Felstead, Greenwillow **oooo**).

Death of a Pet

■ Saying Goodbye to Lulu 2005

(by Corinne Demas/illus. by Ard Hoyt, Little, Brown $ 15.95 **oooo**) If you've ever lost a pet, this book is going to make you cry. Lulu the dog is in failing health; in this tender story her owner, a little girl, is coping with Lulu's inevitable death. Some aspects may be too much for your child; the little girl is brought to say good-bye to Lulu after she's died and then they bury the dog in the back yard. 5 & up.

■ The Tenth Good Thing About Barney

(by Judith Viorst/illus. by Eric Blegvad, Atheneum $12.95 **oooo**) When his cat Barney dies, a young boy deals with his loss by remembering the good things about him. This bittersweet classic says it all. 4–8.

■ When a Pet Dies

(by Fred Rogers, Putnam $5.95 **oooo**) Mr. Rogers talks in clear language about what happens when a pet dies because it is hurt or ill. 4–8.

Holiday Books

Thanksgiving

■ Thanks for Thanksgiving 2005

(by Julie Markes/illus. by Doris Barrette, HarperCollins $12.99 ●●●●) With a warm autumnal feel, Markes chronicles all the things a brother and sister are thankful for in this retro-feeling ode to a traditional family at Thanksgiving. 4 & up.

■ Thanksgiving at the Tappletons'

(by Eileen Spinelli/illus. by Megan Lloyd, HarperCollins $14.99 ●●●●½) From the moment Mrs. Tappleton opens the front door and drops the turkey that slides into the pond, the stage is set for a Keystone Cops comedy. But all's well that ends well, even among a family of wolves. 5 & up.

■ The Thanksgiving Door 2005

(by Debby Atwell, Houghton Mifflin $15 ●●●●½) When an old couple's Thanksgiving dinner is burned by accident, little did they think it would turn into the best Thanksgiving. Quite by chance they go to a restaurant run by an immigrant family. Though they are closed, the grandmother of the family insists on making a place for them both. 4–8. For older readers, see **Molly's Pilgrim** (by Barbara Cohen, Lothrop $3.99).

Passover

■ The Secret Seder 2005

(by Doreen Rappaport/illus. by Emily Arnold McCully, Hyperion $16.99 ●●●●½) Jacques and his father are determined to keep their promise to celebrate Passover in WWII France, where they have avoided being taken away by the "black-boot men." Based on true stories of Resistance fighters, this picture book captures the true spirit of Passover and those with faith and courage, even in a time of darkness. 7 & up.

Kwanzaa

■ Seven Spools of Thread

(by Angela S. Medearis/illus. by Daniel Minter, Whitman $15.95
●●●●●) In a village in Ghana, seven brothers quarrel from morning
to night. Their father says he will leave his possessions to them only
if by sundown they can turn seven spools of colored thread into gold.
Although this is called a Kwanzaa story, it is a timeless tale about
working together for a common good. A memorable *pour quoi*-style
tale with striking woodcuts filled with the symbols of Kwanzaa.
PLATINUM AWARD '01. 5 & up.

Chinese New Year

■ My First Chinese New Year 2005

(by Karen Katz, Henry Holt $14.95 ●●●●)
With festive illustrations, Katz highlights all
the traditions of celebrating the Chinese New
Year from a child's point of view. 4–8.

Christmas

■ Bear Stays Up for Christmas 2005

(by Karma Wilson/illus. by Jane Chapman, McElderry Books $16.95
●●●●) All of bear's friends are desperate to share Christmas with
their friend so they spend the days and nights keeping the bear
awake. There's even a visit from Santa Claus. A charming new
Christmas story with joyful illustrations. 3–7.

■ The Miracle of the Poinsettia

(by Joanne Oppenheim/illus. by
Fabian Negrin, Barefoot Books $16.99
●●●●●) Inspired by an old Mexican
folktale and our own family's love of
Mexico. With nothing to bring to the
baby Jesus, Juanita gives from her
heart with a miraculous outcome.
Understandably one of our favorite
titles, available in English and Spanish and this season in paperback.
6 & up.

■ How Santa Really Works 2005

(by Alan Snow, Atheneum $15.95 ●●●●) Snow's illustrations are deliciously detailed, showing the underground workshop and staff at the North Pole. The CIA, Christmas Intelligence Agency, keeps him posted on who's been bad or good. The only drawback is that the level of detail will be lost on younger true believers. 6 & up.

■ **Santa Claus Is Comin' to Town** *2005*

(by J. Fred Coots & Haven Gillespie/illus. by Steven Kellogg, HarperCollins $16.99 ●●●●) Kellogg creates a joyous and bustling celebration as the town gets ready for Santa. He brings the 1934 classic song to life, capturing the excitement of the season. 3 & up.

■ **Uncles and Antlers** *2005*

(by Lisa Wheeler/illus. by Brian Floca, Atheneum $15.95 ●●●●) A jolly romp as Octavia the reindeer extols the virtues of her seven uncles. A bouncing rhyme with lots of counting mixed in, they all join in once a year to help pull Santa's sleigh. No Rudolph in this version! 4 & up.

Our Favorite Classic Christmas Picture Books

🍭**Dream Snow** (by Eric Carle, Philomel) PLATINUM AWARD '01. 2½ & up.

🍭**If You Take a Mouse to the Movies** (by Laura Numeroff/illus. by Felicia Bond, HarperCollins) PLATINUM AWARD '01.

🍭**Carl's Christmas** (by Alexandra Day, Farrar, Straus & Giroux) 4 & up.

🍭**The Jolly Christmas Postman** (by Janet and Allan Ahlberg, Little, Brown) 4 & up.

🍭**Mim's Christmas Jam** (by Andrea Davis Pinkney/illus. by Brian Pinkney, Harcourt) 4–8.

🍭**The Polar Express** (by Chris Van Allsburg, Houghton Mifflin) 5 & up.

🍭**Santa Calls** (by William Joyce, HarperCollins) 6–10.

🍭**The Night Before Christmas,** PLATINUM '03 and **The Twelve Days of Christmas** (by Robert Sabuda, Simon & Schuster) 6 & up.

🍭**Who'll Pull Santa's Sleight Tonight?** (by Laura Rader, HarperCollins) PLATINUM AWARD '04. 4–8.

Hanukkah

■ Chanukah Bugs

(by David A. Carter, Little Simon $10.95 ❍❍❍❍❍) Each of the eight nights of Chanukah is represented with an amusing and amazing gift box that opens to a twirling dreidel, sizzling latkes, sparkling menorah, and others. PLATINUM AWARD '03. 3–7.

■ Latkes, Latkes, Good to Eat

(by Naomi Howland, Clarion $15 ❍❍❍❍) Borrowing the old folktale device of a bountiful pot that won't stop giving, Howland has spun a tale that's as delicious as a plate full of latkes with sugar on top! 4 & up.

■ Mrs. Greenberg's Messy Hanukkah *2005*

(by Linda Glaser/illus. by Nancy Cote, Albert Whitman $15.95 ❍❍❍❍) Even though it's the first night of Hanukkah, Rachel's mother says they will not make latkes until next week when their relatives come for dinner. Rachel visits her elderly neighbor Mrs. Greenberg and convinces her that they should make latkes. A mess ensues, but Rachel's parents step in and everyone has a special night. 4 & up.

Reference Books for Mixed Ages

Dictionaries

Preschool: Very young children don't really need a dictionary, but their love of words and their exploding vocabulary make books with tons of pictures and labels great for looking at. Most are arranged in categories rather than alphabetical order.

■ The American Heritage Picture Dictionary

(Houghton Mifflin $10 ❍❍❍❍) Nine-hundred-word "pictionary" with words and pictures in alphabetical order. Thematic lists are fun for pre-"reading" and early writing. 4–7.

Early School Years—First to Third Grades: Beginning readers and writers start to use dictionaries with A-to-Z listings and pictures to find words they need. Too big a book will be hard to sift through, so less is best!

■ Scholastic First Dictionary

(Scholastic $14.95 ❍❍❍❍) Easy-to-read definitions with pictures, and the words are used in sentences. 6–9.

■ Macmillan First Dictionary

(Macmillan $14 ●○○○) Illustrated with photos and drawings. Gives plurals of nouns, past tenses of verbs, and defines words with multiple meanings. 6–9.

Later School Years–Fourth Grade and Up: These dictionaries are more complex, with syllabification, pronunciation, and often word histories. They have fewer illustrations and many more words. Both also include maps and biographical and other historical data. For 9 & up.

■ Macmillan Dictionary for Children

(Macmillan $16.95 ●○○○) Updated in 2002 with more color photos. 8–12.

■ Scholastic Children's Dictionary

(Scholastic $17.95 ●○○○) With new and updated entries, this edition has more photos and uses phonetic pronunciation instead of traditional symbols; includes Braille and American Sign Language alphabets and 100 high-tech terms. Also **Scholastic Student Thesaurus** ($15.95 ●○○○). 8 & up.

Encyclopedias

Before making a big investment in an encyclopedia, go to the public library or your child's school. Look at several sets without pressure from a salesperson. Keep in mind:

📖 Most kids won't regularly use an encyclopedia before fourth grade, so don't rush.

📖 Look up the same entry in each set—for example, look at the presentation for "dogs" or "dinosaurs" in each encyclopedia and compare content, style, and illustrations.

📖 Visuals such as photos, charts, and drawings will be very important to your child.

📖 A used edition costs less, but statistics, maps, and other information may be dated.

Following are the best choices:

■ Compton's Encyclopedia or World Book

(Compton's/World Book $420 & up ●○○○) Either of these sets will be used by students from fourth grade through high school. The entries are not super-easy to read, but they are clear and well written, with attractive, colorful illustrations and photos. Both sets are of equal value and the choice is one of personal preference. See Computer chapter for multimedia encyclopedias.

Single-Volume Resource Books

■ How People Live

(DK $19.99 ●○○○) This is the type of book that kids will love poring over. Spectacular photos of children from the African Wodaabe to the Arctic Inuit, the volume is chock-full of juicy factoids that school-age kids enjoy. 8 & up.

■ National Audubon Society First Field Guides

(Scholastic $11.95 each ●●●○) Designed to be used in the field or as a resource at home, each of these handsome books has hundreds of photos, clear information, and a "spotter's card," a quick reference card to identify an animal or plant. Titles include **Birds, Insects, Reptiles, Rocks,** and **Trees.**

■ National Geographic World Atlas for Young Explorers

(National Geographic Society $24.95 ●●●○) Stunning images from space, photos, and handsome physical maps introduce each continent and its people with political maps that zoom in on countries and states. This book could not have existed when today's parents were in school, but it could turn kids into map lovers instead of map phobics!

■ Smithsonian Children's Encyclopedia of American History

(by David C. King, DK $29.99 ●●●○½) This is like a coffee-table book for young history buffs. Visually exciting with photos, art, and photographs all explained with captions and short, crisply written passages. Fun to dive into rather than to read from front to back. 8 & up.

■ State-By-State Atlas

(by Beth Sutinis et al., DK $19.99 ●●●○) Organized by region, this state-by-state atlas presents information about geography, population, industry, famous people, and landmarks. 8 & up.

■ The White House

(by Catherine O'Neill Grace, Scholastic $19.95 ●●●○) An illustrated history of the White House with handsome photos, behind-the-scenes information, and first-hand accounts from many people who work in the "People's House," the 132-room mansion that is a museum, home, office, and setting for so many occasions that live in history. Includes an introduction by First Lady Laura Bush. For those who have visited and the many others who will do so one day. 8 & up.

III • Videos

The golden age of children's videos is over for now. We had a painful job this season sorting through new titles looking for gems that we could recommend. They were few and far between. The good news, however, is that many of our old winners are now available on DVD.

What's in a Name? Many of our past award winners have new entries that have taken dramatically wrong turns, leaving us with the overall warning that name recognition and past performances are not enough to go by when selecting new videos for your kids. Series still need to be viewed one title at a time, otherwise you are apt to come home with a video for toddlers with story lines about aliens, witches, and ghosts (Kipper); or how about a "legend" for 2- and 3-year-olds told by a fairy who comes from a blue moon (Blue's Clues)? We even received a preschool video about a boy who has good parents, nice toys... everything... except a body.

Well, Excuse You! Last year we complained about the abundance of flatulence jokes in movies. We wondered whether there was a public relations campaign under way by the Flatulent Society of America. This year, forget flatulence. How about a movie about an animated doggie poo? (no, joke).

Why No Baby Videos? Developmentally, babies learn from active, real-life experiences rather than from being "plugged in" to passively watching others at such an early age. We believe that a mirror would be more interactive and age-appropriate than a video screen. Reading books and talking about the pictures, or interacting as you sing songs and recite rhymes, will do more to build language than plugging babies into the TV to look at pretty pictures with music. For kids under 2 (and beyond), less is more! We are delighted that the American Pediatric Association has agreed with our position.

More Scare for Your Video Dollar. Entertainment that looks like children's fare sometimes comes laced with a heavy dose of adult-sized violence. While many of us remember watching the Wicked Witch of the West from behind a blanket, most of us were school-age, not three. Some filmmakers seem to forget that young children are still working on the distinction between real and make-believe. Given that many parents use videos as a better alternative to television, it's important to know that videos are not a safe haven.

Positive Choices. What you will find in this chapter are quality music, story, information, and how-to videos that involve kids in active doing. These are arranged from choices for the very young to those for older viewers. Some videos span a broad age range, from preschool to early school years. If you have a child between 4 and 8, look at the choices in Toddlers, Preschoolers, and Early School Years.

A Word of Warning. Like many products directed at children, age labels are often marked too broadly. Parents who fondly remember feature films from their childhood often hurry home with classics, only to find that these are too scary for young children. Videos, like toys, are not "one size fits all."

Screen Your Videos. Whenever possible, take the time to preview videos, or at least watch with your children the first time around. You may be surprised at the number of videos you choose not to watch to the end. Teaching kids to turn off a film because it's just not worth watching is also not a bad lesson to pass on.

Music and Activities

Preschoolers and Early-School-Years Kids

■ **Barney Movin' and Groovin'** 2005

(Lyons Group $16.95 ●●●●) A new Barney meant to encourage your kids to get up off the sofa and dance along. Nothing groundbreaking here, but a classic style Barney video about making your own music that will appeal to fans of the purple dino. Still top rated, **Barney's Musical Castle** (●●●●). If your child has ever been to or dreamed of going to a Barney show, the new **Barney's Colorful World!** will be the next best thing. We have to be honest—we had to mute part of it. Seventy minutes is just too much Barney. These tapes may be preschooler's dream come true, or your 9-year-old's worst nightmare. 2–6. (800) 791-8093.

■ Blue Talks **2005**

(Paramount $12.95 ●●●) It would have been better for Blue to remain speechless. More importantly, the stories about "moon fairies" and far-out fantasy are way beyond the understanding of young preschoolers. The strength of the original Blue concept was right on the mark for preschoolers who loved the magic of helping the host finding the clues. These episodes empowered kids, making them feel very smart. We find a disconnect between the new stories and the audience, who are still sorting out real and make-believe. We also have trouble with **Blue's Clues: Blue Takes You to School** (●●●). Our problem is that the featured color is chartreuse, and the shape of the day, a pentagon. How about starting with green and a triangle? A much better choice is **Blue's Clues Shapes and Colors** (●●●●½). Joe and Blue play a lot of shape-hunting games with some licks of color thrown in. 3–5.

■ Be a Hula Girl

(Kuleana Prod. $14.95 ●●●●●) We were testing a luau craft kit when this wonderful dancing video arrived from Hawaii. Our 8-year-old testers followed every motion and learned how to dance and move to the traditional music. We liked how the instructor kept reminding them to smile! You can buy the video alone, or with a raffia skirt and beads ($24.95). This would be

fun to use for a luau party. 5–9. PLATINUM AWARD '02. (866) 367-4852.

■ Fiesta! BLUE CHIP

(Sony $12.98 ●●●●●) Now available in DVD, a lively Sesame Street video with many songs performed in both English and Spanish, introducing kids to counting, colors, and familiar music with a Latin beat. Also top rated: **Get up & Dance** (●●●●) and PLATINUM AWARD '97 winner **Elmocize** (●●●●●). We have found the **Elmo's World** series to be inconsistent. Our viewers enjoyed **Birthday**

Games & More (●●●●) (once they got past the first frenetic 10 minutes), but found **Elmo's Magic Cookbook** (●●) to fall below the usual high standards set by Sesame Street. We found the dumbed-down content was more irritating than inspiring. 2½ & up.

■ How to Be a Ballerina

(Sony $9.98/$12.95 ●●●●) Now on DVD, young ballerinas can join along with a children's class at the Royal Academy of Dance. From warm-ups, to rehearsing, to a charming performance of scenes from *Sleeping Beauty*, viewers are invited to dance along. A short version of *Sleeping Beauty* is told as film clips show adult ballerinas dancing, but it is the children's performance of the story that will inspire viewers. DVD also includes "How to Be a Ballet Dancer." 5–9.

■ What's the Name of That Song?
2005 PLATINUM AWARD

(Sony Wonder $12.95 ●●●●●) A hit parade of favorite Sesame Street songs, but our favorite moments are Wayne Brady singing "Between," and Patti LaBelle singing the alphabet! Closer in spirit to the original show (with a sense of humor that isn't condescending to kids). 2 & up.

■ Raffi on Broadway BLUE CHIP

(Rounder $19.95 ●●●●) A real musical experience with the "eco-troubadour" singing many old favorites such as "Baby Beluga." We could have done without the pessimism of "Will I Ever Grow Up?" but kids probably hear it as a song of longing rather than doubt. 4 & up. Also classic: **Raffi in Concert** (●●●●). (800) 768-6337.

■ Sing Along Songs BLUE CHIP

(Disney $12.99) Over the years we have found some of the "Sing Along" tapes a better alternative for preschoolers than the feature-length films that are too scary for young viewers. However, these are uneven and sometimes include clips that are not for all ages (our tip: rent before you buy). The newest, **Home on the Range** (●●), was not particularly engaging for our viewers. (The movie wasn't that great either.) **Winnie the Pooh Sing a Song with Tigger** (●●●●) got much higher ratings. We do like the way the words to the songs bounce along the bottom of the screen so kids who can read can sing along. 4 & up.

■ **There Was an Old Lady Who Swallowed a Fly &
More Stories That Sing** 2005

(Scholastic $9.95/$14.95 ●●●●) The art from Simms
Taback's version of **There Was an Old Lady** comes
to life through brilliant animation. Parents (and kids)
will enjoy Cyndi Lauper's narration and singing. The
other two stories to sing: a chorus of penguins in
Antarctic Antics by Judy Sierra and the noisy
hippo, **Musical Max,** by Robert Kraus. 4 & up.

BLUE CHIP **Folk Music Videos**
Three Favorites: **Ella Jenkins Live at the Smithsonian**
(Smithsonian Folkways $14.98 ●●●●) Without gimmicks, here's
a master teacher involving kids in sing-, clap-, snap-, and tap-
along fun! All ages. (800) 410-9815. **Peter, Paul, and Mommy,
Too** (Warner $19.98 ●●●●) From the opening bars of "Puff," the
magic is still here! All ages. **This Pretty Planet: Tom
Chapin Live in Concert** (Sony $14.98
●●●●) Thirteen of his best-loved
songs, such as "The Wheel of the
Water," "Good Garbage," and others with an ecology theme. All ages.

Picturebook Videos

Many wonderful picture books have been brought to life as
videos. Unfortunately, some video makers take the names of
well known books and turn them into Saturday-morning-style
programs. Be sure to look at the **Information, Please** (p.
213) and **Coping** (p. 216) sections for other toddlers' and
preschoolers' videos.

Toddlers and Preschoolers
■ **Angelina Ballerina: The Magic of Dance** 2005

(Hit Entertainment $12.99/$16.99 ●●●½) Many
Angelina story lines have been "notched up" with
more tears, squeals, and edgy moments than usual
this season. It's not terrible, but less would have
been more. In "William the Conjurer," William
uses his father's magic box and thinks he has made
Angelina disappear! In "Angelina and Grandma," a

special tutu that Miss Lilly wore when she was a girl gets ripped by accident. Mother is away, and Grandma is busy getting ready for a friend's party and impatient with Angelina. In "Miss Lilly Comes to Dinner," Angelina is worried about impressing her teacher. Finally, a special day is almost spoiled, thanks to many unpleasant exchanges between sneaky Sammy and gullible William, in "Angelina's Valentine." Between the stories there are live-action clips of young dancers. The new **Lights, Camera, Action** video has the same unnecessary contrived fear and nastiness in two episodes—one with a witch, and another with mice who exclude William. Still top rated, **Angelina Ballerina Friends Forever** and **Rose Fairy Princess,** both PLATINUM winners. (866) 587-1778.

■ **Bob the Builder: The Live Show** ⭐*2005*

(HIT Entertainment $14.99/$16.99 ●●●●) If "yes, we can" is big in your house, then this live-action show will be a hit. When the talking trucks first make an appearance, it is pretty neat. It's a lot like Barney—if you're four, it's really great fun; if you're forty, you'll want to bang your head against the wall. There's also the new **Snowed Under** (●●●●) where Bob and gang go the Bobblesberg Winter Games (we kid you not!) and still top-rated **Building Friendships** (●●●●½). Bob and his crew of talking building machines are featured in four little stories that focus on cooperation, have a small dose of tension, and are not scary. 3 & up.

■ **Caillou At Play** ⭐*2005*

(Warner Brothers $12.95 ●●●●) Caillou is older than Maisy, less noisy than Elmo, and paced just right for young viewers. Playground and friendship issues like sharing and getting along are center stage here. Also recommended, **Caillou's Neighborhood** (●●●●) and **Caillou the Explorer** (●●●●●) PLATINUM AWARD '02, which explored transportation from a child's point of view.

■ **Click, Clack, Moo: Cows That Type**

(Scholastic $9.95/$14.95 ●●●●½) Farmer Brown's cows and hens are on strike. They want electric blankets, or else: no milk or eggs! A prize-winning story translated to the screen, narrated by Randy Travis with down-home music. Still top rated from this series: **Good Night Gorilla** (●●●●) and

Chrysanthemum (❍❍❍❍❍), PLATINUM AWARD '03. Meryl Streep, Sarah Jessica Parker, and Mary Beth Hurt narrate three wonderful picture books by Kevin Henkes. 4–7.

■ Discover Spot

(Disney $19.99 ❍❍❍❍❍) A creative blend of short animated stories featuring Spot and his friends and live action showing real kids doing similar things. For example, when Spot and his friends see a band in the park, they go home to make their own music. Video then features real-life kids trying different instruments. PLATINUM AWARD '01. 3 & up.

■ Make Way for Ducklings 2005

(Scholastic $9.95/$14.95 ❍❍❍❍½) Parents and even grandparents have grown up with Robert McCloskey's three beloved Caldecott Award winners on this video. "Make Way for Ducklings" tells the jolly tale of Mr. & Mrs. Mallard, who find a home for their ducklings Jack, Kack, Lack, Mack, Nack, Ouack, Pack, and Quack. McCloskey's drawings have not been animat-

ed, but they retain superb vitality as the camera pans and zooms in on his jaunty ducklings and their world. There's delicious suspense in "Blueberries for Sal," and summer in Maine is beautifully encapsulated in "Time of Wonder." You'll find two more favorites, "Lentil" and "Burt Dow," plus a Spanish version of "Ducklings" and read-along features that make the DVD version worth the higher price. 4–8.

■ Miffy's Springtime Adventure 2005 PLATINUM AWARD

(Sony $9.98/$12.98 ❍❍❍❍❍) Based on Dick Bruna's picture books, the video includes more than a dozen small stories featuring Miffy and friends. Springtime focuses on the discoveries of the season. These are low-keyed stories, without nervous hype or tension, and include some simple counting games. Just right for older toddlers and young preschoolers.

■ New Friends: Clifford's Puppy Days 2005

(Scholastic $14.98 ❍❍❍❍) There are lots of stories and activities on this DVD based on Norman Bridwell's storybooks. This animated cartoon show has plenty of positive messages packed into the mix. We could have done without the suspense of a story called the "Monster in 3B." Of course there is no monster, but why present the possibility to threes? That said, this is otherwise a pretty good video for preschoolers. 3 & up.

■Kipper Fun in the Sun

(HIT Entertainment $9.99 ●●●●) This series seems to be back on track for the two-and-up crowd with the simple stories and adventures of Kipper the dog and his friends, Tiger and Arnold. Seven short stories include "The Rescue," "Clouds," "The Farm," and "Crazy Golf." We'd pass on last year's **Kipper Imagine That!** (●●●), which included a hunt for scary creatures and other more Saturday-morning-ish cartoon clichés. 2 & up.

■ Big Little Bill

(Paramount $12.95 ●●●●●) Five-year-old Little Bill longs to be a big kid and succeeds in the several episodes presented here. There's none of the usual cartoon frenzy in these videos. Each story reinforces his sense of himself as a big boy who can help with a baby cousin, at the office, and even at a wedding. PLATINUM AWARD '02. Also top rated: **What I Did at School** (●●●●), several episodes centering on Little Bill and his friends at school. 4–6.

■ Little Bear: Feel Better, Little Bear

(Paramount $9.95 ●●●●●) This series continues to be one of the best for preschoolers with age-appropriate stories about friendship and family. **Feel Better, Little Bear** includes four stories about getting the mumps, a pretend picnic, having the flu, and eating too many sweets. Still top rated, **Little Bear's Band; Summertime Tales; A Kiss for Little Bear; Friends; Winter Tales;** and **Goodnight, Little Bear** (●●●●●). PLATINUM AWARD '03. Forget **Little Goblin Bear** (●●), a seasonal attempt at a safe scare with several dream sequences that may be edgy for some viewers. 3 & up.

■ Madeline at the Ballet BLUE CHIP

(Sony $9.95 ●●●●●) Once more they've come up with a new story based on the original characters. This one will have special meaning to the many little ballerinas who long to get their first toe shoes and worry about living up to their dreams of becoming prima ballerinas. Narrated by Christopher Plummer, this one talks to the importance of practice and believing in oneself. PLATINUM AWARD '00. 4 & up.

■ Maisy's Springtime

(Universal $9.98 ●●●●●) Maisy stars in five little seasonal stories about an egg hunt, a bird building a nest, a trip to the farm with baby animals, and some farm songs. PLATINUM AWARD '02. We wish the songs were more tuneful, but we much prefer this to the **Maisy: ABC** video (●●). Maisy, who doesn't yet speak, doesn't need to learn the alphabet! We suggest previous videos such as **Play with Maisy** (●●●●●) PLATINUM AWARD '01, with little slice-of-life adventures with her friends, very slow paced, and just right for young video viewers. 2½ & up.

■ Pete's a Pizza

(Scholastic $9.95/$14.95 ●●●●●) What can you do on a rainy day when you want to play ball? Pete's playful parents play a game of turning Pete into a Pizza— totally pretend—and by the time he's been "cooked," the sun comes out. Charmingly narrated by Chevy Chase. Two more William Steig favorites included: "Dr. DeSoto" and "The Amazing Bone." All three of these are good fun for 4–8s. The extras here are three rather dark stories by Tomi Ungerer. These extras are better suited to older kids who have a solid understanding of real and make-believe. 54 mins. PLATINUM AWARD '04.

■ The Very Hungry Caterpillar BLUE CHIP

(Disney $12.99 ●●●●●) The story of that very well loved, hungry caterpillar has been transformed into a totally magical video! Animation and music have enhanced Eric Carle's beautiful illustrations and given them another dimension while retaining their original beauty. A delicate blend of imagination and information illuminated with great artistry. Closed-captioned. 2–6.

■ Winnie the Pooh Series

(Disney $12.99) In the past we have recommended this series as "kinder and gentler animated cartoons than most of Saturday morning fare." Unfortunately, all recent Pooh videos have gone in another direction with story lines that are too intense for young viewers. For example, in **Tigger-ific Tales** (●), Tigger's so-called friends give him a bath and his stripes disappear—for preschoolers, who typically worry about body integrity, this video is developmentally inappropriate. We still recommend the original videos: **A Blustery Day** (●●●●) and

The Honey Tree (oooo). Closed-captioned. 2 & up.

Story Videos for Early School Years

Some of the videos in this section have pieces that may be enjoyed by older preschoolers, but for the most part these are stories for 5 and up.

■ Dear America Series

(Scholastic $12.95) Based on the award-winning *Dear America* diaries that we have recommended for school-age readers, this series combines history with story in live-action dramas. In **So Far from Home** (oooo), Mary flees Ireland and the potato famine only to struggle for humane work conditions in the textile mills. **Remember Patience Whipple** is the story of a girl who arrived on the Mayflower and keeps up her courage even after she loses her mother. In **Standing in the Light** (oooo), a Quaker girl and her brother are captured by the Lenape and come to respect their new family and its traditions. **A Picture of Freedom** (oooo) is set in the antebellum South, where Clotee, a slave who knows how to read and write, helps other slaves escape. These films are engrossing, but some have content that may be disturbing to younger viewers; for example, there is a whipping scene in **Picture of Freedom.** It's historically accurate, but it's not for young viewers. Similarly, **Valley Forge Saga** includes an off-screen amputation and a birth with sound effects you'd expect. 8 & up. (877) 750-7111.

■ Goodbye, Mr. Chips *2005*

(Masterpiece Theatre/WGBH $19.95 oooo½) Based on James Hilton's novel, this video features Martin Clunes playing the endearing Latin master at an English boarding school. His inept style is transformed by the woman he loves (Victoria Hamilton) and tragically loses. A glimpse into the past and a life that will seem very foreign to young viewers. Also recommended, last year's PLATINUM winner, **The Railway Children** (ooooo). 8 & up. (800) 949-8670.

■ Parents Are From Pluto *2005*

(Sony $12.98 ooo½) Three new Arthur stories address school-aged kids' sometimes mixed emotions about their parents. The title story centers on wanting parents to make a good impression at "Parents' Open House," something older kids are more apt to worry over than

kids in early grades; in "My Dad, the Garbage Man," Francine is not sure she wants classmates to know what her father does. This is well done and good food for talking. "Mom and Dad Have a Big Fight" talks to the big idea that grown-ups sometimes argue and kids often fear their family will fall apart. It's an important idea, but the video slips from real to imaginary situations so glibly that parents may need to help kids sort out the real from make believe in both video and life. **Arthur's Eyes** (●●●●), reissued in DVD format, includes several themes that are meaningful to school-age kids. Poor Arthur can't see the chalkboard and he must come to terms with wearing glasses. "Francine's Bad Hair Day" centers on wanting to look like someone else instead of oneself. "Draw" is an extra story that was not on the original video. Here Francine calls Fern a "mouse" and discovers that name-calling can backfire. These stories stay truer to the original storybooks. 5–8.

■ **Little House on the Prairie** 🌟2005

(Imavision $49.98 each ●●●●) Imagine a whole generation who knows Melissa Gilbert only from infomercials. Feel old? New fans of the books asked, "There was a show?" The first five seasons are available on six CD sets. Fun to see again and share with your kids! 6 & up.

■ **The Snowman** BLUE CHIP

(Miramax/Buena Vista $12.99 ●●●●●) An enchanting fantasy of a snowman who takes a small boy on a flying adventure. A word of warning: one three-year-old dissolved in tears when the snowman melted. A better choice for 4 & up.

■ **Strega Nona & More** 🌟2005

(Scholastic $9.95/$14.95 ●●●●½) A collection of Caldecott award winners includes Tomie dePaola's best loved witch, Strega Nona, and her foolish helper Big Anthony, who is warned not to touch the magic cooking pot. Also, Simms Taback's "Joseph Had a Little Overcoat," the tale of a worn-out overcoat that proves through its many incarnations that "you can always make something from nothing." Similarly, Marcia Brown's "Stone Soup" is an old tale of three clever soldiers who manage to make soup from a stone. The DVD version also includes "The Tale of

the Mandarin Ducks," plus Spanish versions of "Stone Soup" and "Strega Nona," and read-along text. This does not look like a Saturday morning animated feature, but is true to the spirit and art of the award-winning books. Also reissued this year, **Curious George Rides a Bike & More Tales of Mischief** ($9.95/$14.95) 3–8.

Feature-Length Films

■ Brother Bear *2005*

(Disney $29.99 ●●●●) Kenai, trying to avenge the death of his brother, kills the grizzly bear he believes responsible for his brother's death. The spirits then turn Kenai into a bear. Kenai is rescued and befriended by an orphaned bear cub named Koda. Can you guess who killed his mother? In the end, Kenai chooses to remain a bear to be with Koda. Classic Disney. Rick Moranis and Dave Thomas add comic relief as two wandering moose. 5 & up.

■ Cheaper By the Dozen *2005* PLATINUM AWARD

(Fox $29.98 ●●●●●) Steve Martin and Bonnie Hunt star in the latest remake of the classic book about a family with 12 kids. In one of the best casting moves, the older siblings are played by Hilary Duff and Tom Welling ("Superman"); and Asthon Kutcher aptly plays the oldest sister's easy-to-despise boyfriend. Martin's performance is funny but tempered, and with the collection of teen stars, this is a movie that will appeal to a wide range of family members. 7 & up.

■ Ella Enchanted *2005*

(Miramax $26.99 ●●●½) Ella (Anne Hathaway) is cursed at birth to be obedient. Hathaway is known and beloved by girls and 'tweens from "The Princess Diaries." Unfortunately, Ella was not enchanted with a great screenplay. The movie drags and there just isn't the spark you would expect from what should have been a clever romp. Our group of 11-year-old viewers thought it was cute enough, but thought it would be best enjoyed by the "7–9 crowd."

■ Harry Potter and the Prisoner of Azkaban
2005 PLATINUM AWARD

(Warner Bros. $26.99 ●●●●●) We had a very strong division of opin-

ion about the third Potter movie. While most
adults enjoyed director Alfonso Cuaron's liberties
with J. K. Rowling's book, our kid viewers didn't
think it was right! Even with that criticism, they
gave the movie high marks for being entertaining
and we can't wait for the next one! As Harry gets
older, the movies get darker and are not appropriate for younger viewers. The dementors and
the werewolf scene are particularly intense and

make the Wicked Witch of West look like Mary Poppins! 9 & up.

■ The Miracle *2005* PLATINUM AWARD

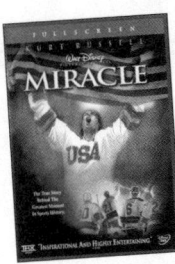

(Disney $22.99/$29.99 ●●●●●) In the tradition of
"The Rookie" and "Remember the Titans," this is
the latest feel-good sports movie from Disney.
While most of the current family movies revolve
around teenage starlets, "Miracle" is one of the few
films that will keep your sons engaged. It's also fun
to revisit a moment most parents remember vivid-
ly. Kurt Russell stars as Coach Herb Brooks, who
dared to believe that the amateur US team could

win the Gold Medal in Hockey. 8 & up.

■ Princess Diaries 2: Royal Engagement *2005*

(Buena Vista $TBA) Anne Hathaway reprises her role as Princess
Mia and has now left America to return to her father's land of
Genovia to take up her proper duties as a princess. But she soon discovers that she is expected to become Queen (and oh, yes, get mar-
ried, too!). Was not ready for screening before press time, but will
surely appeal to the fans of the original. 8 & up.

■ Shrek 2 *2005* PLATINUM AWARD

(Dreamworks $22.99/$29.99 ●●●●○) Can you live
happily ever after? Shrek and Princess Fiona put the
famous fairy tale ending to a test when they go home
to meet Fiona's parents, played by Julie Andrews and
John Cleese. The anxiety-ridden premise of meeting
your in-laws appealed to the grown-ups in the audience. Antonio Banderas as Puss in Boots got high

marks from both young and older viewers. An engaging sequel that
will be playing in living rooms, over and over again. 5 & up.

■ Two Brothers *2005*

(Disney $22.99 ●●½) Two brother tigers from French Indo-China are separated; one goes to the circus, the other becomes a trained killer. They are inevitably reunited, but what will happen next? Oh no, lions and tigers and bears... oh my! Younger viewers found all the shooting frightening; older viewers thought it was boring.

BLUE CHIP and Notable Past Winners: Feature-Length Films

These are widely available films that you'll find in the video store or library. They also are shown frequently on TV, but the video versions lack interrupting commercials—a real plus! Most of these are for early school years and beyond.

- Anne of Green Gables
- Apollo 13
- Babe
- Beauty and the Beast
- Beethoven Lives Upstairs
- The Borrowers
- Cinderella and Cinderella II
- Charlotte's Web
- Chicken Run
- Chitty Chitty Bang Bang
- E.T.
- Finding Nemo
- Fly Away Home
- Freaky Friday
- Gulliver's Travels
- Harriet the Spy
- Harry Potter and the Sorcerer's Stone
- Holes
- Homeward Bound and Homeward Bound II
- Honey, We Shrunk Ourselves
- The Indian in the Cupboard
- The Lion King and The Lion King II

- The Little Mermaid
- Madeline
- Mary Poppins
- Mulan
- My Dog Skip
- The Nutcracker (with Baryshnikov)
- October Sky
- Peter Pan (Mary Martin version)
- The Red Balloon
- Remember the Titans
- The Rookie
- The Santa Clause
- Sarah, Plain and Tall
- The Secret Garden
- Shrek
- The Sound of Music
- Snow White
- Sounder
- Stuart Little and Stuart Little 2
- Tarzan
- To Kill a Mockingbird
- Willy Wonka and the Chocolate Factory
- The Wizard of Oz

Information, Please

Toddlers and Preschoolers

■ Cleared for Takeoff BLUE CHIP

(Fred Levine Productions $14.95 ●●●●●) Fasten your seat belt and get ready for a fast-paced look at commercial aviation that follows a mother and three kids on a trip from start to finish. Interesting information and film footage takes kids behind the scenes at the airport. From the maker of the granddaddy of construction videos, **Road and House Construction Ahead** (●●●●●). BLUE CHIP '96. 2½ & up. (800) 843-3686.

■ Doing Things BLUE CHIP

(Bo-Peep Productions $14.95 ●●●●●) Every video library should have **Doing Things**! With almost no talking or cutesy narrative, it presents kids and familiar barnyard animals going through the routines of the day—eating, washing, and playing. There's something new to see each time you watch. The cast of kids is multiethnic and the music is fun but not intrusive. **Doing Things** leaves the talking to you and your kids. 2 & up. (800) 532-0420.

■ Elmo's World: Families, Mail & Bath Time! *2005*

(Sony Wonder $9.98/$12.95 ●●●●) Elmo, Mr. Noodle, and the rest of his gang give information about how different families can look, how to mail a letter, and how to take a bath. High marks for inclusion of multicultural families and children with special needs. We question why the mailbox needed to fly for "air mail" delivery. As cloying as Mr. Noodle may be to adult viewers, he has big-time appeal with kids. Also recommended, last year's **Wake Up With Elmo** (●●●●½) with tips on sleep, getting dressed, and taking care of their teeth. Live-action film of a first visit to the dentist is especially useful. 2 & up.

■ Toby the Truck

(emaginate $12.99 ●●●●) An animated truck explores the world of trucks. He gets a tour of a firetruck, a concrete truck mixing and pouring, a garbage truck, the inside of an ambulance, tow trucks and more. The information part is live action and moves slowly enough for young viewers to follow. Doesn't rely on slapstick pratfalls to entertain. 2–5.

Early School Years

■ The American Experience: Seabiscuit

(PBS Home Video $14.95 ●●●●●) This is not so much about horse racing as it is about the spirit of those who believed in Seabiscuit, sometimes called the little horse who could. It's really a story about perseverance and riding it through the ups and downs of one's dreams. 10 & up. PLATINUM AWARD '04. (800) 645-4727.

■ The Artists Specials

(Devine Entertainment $19.95 each ●●●●●) Rather than doing biographies of an artist's whole lifetime, these made-for-TV **Artists** series videos zoom in on a short but significant period in an artist's life. They weave fact and fiction in a relationship between an artist and a young person with very human and universal problems. **Mary Cassatt: American Impressionist,** PLATINUM AWARD '01, stars Amy Brenneman. In **Degas and the Dancer,** struggling with debt and his own self-doubt, Edgar Degas inspires a young dancer to believe in herself and her talent. In helping her, he helps himself. For those who love Degas, the ballet, or both, this is not to be missed! 8 & up. (877) 338-4633.

■ Baseball's Greatest Rivalries *2005*

(Major League Baseball $14.95 ●●●●) The video starts with some Red Sox fans shouting "Yankees suck!" and there are the occasional brawls—but our viewers assured me that it was great to see the old players talking about classic moments in baseball and even better when they showed those pivotal moments in America's favorite pastime. For a broader, more historical look back, we recommend **Baseball: A Film by Ken Burns** BLUE CHIP (PBS Home Video $149.98/$179.98 ●●●●●) There is probably no better gift to serious fans than this nine-tape history of baseball. Burns traces the game's history back to the nineteenth century. Film clips of classic moments in unforgettable games are even more memorable as old-time players, commentators, and fans tell about historic games. Borrow this at the library if the price seems steep, but don't miss it! No better way to introduce sports-minded kids to history! 9 & up. (800) 645-4727.

■ Building Skyscrapers BLUE CHIP

(David Alpert Assoc. $19.95 ●●●●●) Kaboom! Down with the old and up, up, up with a new skyscraper in New York City. Step by step from implosions to raising the steel, to concrete oozing out of hoses, here's a ringside seat for watching a building go from foundation to finish. Real construction people, both male and female, answer the questions of a 7-year-old child in a well paced, clearly written film that was shot from many perspectives, including from a helicopter.

■ Families of the World Series 2005

(Master Communications $19.95 each **oooo**) Newest in the series, this year's video is set in Vietnam. Narrated by a child from the featured country, these are low on energy but high on information about the food, work, school, and customs, told from a child's point of view. More like social studies films for school or libraries, these are nevertheless one way to introduce kids to far-away places. Earlier videos cover, among other places, **China, Thailand, Mexico, India, Korea,** and **Israel.** 30 min. 5–11. (800) 765-5885.

■ Look Mom! I Have Good Manners 2005

(Thinkeroo $14.95 **oooo**½) Based on the title alone, we expected this would be a didactic thumbs down. But with its quiz-show format, the hyper-happy show host involves viewers as players with questions that center on table, good health, playground, and school manners. Kids featured are school-aged kids—the audience for this lively and non-preachy video. (800) 477-7811. 6–10.

■ The Magic School Bus Gets Planted

(Kid Vision $12.95 **oooo**) Phoebe gets transformed into a giant vine and needs to learn what she needs to grow. Still top rated: **Magic School Bus Greatest Adventures** ($12.95 **ooooo**), a compilation of best videos that includes **Busasaurus,** a journey back into the time of dinosaurs (PLATINUM AWARD '98); **...Gets Lost in Space** and **...In a Pickle.** The series features the wacky Ms. Frizzle (voice of Lily Tomlin) and her class. Recommended prior winners: **...Getting Energized,** a look at different types of energy; **...Gets Ants in Its Pants,** a trip into the social world of ants; and **The Magic Schoolbus for Lunch,** a journey through the digestive system. PLATINUM AWARD '96. 5 & up.

■ **Popular Mechanics for Kids: Radical Rockets**

(Koch Vision $12.98 ●●●●) Two teens take kids on a visit to NASA and get to try out all sorts of equipment used to train real astronauts. This is an interesting video for kids who are taken with the idea of exploring space. We didn't like **Slither & Slime** (●●●), with too many moments that felt like "Fear Factor," with earthworms slithering over the kids' faces. 7 & up.

■ **Really Wild Animals** BLUE CHIP

(National Geographic/Columbia TriStar $14.95 each ●●●●) A lively blend of splendid film footage, information, and music have made this series a hit with kids. Dudley Moore narrates all three videos: **Monkey Business** looks at animal families, **Dinosaurs and Other Creature Features** explores the mysteries and characteristics of some of the weirdest wildlife, **Polar Prowl** travels from North to South Pole. Closed-captioned. 5–11.

Coping with Real Life

■ **Arthur: The Good Sport**

(Sony Wonder $9.98/$12.98 ●●●●) These are three stories that will appeal to sports-minded kids. In "The Good Sport," Francine has to get over not winning the Athlete of the Year Award. Champion figure skater Michele Kwan (our favorite!) helps Francine see her way to becoming a good sport. In "Muffy's Soccer Shocker," Muffy has to deal with her demanding coach—her dad! "Francine Frensky, Olympic Rider" is a funny story about dreaming of becoming an Olympic equestrienne. 5 & up.

Bedtime Fears

■ **Goodnight Moon and
   Other Sleepytime Tales**

(HBO Kids Video $9.95 ●●●●●) Though toddlers might enjoy the title story, this is not a film for the very young. Through interviews with dozens of real kids, this refreshing film captures kids' typical feelings about dreams and bedtime. Viewers will find comfort in knowing that they are not alone in some of their fears. Laced throughout these wise remarks from kids are Natalie Cole narrating Faith Ringgold's *Tar Beach*, Billy Crystal's telling of Mercer Mayer's *There's a Nightmare in My Closet*, and familiar bedtime songs sung by Tony Bennett, Aaron Neville, Lauryn Hill, and Patti LaBelle. Oh, yes, and *Goodnight Moon* comes to life faithfully with brilliant color and minimal animation, and is read just as it should be, with simplicity, by Susan Sarandon. Save this for kids from 4–7. PLATINUM AWARD '01.

■ Franklin in the Dark

(USA Home Entertainment $12.95 **oooo**) If you're dealing with nighttime "monsters," **Franklin in the Dark** may help. In this little story Franklin is afraid of dark places. Mother Turtle has a story that assures Franklin he is not alone. On the other hand, if you aren't dealing with monsters—don't bring any home. 4 & up.

New Baby in the House
■ Arthur's Baby

(Sony $12.95 **ooooo**) When Arthur learns that he's about to become a big brother, he has mixed emotions about the changes in his life. A second story, "D.W.'s Baby," features the arrival of Baby Kate. PLATINUM AWARD '98. Note: Unfortunately, this series has not been consistently solid. In **Arthur's Tooth** (**o**), there are monsters and spitting contests; in **Arthur Makes the Team** (**o**), the second story, "Meek for a Week," has a fantasy sequence in which Francine "blows her top" and her head actually comes off and lands on a lawn (still talking). We find these images unnecessary for any age, but particularly inappropriate for Arthur's large preschool audience.

■ Three Bears and a New Baby

(Sony Wonder $12.95 **ooooo**) Baby Bear is freaked out when he discovers that the new baby on the way is going to actually live at his house. "But I'm the baby bear! That's my name, Baby Bear!" He reminds his parents that they are, after all, the storybook classic, "The Three Bears," not the four bears. A reassuring choice for older siblings who may be ambivalent about pending new arrivals. PLATINUM AWARD '04.

Going to School

■ Arthur's Famous Friends

(Sony $12.95 ⦿⦿⦿⦿⦿) This is one of our favorite Arthur videos. Each of the three stories features a guest visitor whose voice is used with animated images. In the first segment, Mr. Rogers comes to visit, but Arthur thinks Mr. Rogers is for babies and is surprised to discover that his friends want to meet their old friend. In the second story, poet Jack Prelutsky comes to the local library for a poetry contest and recites some of his own verse. There's some gratuitous gross-out verse in this segment that we could have done without, but kids will find it funny. The third episode, with Yo-Yo Ma, centers on a debate about jazz vs. classical music. PLATINUM AWARD '01. 5 & up.

■ Spot Goes to School

(Disney $14.99 ⦿⦿⦿⦿) There are some real stories here that preschoolers will relate to. Spot's first day at preschool gives a reassuring glimpse of a typical day of playing with friends and paw painting. On the same tape is "Spot at the Playground," which reinforces ideas of taking turns and safety without preaching. Also recommended: **Where's Spot?** and **Spot Goes to a Party.** PLATINUM AWARD '95. 2 & up.

Potty Videos

There are no magic bullets, but these may be helpful reinforcements. Of course, don't be upset if your reluctant potty user leaves the room when you put these tapes on!

■ Potty Power *2005*

(Thinkeroo $14.95 ⦿⦿⦿½) Toddlers who are on the threshold of "potty power" will relate to the kids in this video who demonstrate all the things they as big kids can do—including "going potty." An amiable young woman sings and speaks along with an animated roll of toilet paper—sounds a bit hokie, but comes across as age-appropriate and not preachy. No miracles promised, but it couldn't hurt! (800) 477-7811. 2½ & up. Also recommended: **It's Potty Time** (A Vision $19.98 ⦿⦿⦿⦿). Developed by the Duke University Medical Center, this "story" features kids of many ages getting ready to go to a party.

Safety

■ Big Bird Gets Lost BLUE CHIP

(Sony $12.95 ●●○○○) In this episode of Sesame Street's *Kids' Guide to Life* series, Maria takes Big Bird shopping. The bad news is that Big Bird gets lost; the good news is that Maria has taught Big Bird and viewers a catchy song for remembering their phone numbers as well as how to find help in the store. A nonthreatening and valuable video with guest star Frances McDormand. 3–7.

Other Issues
Staying Healthy

■ Arthur Goes to the Doctor

(Sony $12.95 ●●●●●) There are several health-related stories in this excellent video. In the first story Arthur cuts his knee and is afraid to tell his parents. It's D.W. who helps him do the right thing. In the second story D.W. gets poison ivy; and the third story features Buster and his asthma. This informative film includes a live-action visit to a doctor about asthma. PLATINUM AWARD '02. Still top rated: **Arthur's Eyes** ($12.95 ●●●●), a video that may help kids who are getting used to needing glasses. 4–8.

■ A Trip to the Dentist Through Pinatta's View

(Boggle-Goggle $14.95 ●●●●) Move over, Oprah! Pinatta, a lively talk show star/puppet, hosts a preschooler and her mom on the subject of going to the dentist. Practicing is one way to overcome fears about a first trip to the dentist, and this includes a nice blend of live-action footage with puppets. 3 & up. (440) 984-3367.

Honesty
■ Telling the Truth

(Sony $12.98 ●●●●) Telly makes the mistake of telling a lie to impress his friends and then has to live with the consequences. Dennis Quaid makes a guest appearance and helps Telly face up to the truth. An age-appropriate retelling of "The Boy Who Cried Wolf" parallels

Telly's predicament. From the *Kids' Guide to Life* series. Also, **Learning to Share,** with Katie Couric. Closed-captioned 4–8.

Science and Ecology

■ Earth Stories Paleontology Vol. #1

(Mazon Productions $19.95 ●●●●●) Chip, the talking rock hammer, is your animated host through this engaging introduction to paleontology. Really most appropriate for upper school (9+). Excellent graphics explain complicated concepts. Live action of digs in Argentina and Illinois are also included, and show the amazing process of fossil hunting. This is the type of film you only wish your Earth Science teacher had had! 30 mins. PLATINUM AWARD '04. (800) 332-4344.

■ The Inventors' Specials

(Devine Entertainment $19.95 each ●●●●●) An excellent series about famous scientists introduces young viewers to the past with an

artful blend of fact and fiction. Each film pairs a well-known scientist with a young person—and both learn much from each other. **Marie Curie** (PLATINUM AWARD '01) is an exciting tale of two sisters whose lives cross paths with Madame Curie during World War I. **Edison** (PLATINUM AWARD '01) opens with a chase scene as a runaway orphan boy literally runs into the scientist's lab, where he becomes an apprentice. A wonderful period piece! Also top rated: **Einstein: Light to the Power of 2,** which portrays a bigoted teacher, a young black girl in the fifties, and the world-famous scientist who befriends her. 9 & up. (877) 338-4633.

■ Playtime With Ahpun & Oreo

(Alaska Postcards $14.95/$19.95 ●●●●½) There's nothing cutesie about this film featuring two bear cubs who were orphaned in the wild and raised in the Alaska Zoo.

In the wild, one would never be able to see a polar bear and brown bear playing together, but these two playful cubs can be seen growing into yearlings through the magic of video. The pace is moderately slow, but the film footage is interesting and likely to keep kids entertained and informed. 2½–7. (800) 248-2624.

Holidays

Christmas, Chanukah, & Kwanzaa

■ Angelina Ballerina, The Show Must Go On *2005*

(HIT Entertainment $12.99 ●●●●) It's Christmas in Mouseland and Angelina wanted to be the star of the show. But, alas, she dances better than she sings and ends up cast as the mean old stepmother in Cinderella. This is the first feature-length special (50 mins.) and the best of this year's Angelina videos. 4–8.

■ Elf *2005* PLATINUM AWARD

(New Line Home Entertainment $22.99/ $29.95 ●●●●●) Starring Will Ferrell as the man who grew up at the North Pole, thinking he was an elf. He heads to New York to seek out his father, a Scrooge-inspired character played by James Caan. Ferrell is great at the physical humor that appeals to kids; adults also didn't mind this family fare with a memorable performance by Bob Newhart as Papa Elf. 9 & up.

■ Bob the Builder: A Christmas to Remember

(HIT Entertainment $14.99/$16.99 ●●●●½) Bob's brother Tom is coming home for the holidays and Bob is thrilled. But Bob is busier than ever getting the city lights, tree, and park ready for the Christmas concert. Tom misses the last boat, but all's well that ends well. Sir Elton John is a featured guest, appearing as an animated character in the show. 50 mins.

■ Sesame Street Celebrates Around the World

(Sony $14.95 ●●●●) If you lived in Portugal, you would celebrate the New Year by making wishes and eating 12 grapes, one for every month of the year. With music and humor, Big Bird and friends introduce viewers to children and customs in many parts of the world. Also, **Shalom Sesame Chanukah** (●●●●), **Jerusalem Jones and the Lost Afikoman**(●●●●), and **The Aleph-Bet Telethon** (●●●●). 4 & up.

Noteworthy Catalogs

Big Kids Productions (800) 477-7811
Music for Little People (800) 409-2457
PBS Home Video (800) 645-4727
WGBH (800) 949-8670

Noteworthy Websites

amazon.com
bigkidsvideo.com
musicforlittlepeople.com
reel.com
www.shopPBS.com

IV • Audio
Great Music & Stories

Music Exploration. Audiotapes and CDs are a great way to introduce children to a broad range of music such as folk songs, marches, classics, and show tunes, that they might not hear on the radio. These musical explorations are opportunities for dancing, conducting, drawing while listening, and even daydreaming.

Story Power. Listening to stories told on tapes can help beginning readers as they follow along in a book. Simply listening to longer books provides food for the imagination—to make one's own pictures from the spoken word. Children enjoy and understand stories well beyond their reading level and readily do so when no adult is available to read with them. For quiet or sit-down travel time, few take-alongs are as valuable as some well selected audio stories.

Criteria. In testing new products, we continue to reject "children's music" that is preachy, overproduced, and in many cases, condescending to young listeners. Our ultimate test is still whether we can stand being in a car with it or whether someone in the driver's seat or car seat screams, "Turn it off!"

Shopping Tips. We also recommend that you share your favorite music, whether it be contemporary, folk, jazz, classical, or show tunes. If you're enjoying the music, chances are it will be contagious.

We have listed the prices for tapes first and then for CDs, if available. Large music stores carry products of major companies such as Disney, CBS, and Sony Wonder. We have provided phone numbers and websites to help you locate titles from smaller recording companies that sell directly or through catalogs.

Music

Lullabies and Songs for the Very Young

■ All the Pretty Little Horses

(Randa Records $15.95 ●●●●½) A very traditional collection of 14 lullabies from Gershwin to "Rock-a-bye Baby." Miranda Russell's voice is as smooth as satin and the variety of instuments—flutes, guitars, harpsichord, and bass—all add to the richness of this recording. www.mirandarussell.com.

■ American Lullaby

(Ellipsis Arts $15.98 ●●●●●) A special collection of lullabies from American folk, country, and gospel traditions, sung by the best in children's music including Maria Muldaur, Bill Staines, Cathy Fink and Marcy Marxer, Sweet Honey in the Rock, and Susie Tallman. Songs include "Prairie Lullaby,"

"Hush Little Baby," and "My Creole Belle." PLATINUM AWARD '04. (800) 788-6670.

■ At Quiet O'Clock BLUE CHIP

(Sally Rogers, Rounder $8.98 ●●●●●) These lullabies are just the ticket for a quiet time—whatever the hour might be. With guitar, dulcimer, or piano as accompaniment, this wonderful collection of traditional and original lullabies by award-winning vocalist Sally Rogers is still our favorite! Trust us, this is a must-have for all new babies (and their parents). (800) 768-6337.

■ Baby Einstein: Lullaby Classics ⭐2005

(Buena Vista $9.98 ●●●●) We're not usually big fans of synthesized music, but this is a pleasing collection that includes selections by Mozart, Beethoven, Chopin, Dvorak, and others. Also, **Baby Vivaldi** (●●●●) and **Baby Galileo: Concert for Little Ears** (●●●●).

■ Dreamland

(Putumayo $15.98 ●●●●●) Soothing lullabies from many lands sung with authentic instruments in the language of each land. Songs from Brazil, Madagascar, Canada, Scotland, Japan, Argentina, and more. Perfect for snuggle-down time. All ages. PLATINUM AWARD '04.

■ Dream with Me Tonight

(Sandman Records $12.98 ●●●●●) Melodie

Crittenden's beautiful voice makes you want to find your blankie and get cozy. The original music composed by Lanny Sherwin is lovely and right on target for setting the mood for bedtime. From the title song "Dream with Me Tonight" to the instrumentals at the end of the recording, this will do the trick for naptime (just be careful that you don't fall asleep too!). PLATINUM AWARD '03. Also, **Dream With Me Tonight (Volume 2)** features Gene Miller. The title song is our favorite. Miller's voice is calming but one song sounds too much like the last. www.echomusic.com.

■ Goodmorning Guitar 2005

(Homesong Media $9.98/$14.98 ●●●●●) The reissue of the PLATINUM AWARD-winning Ray Penney's classical guitar recording is just right for dancing, painting, reading, or just plain daydreaming. Pure and pleasant mix of classic and folktunes to enjoy—sing along if you like, but most of the selections are simply for your listening pleasure. (631) 728-4483.

■ Pocket Full of Stardust

(Rounder $8.99/$12.99 ●●●●●) Consistently, Cathy Fink and

Marcy Marxer can be counted on for humor and musicality that you and your child will enjoy. This entry opens with some pretty lively fare for sleep time, but it calms down as the tracks proceed, almost mirroring the way we unwind slowly at the end of the day. Save this for older kids, not toddlers. PLATINUM AWARD '03. Still top rated, **Pillow Full of Wishes.** (800) 768-6337.

■ The Sun Upon the Lake Is Low BLUE CHIP

(Mae Robertson & Don Jackson, Lyric Partners $10/$16 ●●●●●) A collection of glorious traditional and contemporary folk songs—a soothing way to end any day. Includes, among others, "Circle Game,"

"Michael Row Your Boat Ashore," and "Gaelic Lullaby." Also top rated, **All Through the Night.** (800) 490-8875.

Music for Moving, Singing, and Dancing

■ Celebration of America

(Music for Little People $15.98 ●●●●) A
blend of folk songs, patriotic marches, and traditional patriotic music performed by a wide
range of well known artists including Linda
Ronstadt ("Back in the USA"), the Weavers
("This Land is Your Land"), and the American
Philharmonic Orchestra ("America the

Beautiful"). A feel-good collection just right for a 4th of July celebration! (800) 409-2457.

■ Classic Nursery Rhymes 2005

(Rock Me Baby Records $16.99 ●●●●●)
"Skidamarink," "I'm a Little Teapot," and "All
Around the Mulberry Bush" are among the 37 clas-
sics Susie Tallman performs with stylish wit and
energy. PLATINUM AWARD '03. New for 2005,
Children's Songs (●●●●), a collection of 38
best-loved traditional songs and rhymes in
English, Spanish, and French. (415) 255-4719.

■ Come and Make a Circle 2005

(Peachhead Productions $15.99 ●●●●) Susan Salidor combines eight
previously released songs with twelve new songs and fingerplays that
are sure to be favorites for home and cirlce time fun. Lyrics include
playful suggestions for moving to the music using fingers, toes, and
their whole bodies to a variety of multicultural songs. 3 & up.

■ I Sang It Just for You 2005

(Music by Mary Kaye $15 ●●●●) A collec-
tion of refreshingly original music sung by the
composer. Her songs have humor, a variety of
styles, and don't talk down to kids. You won't
mind listening to this—with or without
them.

■ Inside Out

(Rounder $10.98/$15.98 ●●●●) It may be inside out, but it's totally
right side up for getting kids up and moving to samba, rap, swing, and

reggae beats. Jessica Harper's lyrics are child centered, her music is crisp and refreshing. Still top rated, **Rhythm in My Shoes,** PLATINUM AWARD '01. 2½ & up. (800) 768-6337.

■ Raffi: Let's Play

(Rounder $12.98 ●●●●●) This celebrated children's composer and performer hasn't lost his touch. This collection includes both original music and well known songs, including "Yellow Submarine" and "The Eensy Weensy Spider." Jane Goodall contributes sound effects of chimp sounds in Raffi's tribute song to her work. PLATINUM AWARD '03. (800) 768-6337.

■ Nancy Cassidy's Kids' Songs **2005** PLATINUM AWARD

(Klutz $21.95 ●●●●●) One of the brightest new recordings in an otherwise lackluster year of children's audio is Cassidy's strong collection of classics, including "She'll Be Coming 'Round the Mountain," "Apples and Bananas," "Day-o," and "This Little Light of Mine." This two-CD set comes with a sing-along songbook (a real plus when you don't remember all the words!). 2 & up.

■ Ragtime Romp

(Music for Little People $9.98/$15.98 ●●●●●)

Put on Ric Louchard's collection of Scott Joplin and watch your child's eyes open wide. From "Elite Syncopations" to "The Ragtime Dance" to "The Entertainer"—it's never too early to introduce kids to this part of America's musical heritage. PLATINUM AWARD '02. (800) 409-2457.

■ Sing Along with Putumayo **2005** PLATINUM AWARD

(Putumayo Kids $15.98 ●●●●●) What a spirited collection of folk and blues classics! Arlo Guthrie opens the festivities with "Bling-Blang," and the quality of the singers and selections never lets up! You'll hear Taj Mahal with "Don't You Push Me Down"; Dan Zane doing "Bushel and a Peck"; Rosie Flores singing "Red, Red Robin"; and so many more. (888) 788-8629.

■ Songs from the Street

(Sony $49.98 ●●●●●) The Street is Sesame. Need we say more? Parents, themselves old Sesame Streeters, will relish hearing their old favorites in this three-CD box set featuring over 63 remastered tracks with performances from the past 35 years PLATINUM AWARD '04. All ages.

■ That's What Kids Do!

(Building Block Music $15 ●●●●●) Here's an original musical with the feel of a kids' version of "A Chorus Line." Players from 4 to 14 sing their stories in a sassy variety of musical styles with lyrics that are often funny, sometimes wistful, and always entertaining. We saw the show live and are proud to say this was composed, produced, and played by five members of our family! PLATINUM AWARD '02. (800) 842-7664.

■ Under a Shady Tree

(Two Tomatoes Records $14.99 ●●●●●) Laurie Berkner is back with a happy collection of original music and a bright voice to match. Berkner strikes just the right balance of creating music for children, and displaying a strong musical quality that will appeal to parents as well. PLATINUM AWARD '04. All ages.

■ Wiggle Waggle Loop-de-Loo! ⬛2005

(Kindermusik $25.95 ●●●●½) An appealing music kit with a board book to share, a CD with both lively and soothing music, and a jolly-looking velour bumble bee with crinkle wings and quiet jingle inside. Dance to the music with your babe in arms, share the lilting language of the book and songs. 6 mos. & up. (866) 376-9123.

Folk Tunes for All Ages

■ Bill Staines' One More River

(Red House Records $8.98/$17.98 ●●●●) If you are a folk music person, you'll need no introduction to Bill Staines. This isn't a collection of cutesie songs chosen for the kiddies. It's honest-to-goodness music— some somber, some classic, some less familiar, and all joyful. Accompanied by everything from banjoes to violins, congas to penny whistles, guitars to bass. (800) 695-4687.

■ Bright Spaces

(Rounder $10.95/$15.95 ●●●●●) A must-have collection of wonderful songs sung by the best in children's music. The voices of Arlo Guthrie, Woody Guthrie, Jessica Harper, Dave Mallett, Cathy and Marcy, and Sweet Honey in the Rock are brought together for this collection to benefit homeless children. Between Woody Guthrie's "This Land Is Your Land" and Dave Mallett's "Garden Song," all seems right with the world! PLATINUM AWARD '02. (800) 768-6337.

■ Family Fare: Folk Songs for Children and Their Families

(Elm Hill $15 ●●●●●) You're going to love this lively collection of songs by Woody Guthrie, Pete Seeger, and other traditional favorites plus many original songs with catchy lyrics and a sense of humor. Accompanied by guitar, banjo, autoharp, dulcimer, and harmonium, and all played and sung by the talented Ellen Edson. A gem that's destined to be a sing-along hit! PLATINUM AWARD '02. (603) 336-7796.

■ Folksongs and Bluegrass for Children

(Rounder $10.98/15.98 ●●●●●) From the minute this disc starts spinning, you'll be singing along and tapping your foot! Phil Rosenthal's collection starts with "The Train Song" rolling down the track, and on to "In the Jungle," followed by such well loved songs as "Six Little Ducks," "The Paw Paw Patch," "Mama Don't Allow," and "Aiken Drum," among others. A winner! (800) 768-6337.

■ Kids, Cars & Campfires

(Red House Records $15 ●●●●●) If you are going to buy one recent collection of folk tunes, this is it. Bill Staines, Tom Paxton, Sally Rogers, the Chenille Sisters, and other great singers combine forces—the only thing missing is the marshmallows! Songs include "Froggie Went a Courtin'," "Little Brown Dog," and "Your Shoes, My Shoes." PLATINUM AWARD '02. (800) 695-4687.

■ Little Johnny Brown

(Smithsonian Folkways $10/$15 ●●●●) With this reissue of a collection from the early '70s, a new generation will enjoy Ella Jenkins, the ultimate songsmith for the young. Features Ms. Jenkins interacting with her young audience with such songs as "Miss Mary Mack" and "Head, Shoulders, Knees and Toes." These are classic folk songs with plenty of repetition and easy sing-, clap-, and tap-along fun. (800) 410-9815.

■ O Mickey, Where Art Thou?

(Disney $18.98 ●●●●) The leading Bluegrass singers are included in this collection of classic Disney songs with their own special twang. Songs include "Circle of Life," "Zip-A-Dee-Doo-Dah," and "When You Wish upon a Star." If you love bluegrass/country and Disney, this one's for you. All ages.

■ Pete Seeger American Folk, Game & Activity Songs for Children BLUE CHIP

(Smithsonian Folkways $15 ●●●●●) Roll up the carpet and get ready to dance! You'll have a library of the best-loved folksongs and games with this reissue of Seeger's classic *American Folk Songs for Children* and his *American Game and Activity Songs for Children*. Accompanied by his banjo, Seeger sings 22 well loved tunes such as "Bought Me a Cat," "Shoo Fly," "This Old Man," "Skip to My Lou," and "Clap Your Hands." 3–7. PLATINUM AWARD '01. (800) 410-9815.

■ Sweet Dreams of Home

(Magnolia Music/Lyric Partners $10/$16 ●●●●●) Mae Robertson and Eric Garrison's eclectic collection of contemporary folk music in appreciation of the concept of "home" includes songs ranging from Graham Nash's "Our House" to David Byrnes' "This Must Be the Place." PLATINUM AWARD '00. (800) 490-8875.

■ This Land Is Your Land BLUE CHIP

(Rounder $10.98/$15.98 ●●●●●) Introduce your kids to the music of Woody and Arlo Guthrie as they sing such classics as the title song, "So Long, It's Been Good to Know Yuh," and "Riding in My Car. " (800) 768-6337.

Multicultural Music

■ Cajun

(Putumayo $15.98 ●●●●●) From the first note, you're transported to

the bayous of southwest Louisiana. It's almost impossible to sit still while this collection of Cajun music is on—fun for kids to move to! PLATINUM AWARD '02. (888) 788-8629. Also top rated, **Le Hoogie Boogie: Louisiana French Music for Children** BLUE CHIP (Michael "Beausoleil" Doucet et al., Rounder $10.98/$15.98). (800) 768-6337.

■ **Still the Same Me**

(Sweet Honey in the Rock, Rounder $10.98/$15.98 ●●●●●) Once again this superb African American ensemble gives us an inspired collection of songs and improvisations. Featuring only their voices and percussion instruments, this is a listening treat for the whole family that will move your spirit and your whole being! PLATINUM AWARD '02. (800) 768-6337.

Introducing the Classics

While there has been a great deal written about the "Mozart effect," you should know that even the researchers who did the original study did not work with babies—and are generally dismayed at the marketing that has been spun around their research with college students. That said, listening to classical music is a treat. If you have your own collection, experiment and see what your child enjoys at different times of the day. Here are some collections:

■ **Beethoven's Wig 2** ⬛2005⬛ PLATINUM AWARD

(Rounder Kids $12.98 ●●●●●) Brava! Brava! Lighthearted LOL lyrics are set to classics by Bach, Schubert, Vivaldi, Strauss, Brahms, Grieg, and others. Richard Perlmutter has done it again—linking familiar music with witty ditties and each composer's name! Like the original **Beethoven's Wig,** PLATINUM AWARD '03, this is an amusing symphonic romp in the spirit of PDQ Bach for young audiences. (800) 768-6337.

■ **Classical Child**

(MetroMusic $15.95 ●●●●●) Selections are by turns as playful as "Papagena!" from *The Magic Flute*, as powerful as the "Anvil Chorus" from *Il Trovatore*, and as heavenly as the "Flower Duet" from *Lakme*. What a splendid way to introduce young listeners to the opera!

PLATINUM AWARD '01. (888) 433-4408.

■ H.M.S. Pinafore BLUE CHIP

(London $14.96 ●●●●●) Part of every child's musical experience should include the sparkling music of Gilbert and Sullivan. *H.M.S. Pinafore* is always a good place to start.

Stories: Audio/Book Sets

Most storybooks published in audio form already have been well received as stand-alone books. Add music, sound effects, and a well known narrator, and a good thing just gets better! These combined forms of media can do a lot to promote kids' positive attitudes and appetites for books and reading. Here are some of the best tickets to pleasurable and independent storytimes. Some are just audio; others are packaged with book and audio.

Preschool Stories

■ Blueberries for Sal

(by Robert McCloskey, Puffin $7.99 ●●●●) In this classic mix-up, a mother bear and cub get separated, as do a human mother-and-child duo. All's well that ends well. This no-frills set has no big-name stars, but beginning readers can follow the text or flip the tape for lively activity songs related to bears and berries. This series includes many other classics. 3–7.

■ If You Take a Mouse to the Movies

(by Laura Joffe Numeroff/illus. by Felicia Bond, HarperFestival $11.95 book & tape ●●●●●) The amusing circular story of what happens if you take a mouse to the movies is now available in a book-and-audio set. Narrated by Jason Alexander. The story is followed by "Mouse's 12 Days of Christmas" and other mouse Christmas carols. PLATINUM AWARD '02. 3–7.

■ Tell Me a Story Series BLUE CHIP

(HarperChildren's Audio $7.95 ●●●●) Many best-loved classics are available in inexpensive paperback-and-audio sets. These make good take-along travel treats and great gifts, and are an excellent way to build your child's listening ability and personal library. Bring home a mix of classics such as **Caps for Sale,** by Esphyr Slobodkina, **Dr. DeSoto Goes to Africa,** by William Steig, and **Dinner at the**

Panda Palace, by Stephanie Calmenson.

Early School Years

Not all story tapes are equal. A solo narrator holding a listener's attention for several hours is no
small feat! Here are the best new and BLUE
CHIP choices:

■ Artemis Fowl series 2005

(Listening Library $28 each ●●●●) Fans of the
adventures of criminal-minded young Artemis
Fowl and his run-ins with the fairy world, will
enjoy listening to Nathaniel Parker's narration.
All three books are now available on CD. 9 & up.

■ Carnival of the Animals 2005

(adapted and narrated by John Lithgow/illus. by Boris Kulikov, Simon
& Schuster $17.95 ●●●½) Lithgow wrote and narrated a story that
was inspired by Camille Saint-Saëns' composi-
tion. (It was performed by the New York City
Ballet.) The included CD is a recording performed by Chamber Music Los Angeles.
Lithgow is always enjoyable to listen to and
Kulikov's illustrations are engaging—but it will
be a hard sell to your average 8 year old.

■ Stories in Music: Mike Mulligan and his Steam Shovel 2005 PLATINUM AWARD

(Simon & Simon $16.98 ●●●●●) More than a recording of a beloved
storybook, this is a musical happening with original symphonic music,
á la *Peter and the Wolf*, plus some jazz and ways of listening for the
whole family to enjoy. 6–9. (800) 419-2409.

■ The Chronicles of Narnia BLUE CHIP

(by C. S. Lewis, HarperChildren's Audio $11.95 each/$50 set
●●●●●) There are seven tapes in this notable collection—each can
stand alone. Narrated by Ian Richardson, Claire Bloom, Anthony
Quayle, and Michael York. Together, they tell the whole story of the
magic land of Narnia. 9 & up.

■ Harry Potter and the Order of the Phoenix

(Listening Library $25 tapes/$28 CDs ●●●●●) We wish Jim Dale
could read all books on tape. He doesn't just read them, really, he performs them with such energy that our testers looked forward to get-

ting back into the car to hear the next install-
ment! For kids that find an 800+ page book a little daunting, here's a great way to experience the
world of Harry Potter. 26 hours & 30 minutes of
listening. Age: late school years, 'tweens, teens.
Still top rated, the first three audio books in the
series. PLATINUM AWARDS.

■ Number the Stars *2005* PLATINUM AWARD

(Listening Library $25 ●●●●●) Blair Brown brings many voices to
Lois Lowry's suspenseful novel set in Denmark during WWII when
the Danish resistance protected their Jewish neighbors and managed
to smuggle them out of the country to Sweden. Lowry tells this chapter in history through the friendship of two ten year olds—one who
must leave, and the other who is forced to find courage inthe face of
true danger. 9 & up.

Audio and Electronic Equipment

COMPARISON SHOPPER
Cassette and CD Players, Recorders & More

The classic **Fisher-Price Tuff Stuff
Tape Recorder with Voice Warp**
(Fisher-Price $34.99 ●●●) did not get
great feedback as a result of the new warping
feature. Testers liked the sturdy quality of the
machine but complained that the warping
voices (monster, robot, alien, bunny) did
not work well and detracted from the product.
This product was being redesigned as we went to press.
Fisher-Price Tuff Stuff Stereo CD Player *2005*
(KIDdesigns $59.99 ●●●●) is a hefty player with safety lock
that young kids can't open independently.
Sound quality is very good and has a sing-
along detachable microphone (you need
to put your mouth on it to make it work
best) and volume limiter. Adaptor is not
included. 4 & up. Also available, the same
basic machine but with a Barbie Motif.
The **Barbie Sing with Me CD Player**

($59.99 ●●●●) has the same sturdy barrel shape with excellent sound quality. Also comes with plug-in mike and CD—we tested it with James Taylor and it's fine. 4 & up. (888) TOP-TOYS. **Disney Personal CD Player with Digital AM/FM Tuner** (Disney $49.99 ●●●●) is a good choice for a first CD player, and comes in either the classic Disney red or with a princess motif. The **Boombox** ($49.99) from this line has a nice sound quality but the play buttons are not very clear. Hands down the best product in Disney's line is the **Motorola Disney Classic Cordless Phone** ($49.99 ●●●●½), which combines Motorola quality with the spirit of Disney (when the phone rings it plays the theme from Mickey Mouse).

Party Time

■ **Barbie CDG Karaoke Tape Recorder with Wireless Microphones** *2005*

(KIDdesigns $99 ●●●●½) Really cool—this plays both CDs and tapes, and can record. Lyrics are displayed on the TV and kids can sing along with two cordless microphones. Loaded with top pops from current 'tweens idols. 6 & up.

■ **My Photo Booth** *2005*

(Girl Tech $44.99 ●●●●½) If you're having a party, this new oversized camera will be a fun activity. Have everyone say, "Cheese!" into the large mirror, and you'll get an instant Polaroid picture. Comes with one pack of Polaroid Instant i-Zone Film. 8 & up.

Online Resources

• **www.amazon.com**
• **wwwmusicforlittlepeople.com**
• **www.rounder.com**

V • Computer Software/CD-ROM

In this chapter we have included the best software we have reviewed, plus titles marked **PREVIEW 2005,** which were not ready to be tested in their final form, but which looked promising. Please consult our website (www.toyportfolio.com) for up-to-the-minute software reviews, plus the Platinum Software Award winners. (Editors' note: TBA—"to be announced"—indicates that a price has not yet been announced.)

About our selections

We spend the year going through stacks of computer software and video games looking for the very best: software that enhances creativity, stimulates thinking, and enables children to express themselves in new ways. These aren't necessarily the ones you'll find pushed at the local computer store. A great deal of software promotes sexual stereotypes and is violent. Even more software is just mediocre mind rot. Too often, software companies rely on the marketing appeal of licensed characters to sell what amounts to the same game over and over again. This is most prevalent in software called "activity centers," and has spread to so-called educational software. The dirty secret of the software industry is that most children's software consists of a handful of arcade games and activities (match game, coloring book, jigsaw puzzle, connect the dots) recycled countless times. You may have bought 10 software packages this year that all have the same activities. Not all our selections have the same marketing money behind them as the bestsellers, but we think that our picks deliver the kind of quality experience you'll want for your child.

Trends

Has Educational Software Dropped Out of School?

Most major players in the once flourishing educational software market (Microsoft, Knowledge Adventure, The Learning Company, DK) have virtually abandoned the field this year. As we went to press, only Scholastic had announced a new educational program (**Dragon Tales: Learn & Fly with Dragons,** a numbers and logic activity set). This dearth means excellent pricing on bundles of "older" recycled educational software—sometimes you can get three or four award-winning titles in a single box. Look for bargains from repackagers like Topics Entertainment (www.topics-ent.com).

Electronic Learning Platforms Challenge Computers

Buying a thousand-dollar computer system for your four year old to learn the alphabet on is overkill. But you may be rightly reluctant to share your computer (and its valuable data) with your preschooler. Fortunately, there are options for young kids that are cheaper and have the added benefit of portability.

■ Leapster

(LeapFrog $79.99 ●●●●½) Looks like a GameBoy on steroids, but the resemblance is only skin deep; the two platforms are designed for different markets. Leapster is designed primarily as a learning system for kids 3–8; the Gameboy is primarily an entertainment system for 'tweens and teens. The screen on the battery-powered, portable Leapster is larger, with control coming primarily from oversized buttons and a touch-sensitive screen. The content is grade-based, offering lots of good opportunity for drill and review. This platform takes off where educational software for the PC ended—providing most of the value at a fraction of the cost.

■ Leap Pad Plus Writing Learning System

(LeapFrog $59.99 ●●●●½)

■ Powertouch Learning System

(Fisher-Price $49.99 ●●●●)

Both use interactive electronic workbooks. Eschewing the "cartoon-ish" approach that has typified much of children's software in favor of a book-oriented approach results in more time being spent in "practice" and interaction than in passive viewing. The "books" are touch sensitive, and some models offer voice recording and even simple writing recognition. We are happy to note that both companies are beginning to use award-winning storybooks rather than just licensed characters, though not all the titles are created equal. The platforms offer great promise and appealed to our testers.

■ V.Smile

(Vtech $59.99) A console that plugs into the television and specializes in drill-and-review games that usually borrow from arcade formats. Includes four games (shape, color, number recognition, letter order) that were similar to the type of activities previously found in children's computer programs. Before judging this platform we'll want to see more software—the line-up relies heavily on licensed characters (Disney, Spiderman, Scooby Doo).

■ InteracTV

(Fisher-Price $39.99) Promises to allow kids to plug the console into their DVD and interact with their favorite episodes of *Blue's Clues*, *Dora the Explorer*, *Barney*, *Sesame Street*, and *Sponge Bob*. Each DVD will include 100 interactive games. Kids will respond to questions via a wireless controller. Targets the 3 & up crowd, but was not available for testing.

■ Etch-A-Sketch ETO THUMBS DOWN

(Ohio Arts $34.99 ●●)

■ Crayola My First TV Play System THUMBS DOWN

(Techno Source $19.99 ●●½)

Although we were enticed by the idea of stand-alone electronic art sets that plug directly into the TV, you'd be better off giving your kids a good set of crayons and some paints. The Crayola gadget has a coloring book and games, though on our unit only the coloring book portion was working; there wasn't much room for open-ended creativity. The Etch-A-Sketch ETO, on the other hand, is all about open-ended drawing, but the controls are not intuitive and there is no on-screen help. 4 & up.

Move Your Body: Feel the Beat

One of the best new movements (if you'll pardon the pun) is the emergence of games that encourage kids to use their whole body. The object of most of these titles is to have a body part hit the right spot to the beat as directed by the game. The games are hardware driven: Because they use a digital camera, EyeToy-enabled games (available only on PS2) actually put the player onto the screen and into the action; the other approach (sometimes combined with the EyeToy) is a pad on the floor that acts as a giant game controller. Our testers found the EyeToy games easier to play; but the dance pad games were particularly fun and challenging for older gamers. In the case of the EyeToy, the camera is sold bundled with the initial package; the dance pads are usually sold separately—we like the **MadCatz Beat Pad** (Mad Catz $19.99). Here are some of our favorites for each platform:

EyeToy Games

■ EyeToy

(Sony $49.99 ●●●●●) Shipping with the camera, this package contains a collection of arcade-inspired games that will get everyone up and moving. There is also a zone where younger kids can simply watch themselves on TV playing in an interactive virtual environment with balloons, leaves, and snowflakes. PLATINUM AWARD '04. 3 & up.

■ Groove *2005* PLATINUM AWARD

(Sony $29.99 ●●●●●) As in most dance games, you have to move to the beat, but here there are special bonuses since the camera can see you! Dance well and you'll actually begin to glow or leave trails of shimmering colors. Our favorite feature: the game takes still and video clips of the players that are great fun to watch in instant replay.

■ AntiGrav *PREVIEW 2005*

(Sony $TBA) Ever wonder what it felt like to be a character in one of those Sonic-like action mazes? Now you can "ride" the game. The EyeToy puts you onto a futuristic skateboard rollercoaster; you must use your whole body, grabbing rings as they whiz by.

■ Nick Toons Bowling *PREVIEW 2005*

(THQ $TBA) This game promises to evaluate your bowling form with the EyeToy.

■ Sega Superstar *PREVIEW 2005*

(Sega $TBA) Similar to the original EyeToy games, this collection of mini-games will feature characters from the Sega franchises like Samba De Amigo and Sonic the Hedgehog. We have some concern, however, that some of the characters and themes from "House of the Dead" and "Virtua Fighter" may be inappropriate for younger players, even if the game receives an "E" rating.

Dance Pad Games

■ Dance Dance Revolution Extreme *PREVIEW 2005*

(Konami $50) This series continues to pump out delightfully difficult dance challenges featuring hot, current songs. The new version will mix EyeToy and DancePad support. The difficulty factor makes this game better for kids 10 & up.

■ Shark Tale *PREVIEW 2005*

(Activision $TBA) While most dance games aim at 'tweens, Activision has included dancing as a mini-game in its suite of mini-games based on the movie.

■ Athens 2004 *PREVIEW 2005*

(Sony $TBA) Inspired by the Olympics? Use your feet to control the action of the athletes in 25 track and field, aquatic, and equestrian events. Set up four dance pads with a multi-tap accessory and you're ready for a 21st-century gym class.

And still other ways to get your kids moving:

■ Donkey Konga *PREVIEW 2005*

(Nintendo $49) The year's most novel "feel the beat" controller comes from Nintendo: a bongo drum! There are at least two games planned for it; the first is a straight music game where you have to hit on the beat with the correct combination of left, right, and both together hand motions (a built-in mike even listens for clapping!). Next year Donkey Konga will feature a Donkey Kong-like adventure/maze game that will be optimized to be controlled by bongos!

■ SSX Snowboarder

(Radica $49.99 ●●●○) Snowboarding games have been around for years, but this is the first stand-alone game to incorporate a "stand-on" snowboard controller. Testers said that game play was easier to master than on comparable PC/Xbox and PS2 systems, making it appropriate for the younger demographic at which it is aimed. 8 & up

■ Karaoke Revolution 2 *2005* PLATINUM AWARD

(Konami $50 ●●●●●) Konami knows how to throw a good party—witness the popularity of the Dance Dance Revolution Series. Now they've taken the Karaoke craze to the next level with a game that monitors how well you sing. The closer to pitch and rhythm, the more the crowd cheers. As you advance in the game, the venues get bigger and more exciting. Still top rated, **Karaoke Revolution,** PLATINUM AWARD '04.

Retro Gaming

Everyone is bringing out cloned versions of games from the dawn of the video age. Nintendo shipped a slew of retro games together with a Gameboy Advance SP molded to look like an old NES controller (**Classic NES Limited Edition,** Nintendo $99.99). Microsoft is bringing retro-spirit to Xbox with **Xbox Live Arcade** ($39.99 for the Xbox subscription): a virtual destination where casual gamers will be able to play puzzle games as well as classic video games such as "Galaxian" and "Dig Dug." Atari: The **80 Classic Games** (Atari $19.99/PC) is another way to get the retro-feeling. If you've got that retro-fever, but don't want to invest in an expensive console, Jakks Pacific puts the goods in a series of battery-operated, joystick-popping, stand-alone platforms that deliver on what they promise: faithful reproductions of old-school games. The question remains, do these old low-res quarter-eaters have an appeal beyond twenty-somethings looking for a dose of nostalgia?

Not all retro-games are created equal. Our favorite is **Arcade Legends: Tetris** (Radica $24.99 ●●●●●), a stand-alone two-controller game that plays five versions of the classic block building game. Its unique controller makes Tetris more intuitive than any version we've played. 9 & up.

On the other hand, the "M" (for "mature") **Midway Arcade Treasures** (Midway $19.99/Xbox) with multiple versions of "Mortal Kombat" is decidedly not kid-friendly.

The Next Next-Generation Consoles

With the PS2, Xbox, and Game Cube coming to the end of their cycle, the usual players have all begun gearing up for the hype machine that will accompany the release of electronic entertainment. When the next next-gen consoles are released in 2005–06 they will feature better graphics and faster processors. Most will undoubtedly also attempt to become the centerpiece for all your media: music, videos, photos, as well as games. In the near-term, this means reduced prices for the current crop of game consoles.

Taking it With You

Twenty-five percent of every dollar spent in gaming is spent on GameBoy products. The popularity of the GameBoy is a mixed blessing. They can make long trips and waits at the doctor's office easier, so strong is their nearly hypnotic attraction. So many parents tell us that kids can "fall into" the GameBoy, it swallows up all their time, attention, and willingness to do other things. Since most games on this platform fall into one or another kind of kick, hit, shoot, or punch activity, the value of this "addiction" is questionable. Now, Nintendo and Majesco intend to launch a series of cartoon-content videos that will play on the Gameboy. These cartridges will hold about 45 minutes of non-interactive cartoons, making the Gameboy even less interactive.

'Tweens will be clamoring for the new **Leaf Green** and **FireRed Pokemon** games, which will include a wireless transmitter that will enable some games to be played head-to-head without a gamelink wire. Hip Games (www.hip-games.com) will also be launching a separate wireless transmitter that will let kids send wireless (instant messaging) messages at even greater distances. At least these devices have a social component—but if our experience holds true, instant messaging and trash talking (and attendant ill will) are not entirely great developments, particularly where the conversation (as here) can't be easily monitored by parents.

Families that have heavily invested in Gameboy should look into the **Gameboy Player** (Nintendo $49.99 **2005** **Platinum Award**), an adapter that lets most of the game carts play through the TV using a GameCube.

Next Generation Portables

Nintendo, which has had a virtual monopoly on the portable market, will face stiff competition this year from Sony, which will be introducing the **Playstation Portable** or **PSP.**

Not to be outdone, Nintendo will release the **Gameboy DS,** a double-screened model with a touch-sensitive screen, microphone, more powerful processor, and more memory. Those old Gameboy titles will continue to work on the new platform and although Nintendo will continue to produce the older Gameboy model, we suspect that Nintendo hopes it will eventually be replaced by the newer one. The Gameboy DS has wireless connectivity, allowing for untethered multi-person play. The games we have previewed were fun and innovative, taking advantage of the hardware's unique feature set. For instance, in **Pac-Pix,** you draw the classic Pac-Man shape on the screen and these, in turn, become animated characters in a maze you draw! In many games the second screen is used to display map information or an "external" view of the action. We also liked **PictoChat,** which enables up to 16 people to exchange instant messages and drawings wirelessly. The bottom screen shows a standard keyboard, while instant messages from other users appear in the top screen. Players can not only exchange text and pictures, they can also modify the pictures and send them back!

Sony's sleeker entry into the portable play market, the PSP, will appeal to 'tweens, teens, and adults. Part gaming machine, part media center, it is being billed as the next-generation walkman with the processing power of a PS2. At initial launch we expect that more titles for kids will be available on the Gameboy DS; but the future of portable entertainment may lie in the Sony PSP. Nintendo, as always, will have to rely on carving a niche in younger gamers with their appealing **Pokemon** and **Mario** franchises.

Internet Games

Most new games have some Internet component, and we know many children (and adults) who love to play online. We are more concerned than ever, though, about the risks online play holds for kids, and urge you to restrict and supervise online access. Online predators and sociopaths are not merely Internet myths, they exist in real life in abundance. We have also seen kids become addicted to this kind of online game play. Of course, the same can be said for instant messaging and surfing. Once kids get started with these activities, you will find yourself having to supervise them more.

Massively multiplayer games are virtual online worlds where players often do more than just "fight"; they live, have occupations, homes. Of course, each universe has its own spin. The big news in the **Star Wars Galaxies** game, for instance, will be an expansion pack that focuses on the spaceship aspects of the universe. The problem with these online worlds is that there is very little supervision online to protect kids. You need to be the one to exercise supervision and discretion.

Internet gaming will come to the major gaming consoles this year. The Xbox, which comes with a built-in Ethernet port and hard disk, was designed from the outset as an online-ready device. **Xbox Live** from Microsoft hosts online games for the Xbox. Users purchase a starter set that comes with a microphone/headset. This allows players to talk to each other while the games are running and also to give voice commands! Voices will be "masked," or altered, so that other users won't be able to know how old you are or whether you are male or female. This will give some protection to kids playing online, yet caution is always in order. Xbox Live will be a broadband service only. In other words, if you live somewhere that doesn't have cable or DSL service, you will be out of luck. The impact of this on gamers who can get on line is that service will be fast—everyone will be playing at the same high speed. This will make games play better and interruptions by unstable phone lines less likely.

Sony, on the other hand, has adopted a decentralized model for online gaming. They offer add-on modules for PS2 that has an Ethernet port or a modem, though many games require the faster Ethernet port and Broadband access.

Diaperware

Do babies and toddlers need to become computer users? We don't think so! Kids who are still in diapers need people to interact with them—people who talk, sing, and play patty-cake and peekaboo. Pushing buttons or looking at a screen does not replace baby's need to move and explore the real world of objects they can touch, taste, bang, and experience with all their senses. Most computer programs for kids under 4 are little more than cartoons with little meaningful value. Sure, kids will like pushing the keys on your computer and making something happen. But you don't need to buy special software for that! This is an example where less will be more! Leave diaperware in the pail.

Software for Younger Users

Storybook Software

Animated eBooks from Brøderbund are great to give as a "first" software experience for kids who aren't yet reading. Unfortunately, this line is not producing any new titles; but we've found them in some stores and online at great prices. Still highly recommended are these BLUE CHIP winners, which you may be able to find significantly discounted: **The Cat in the Hat, Green Eggs and Ham, Just Grandma and Me, Arthur's Teacher Troubles,** and **Arthur's Computer Adventure.** 5 & up. Win/Mac.

■ Alphabet

(Tivola $30 ●●●●●) This program rightfully claims a place in the hall of fame of great children's software. Twenty-six artistically designed screens based on letters in the alphabet entice kids to enter into a collaborative artistic enterprise. Difficult to explain in a few words, the activities remind us of the experience of running through a room full of confetti and watching how the eddies make the colors stir in fascinating patterns. Here, instead of running, you catalyze the action by using the mouse or keyboard or a microphone. There are no quizzes, right answers, or grades. This is truly an open-ended artistic, visual, and musical experience. Our only criticism is that the letters are pronounced in a British style, so Z is called Zed. 3 & up. PLATINUM AWARD '02. (877) 848-6520. www.tivola.com.

Thought-Provoking Programs

Simulations and games develop thinking skills and often expose children to information they might otherwise be resistant to spending time on in more "traditional" settings.

Music Games

■ Morton Subotnick's Making Music
2005 PLATINUM AWARD

(Viva Music $29.99 ●●●●●) Most music pro-
grams seem written by strict piano teachers;
they tend to be about learning the rules and
not much fun. Morton Subotnick, one of the
playful pioneers of electronic music, has rede-
fined the genre with his rich musical games and
activities designed to turn your children on to the idea of making music
and becoming better listeners. PC/Mac. 8 & up. www.viva-media.com.

■ Music Ace Deluxe

(Harmonic Vision $49.99 ●●●●) A classroom-style program that
teaches the fundamentals of music notation. It is chock-full of information, but the approach is pedantic and not very compelling. 10 &
up. www.harmonicvision.com.

Computer Puzzlers

■ I Spy Game Boy Advance

(Scholastic $30 ●●●●●) It might be the best Gameboy title ever.
Here are four games that are entertaining and thought provoking.
Each activity has a logic component, yet it still remains true to the
rapid-fire, arcade experience that kids expect from the GBA. In some
puzzles, objects have to be classified and sorted: animals with animals,
baseballs with bats, and, of course, there are classic I-Spy riddle puzzles as well. PLATINUM AWARD '03. 5 & up.

■ I Spy Spooky Mansion Deluxe
2005 PLATINUM AWARD

(Scholastic $29.95 ●●●●●) The I Spy Series is consistently among
the best software titles of the year. Like others in the series, it is
exemplified by age-appropriate puzzles that develop logic and visual
perception. Kids can make their own puzzles as well as get good practice at following oral directions. There are also puzzles that slip in
sight-word recognition. Kudos for showing how creative children's
software can be without resorting to licensed characters, cutesy voices, and overused activity center games. In short, this software respects
its audience. 5–9. Win 95/98/Mac. (800) 724-6527.

■ StarFlyers Alien Space Chase
StarFlyers Royal Jewel Rescue

(The Learning Company $25 ●●●●) Each title in The Learning

Company's newest "thinking game" series contains 8 games and 12 printable activities, and has three levels of difficulty. They develop logical reasoning, problem solving, hypothesis testing, sequencing, estimation, and spatial relationships. Each story springs from the imagination of protagonist Katherine Cadell, aka Katie Cadet, who has a knack for turning everyday mishaps into make-believe sci-fi adventures. 5–8.

Adventure Games

Most children's adventure games work like interactive cartoons. The object is to solve puzzles, collect objects, and work toward a final goal. Although popular, these can be real time drains with limited intellectual value. Many feature suspenseful themes and implied violence that may be too intense for their intended young audience. Just as bad, they tend to rely on the same type of puzzles from one game to the next with only the licensed character differentiating one from the other.

Simulations

Simulations let players experiment with grown-up activities without having to take responsibility for real-world consequences. Not all simulations are appropriate for kids, regardless of what rating they may receive from the ESRB. Much of the highly anticipated **Sims 2** revolves around courting and sexual behavior (including adultery). For the record, the game looks innovative, funny, and creative—for adults. But it is not a kid friendly sim.

■ Roller Coaster Tycoon 3   *2005*   Platinum Award

(Hasbro $39.95 ○○○○○) RollerCoaster Tycoon puts you in charge of every aspect of an amusement park, from roller coaster design to the price of cotton candy. New to the 3D version: You can actually ride the coasters you create and stroll through your park. Though the subject matter seems "light," the game is a learn-by-doing lesson on subjects as diverse as physics and economics. Platinum Award '00. (800) 400-1352, www.atari.com. If your computer is not recent enough to run RCT3, still highly recommended is **RollerCoaster Tycoon 2,** Platinum Award '01.

■ Zoo Tycoon 2   *2005*   Platinum Award

(Microsoft $TBA ○○○○○) Microsoft synergizes the mix of gaming and "educational content" in its 3D-enabled zoo simulation. Kids landscape the zoos, design the exhibits, and must care for the animals. The animals thrive if you provide them with the right food and habitats, so it is important to read up on them in the included online reference. Most impressive are the realistic animations of the animals.

■ Flight Simulator BLUE CHIP

(Microsoft $TBA) Featuring historic aircraft from Kitty Hawk to the Spirit of St. Louis, the latest version of this classic is realistic and challenging. Since the days of thick manuals that explain how to fly seem to have become as outdated as biplanes, we recommend you give a try to this program with a book/guide that lays out the process of running the simulator in greater detail. Your child will learn the value of nonfiction reading as a means of gaining control of their world. 10 & up. Win. www.microsoft.com.

Classic Games

Computer versions of board and word games provide ways for kids to hone their strategy skills and solve the problem of how to play when there's no one to play with. They are also valuable resources for physically challenged kids who can operate a computer, but have trouble manipulating the pieces of a game set.

■ Hoyle Kids Games

(Sierra $29.95 ●●○○○) Over the years we've recommended many of the Hoyle titles even though they had not specifically been designed for kids. Classic games develop good thinking skills and the computer provides a ready opponent. Now, Sierra has taken some of the best classic games and given them kid-friendly treatments. There are goldfish playing tic-tac-toe and a checkerboard populated by frogs that give a whole new meaning to "jumping" pieces. Unfortunately, the battleship game is point and click, and it does not implement the board game's system of calling out coordinates (a good math concept), instead focusing on missile launches and explosions. PLATINUM AWARD '01. 5–12. Win 95/98/Mac. (800) 757-7707, www.sierra.com.

■ Learn to Play Chess with Fritz and Chesster 2005
PLATINUM AWARD

(Viva $29.99 ●●●●○) The fundamentals of chess are taught with adventure and arcade games in this European import. 8–13.

www.viva-media.com. Also recommended: **Majestic Chess** (Sierra $19.99 ●●●○), which, despite superior graphics, has been reported to suffer from installation problems.

■ Fritz 8 ★2005★ Platinum Award

(Viva $39.99 ●●●●●) Once you've learned the fundamentals of chess, it is time to take on the big guns. Fritz 8 is the most powerful game of chess that you can find on a PC. It will teach you, analyze your game, and provide a constantly improving challenger to play against. 10 & up. www.viva-media.com.

Sports

Some of the most fun games to play with your child on the computer are sports titles. The computer levels the playing field, and might even give a slight advantage to kids. Most require reading (of the manual) to learn to play properly, and strategic thinking. Compared with most action computer games, these are the least violent. New this year are many sports titles on game platforms designed for younger players.

■ Backyard Sports Series Blue Chip

(Humongous $19.99 each ●●●●●) These classic sports games feature all the real teams of the professionals and child versions of many of their stars, such as Mark McGwire and Sammy Sosa. This yera the characters will be rendered in 3D on the PC. Platinum Award '01. 5–10. Win/Mac/GameCube/PS2, (800) 499-8386, www.humongous.com.

■ Electronic Arts Sports Titles Blue Chip

(Electronic Arts $29.95 & up ●●●●●) The best sports titles for kids 10 and up come from Electronic Arts and the biggest news in sports gaming is that they will now be available for Xbox. Now you'll be able to play Madden NFL online with Xbox Live. Top titles: **FIFA Major League Soccer, Triple Play, Madden NFL,** and **NBA Live.** (877) 324-2637, www.ea.com.

Golf Games

■ Mario Golf *PREVIEW 2005*

(Nintendo $49)

■ Hot Shots Golf Fore! *PREVIEW 2005*

(Sony $49.99) Golf games are big this year. Mario Golf and HotShot Golf will take a decidedly cartoonish, miniature golf approach. Since both are exclusive to their platform, your choice will likely be determined by which console you own. 7 & up. www.nintendo.com/ www.sony.com.

■ **Qmotions Golf Simulator** ★2005★ PLATINUM AWARD

(Qmotion $250 ●●●●●) Qmotions Golf Simulator is a hardware/software combo that comes with EA's **Tiger Woods Golf 2004.** Plug this device into the computer and then use your regular golf clubs to hit the tethered ball. Amazingly, you'll see Tiger strike the ball as you did. Because this title uses real golf clubs indoors, you'll need to supervise and exercise caution. 12 & up. www.qmotions.com.

Racing Games

Racing titles for kids have been produced by nearly everyone with a license: Mickey, Kermit, and Bugs Bunny all have arcade racers. Nearly every one is a clone of the other: small carts racing around a track firing various weapons. Yes, these programs make a game out of road rage. We prefer racing games that focus on sport, rather than gunfire.

■ **Gran Turismo 4** *PREVIEW 2005*

(Sony $TBA)

■ **Forza Motorsport Racing** *PREVIEW 2005*

(Microsoft $TBA) It may take a photo finish to determine the best racing game of the year with these two titans vying for bragging rights. The GT series is known for ultra realistic models of hundreds of hot cars; Microsoft is aiming at a similar design with arguably better hardware to support the action. www.sony.com; www.xbox.com.

Robotics

Kits that let children build robots are more than construction sets. They also teach programming and logic.

■ **Lego Mindstorms**

(Lego Systems $99 & up ●●●●●) Every product in this series could qualify as one of the greatest gifts a kid could get. At the heart of each system is a microprocessor block into which kids can plug sensors, motors, and Legos. The **Robotic Invention System Version 2** ($199, 11 & up) has the most parts and requires a personal computer. Lego's lower-priced kits, the **Droid Developer Kit** (PLATINUM

AWARD '00) and **Mindstorms Robotics Discovery Set** (PLATINUM AWARD '03) ($99 and $149 each), dispense with the personal computer and permit direct programming of the robot via a built-in keypad. 9 & up. Win.

Creativity Software

Word Processor
■ **Creative Writer 2** BLUE CHIP

(Microsoft $34.95 ●●●●●) This is the best word processor for late-elementary-school kids. Children can make the program their own by selecting custom thematic borders and sound effects. More than a word processor, Creative Writer 2 sparks the imagination with evocative clip art and activity projects such as cards, banners, and even web page building. 8 & up. Win. (800) 426-9400, www.microsoft.com/kids.

Painting on the Computer
■ **Disney's Magic Artist Deluxe**

(Disney Interactive $29.99 ●●●●●) Disney's Magic Artist Deluxe is must-have software. This art creation program features an incredible array of media: Drizzle Tool splatters paint, Image Spray paints with animated "stamps," Glitter Pen paints shimmering glitter—there are many more. You can drop virtual crayon shavings onto the canvas and then "iron" them down. The program can be used to create abstracts (it is great fun just to explore the toolbox), edit photos, or even create animated flip-books. PLATINUM AWARD '02. Age: 3 & up. Win/Mac. www.disneyinteractive.com.

The Three Rs: Reading, Writing, and RAM

Schoolhouse Grade-Based Software
When the school day is over, kids want an alternative, not more school fare. There is room for software that aims at skill mastery, but unless you offer your children a balanced diet of more interesting software they will soon turn away from the computer. We are also concerned that kids will be confused if the school is using one methodology and the software is using another. Some schools, for instance, emphasize phonics, while

others do not. For this reason we strongly recommend that you speak to your child's teacher before buying a lot of "educational" software that may be confusing.

The activities in these titles tend to be very similar, and the distinguishing factor tends to be the licensed characters, rather than the way ideas are presented. Drill and review tends to be the focus, rather than explanation and exploration.

■ Blue's Clues Preschool

(Atari $19.99 **○○○○**) Joe, the host of "Blues Clues," makes his CD debut on this disk. It is also the first Blues Clues program to follow a curriculum-based set of activities. In addition to the computer-based learning games set in Blue's neighborhood, there are also printable activities to play away from the computer. 3–5. Win/Mac. www.atari.com.

■ JumpStart Advanced Preschool
■ JumpStart Advanced Kindergarten
■ JumpStart Advanced 1st Grade
■ JumpStart Advanced 2nd Grade BLUE CHIP

(Knowledge Adventure $29.99 each **○○○○½**) New to this venerable series is a help system that is designed to respond to the different ways kids learn. At the beginning of the program is an activity that gives the computer an idea of the kind of examples that will make most sense to your child. Seven modes of learning (for example, word problems, pictographs, audible clues) are used to illustrate ways to solve a problem. This is a big step forward for the JumpStart series. Win/Mac. www.knowledgeadventure.com.

■ Pencil Pal Software Preschool
■ Pencil Pal Software Kindergarten
■ Pencil Pal Software First Grade
■ Pencil Pal Software Phonics

(School Zone Interactive $19.99 **○○○½**) All of these disks come bound in printed color workbooks, which, with their emphases on "ditto"-style worksheets, set the tone of the "drill & review"-type activities contained in both workbook and disk. The primary "learning" activities in each disk are sets of drills appropriate to its particular age level and topic. A collection of accompanying supporting activities is essentially the same from one set to the next (connect the dots, coloring book, movie clips). Win/Mac. www.schoolzone.com.

Language Skills

■ Jumpstart Study Helpers Spelling Bee

(Knowledge Adventure $20 ●●●●●) Jumpstart takes the tedium out of learning a list of spelling words with this arcade-influenced drill game. You'll type your child's weekly spelling words into the computer and the program will automatically turn them into rapid-fire drill exercises that play like arcade games (to keep kids motivated). Not only does the program test for correct spelling, it also checks for common spelling mistakes. PLATINUM AWARD '04. Win/Mac. www.knowledgeadventure.com.

■ Reader Rabbit Learn to Read with Phonics Series

(Riverdeep $25 ●●●●) While we found the early Reader Rabbit titles too sweet for our liking, the latest editions offer excellent opportunities for kids to practice letter recognition, sounds, and phonics. Thirty mini-books (with follow-up reading comprehension questions) give kids exposure to many types of writing, including newspapers, journals, and stories. (3–8) www.riverdeep.com.

Math

■ Math Missions

(Scholastic $TBA) Scholastic breathes new life into children's math software with two new Math Mission titles that blur drill, arcade, and simulation genres. Solving math problems gives kids money to build up their game arcade. The better the arcade, the more money they make (and the better games they can purchase). But, occasionally, the kids might want to close the doors of the arcade and play some of the games themselves. 5 & up. Win/Mac. www.scholastic.com.

■ Mighty Math Series BLUE CHIP

(Riverdeep $29.95 each ●●●●●) Among the best children's software ever, this series has been brought out of retirement by Riverdeep. Available primarily online, the Mighty Math series champions learning through exploration and favors independent thinking over drill and review. 5 & up depending on title. Win/Mac. www.riverdeep.com

Science

■ Digital Blue QX3 Microscope

(Digital Blue $99 ●●●●●) A dazzling demonstration of how creative and empowering computer technology can be, this mates a computer-connected video camera to a microscope. The result: kids can take time-lapse movies of growing crystals, watch bugs scurry about inside little viewing bubbles, or take video snapshots of microscopic worlds for inclusion in reports. The optics give better images than any home microscope we've seen to date. This product was discontinued, but is still available online. It is worth searching for. Previously sold as the IntelPlay QX3, PLATINUM AWARD '00. 10 & up. Win. www.playdigitalblue.com/www.intelplay.com.

■ Meade Autostar Suite *2005*

(Meade $149 ●●●●) This package lets you take photos on the computer with your Meade Autostar-enabled telescope. Since this setup requires setting up an expensive telescope and laptop outside, it is not as versatile and kid-friendly as the QX3. Still, its power to bring back amazing pictures of the night sky makes it an impressive tool for young astronomers. 12 & up with parental supervision. www.meade.com.

■ I Love Science

(DKI $19.95 ●●●●) Less of a "game" and more like a visit to a hands-on science museum, this disk is packed with useful facts and hands-on experiments in chemistry, biology, and physics. 7–10. (888) 342-5357, www.dk.com.

■ My First Amazing Science Explorer

(DKI $29.95 ●●●●) If your child has entered the stage when she only wants to know "Why?" then this is the program she needs! Using hands-on experiments and demonstrations both on and off the computer, it sets the stage for a lifetime of interest in science and the world around us. 5–9. Win/Mac. (888) 342-5357, www.dk.com.

Foreign Language

■ Mia's Language Adventure *2005*

(Kutoka $20.00 ●●●½) Our testers loved the graphics, but complained about the pace of this adventure. Along the way to solving the mystery of Grandma's kidnapping, kids learn many words in French or Spanish. 6–10. Win/Mac. www.kutoka.com

PREVIOUSLY RECOMMENDED: **Dora the Explorer: Backpack Adventure** and **Dora the Explorer: Lost City Adventure** (Atari $19.99 each ●●●●) and **KidSpeak 10-in-1 Language Learning** (Transparent Language $49.95 ●●●●).

Reference Titles

■ Encarta Reference Suite Blue Chip

(Microsoft $74.95 ❍❍❍❍❍) The undisputed champion of home reference titles! On one DVD you get an atlas, encyclopedia, quotations book, dictionary, thesaurus, and the best report organizer on the market. There is no product that offers greater value on the personal computer or that better demonstrates the potential of multimedia in education. Also available on CD. ***PREVIEW 2005:*** Now Encarta will feature an optional interface and special collection of articles especially for elementary students. (800) 426-9400, www.encarta.com.

■ American Reference Library

(World Book $89 ❍❍❍❍) More than 110,000 pages of presidential papers, Supreme Court cases, the US Congress Collection, and more are included on one compact disc. 10 & up. Win/Mac. www.worldbook.com.

PREVIOUSLY RECOMMENDED: **World Book Encyclopedia** (World Book $28 & up. 10 & up. Win/Mac.) **The Complete National Geographic** (Encore $119.99. 10 & up. Win/Mac.)

This chapter was written, byte by byte, by Technology Editor James Oppenheim. James is a computer consultant, attorney, and father of two avid computer users.

VI • Using Ordinary Toys for Kids with Special Needs

Our continuing goal is to suggest products that are entertaining and to provide useful tips for getting the most play and learning value out of toys. We also know that children enjoy playing with products that are like their siblings', cousins', or neighbors'. By adapting ordinary toys, we can help put special needs kids' play lives into the mainstream.

Most toys have more than one use and will provide various kinds of feedback for children with different kinds of disabilities. Although we have used the headings *infants*, *toddlers*, and *preschoolers*, age guidelines are blurred, since conventional age labels will be less meaningful for children with significant developmental delays. For children with visual or hearing impairments, learning to make effective use of other senses is essential. Similarly, those with motor impairment need products that are easy to activate and that motivate exploration. Many toys are chosen because they are especially easy to activate physically and because they provide interesting sensory feedback.

While all the new products here are highly recommended,

the most outstanding products selected for these pages have received our SPECIAL NEEDS ADAPTABLE PRODUCT (SNAP) AWARD for 2005. It's our hope that bringing attention to these products will serve kids and motivate manufacturers and publishers to become more aware of children with disabilities who, like all children, need quality products.

Be sure to check out our database! We've put our database of SNAP AWARD winners from past years on our website at www.toyportfolio.com.

Infants and Toddlers

All the toys in this section were selected because they provide plenty of sensory feedback. Some of the best toys for infants and toddlers need little or no adapting.

Note: Reviews of top-rated basics are in the Infants and Toddlers chapters and also will be of interest. Here we have focused on products that are adaptable, easy to activate, or loaded with sound, light, texture, or motion.

BASIC GEAR CHECKLIST FOR INFANTS AND TODDLERS

✓Mobile	✓Fabric blocks	✓Teethers
✓Musical toys	✓Soft huggables	✓Floor toys
✓Crib mirror	✓Manipulatives	✓Balls
✓Fabric rattles	✓Bath toys	✓Infant seat

■ Gymini Super Deluxe Electronic Lights & Music 3-D Activity Gym

(Tiny Love $65 ○○○○○) All new graphics, lights, music, and a mirror have been added to this play mat. We were afraid the sound and lights would be over the top, but they are quiet and soothing with a choice of classical or nursery music. Like the original, this has two arches and dangly toys for gazing at and batting. SNAP AWARD '03. Also top rated, **Baby's Wind Chimes** ($11 ○○○○½), an add-on for baby to kick. Has a pleasing sound quality. (888) 846-9568.

■ Me in the Mirror

(Sassy $14.95 ●●●●) This wedge-shaped mirror (9½")
has no music, but does have a place for adding your
own photo. Can also be used as a tummy time floor
toy. (800) 323-6336.

■ Symphony in Motion Deluxe

(Tiny Love $45 ●●●●●) This award-winning mobile
now comes with a remote control so you can turn the music
on from a distance. Unlike most mobiles, this innovative offering has more visual interest of several kinds:
it tips as it spins, causing objects to shift their posi-
tions in interesting ways; it also pauses, and the start-
and-stop motion adds another kind of interest; small
shapes slide on the arms of the mobile and make small
clicking sounds as the musical mobile turns. The sound
quality on this mobile is better than most, and it plays several classical
music selections. (800) 843-6292.

Making Things Happen

■ Classical Stacker 🏆2005

(Fisher-Price $10 ●●●●●) This prior SNAP Award-
winning stacker is reintroduced in new colors. Star
rings fit on the post in any order (a plus). Post has
magical lights that wink and play music when top
is pressed. Sound quality is not excellent, but it is
a long-term favorite. (800) 432-5437.

■ Crawl-Along Wobbler 🏆2005 SNAP AWARD

(Fisher-Price $12.99 ●●●●●) Motivate tots to move with this wob-
bly rolling toy. A simple bat sends two
wobbling disks rolling forward, activating some lights and sounds (none of
which are overwhelming) and a spin-
ning rattle. It plays three jazzy tunes
(and has two volume levels). The tex-
tures on the disks, the ribbons, and the clacking beads make this a
sensory delight. (800) 432-5437.

■ Earlyears Soft Busy Blocks

(International Playthings $15 ●●●●½)
These have been scaled down in size and are
easier to grab than the originals. The set of

four fabric blocks has interesting textures and patterns and a quiet sound in each block. **Activity:** Sit on the floor, put one or more blocks on your head or shoulder, and encourage your tot to knock 'em off! (800) 445-8347.

■ Lamaze Sing & Spin Bugs

(RC2/Learning Curve $24.95 ●●●●●) This is a fun toy for developing motor skills as kids put on and take off the dancing bugs from the musical platform with crinkle fabric petals. A single big button activates the music and bug dance and provides a lesson in cause and effect. An innovative toy that gives kids a sense of being in charge and makng things happen. **Activity:** Put & Take Game. With children who are working on colors, use color words to call for adding or taking away the red or blue or yellow dancing bug. SNAP AWARD '04. (800) 704-8697.

■ Tap & Twirl Top 2005 SNAP AWARD

(Fisher-Price $12.99 ●●●●●) "What a great toy!" wrote our tester parent. Kids enjoy hitting the green top that activates the jazzy music, lights, and movement on the saucer-like floor toy, which also has interesting ribbons on it for little fingers to explore. Great lesson in cause and effect. High marks for adjustable volume level. Takes 3 AA batteries. Also great fun, **Swirlin' Saucer** ($12.99 ●●●●) comes with three over-sized plastic balls for picking up and dropping into the "swirling" open top. (800) 432-5437.

■ Poppin' Push Car 2005

(Sassy $6 ●●●●½) Push this little car forward and the popping beads (safely enclosed in the dome roof) make a pleasing sound. Pull the car back and when you let go, the car zooms forward. One of the best toys of the season! Just right for floor-time play. (800) 323-6336.

■ Roll & Rhyme Melody Block

(LeapFrog $20 ●●●●●) Turn this 6" fabric block and it either plays music or says a rhyme about the animal featured on the topmost face. There are a small mirror, peek-a-boo leaves that open to reveal a parrot, a polar bear that slides on the snow, a fox that pops in and out of its den, and a lion with a satiny mane. Fun for rolling as well as exploring its textures and sounds. SNAP AWARD '04. (800) 701-5327.

Manipulatives

■ Musical Pop-tivity Table *2005*

(Fisher-Price $19.99 ❍❍❍½) A very classic activity table with lots of buttons to push, dials to turn, and big beads to spin. A push on the big red button activates music and popping beads. (800) 432-5437.

■ Peek a Blocks IncrediBlock *2005*

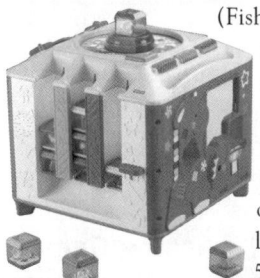

(Fisher-Price $19.99 ❍❍❍❍½) Tots loved standing up to play activities on each side of this huge block. Best fun, push a button and stacks of see-through blocks go kaboom! Or put single blocks on top of a spinner that says the name of the object inside the little block. Develops language as well as dexterity. (800) 432-5437.

■ Musical Stack & Play *2005* SNAP AWARD

(Tiny Love $19.95 ❍❍❍❍❍) An elephant stacking toy with a place for dropping balls in its top. The balls come out at the base with some fanfare (lights/sound) but not too loud. Testers liked the soft fabric rings for stacking, but really spent most of the time playing with the plastic balls. (800) 843-6292.

■ Lego Quatro *2005* SNAP AWARD

(Lego Systems $9.99 & up ❍❍❍❍❍) This year there's a bigger brick (twice the size of Duplos and four times the size of standard Legos!). Made of a softer, easier-to-grasp material, we suggest that more *is* better, so start with the **Large Quatro Bucket** ($19.99/75 pieces; $14.99/50 pieces ❍❍❍❍❍). **Activity:** Sort the blocks by color, building towers or trains of red, yellow, or green. Which tower is taller? (800) 233-8756.

Preschool and Early School Years

As children grow, they need a rich variety of playthings to match their expanding interests and abilities.

⊙ BASIC GEAR CHECKLIST
FOR PRESCHOOL AND EARLY SCHOOL YEARS

✓ Construction toys	✓ Art materials
✓ Sand and water toys	✓ Big-muscle toys
✓ Musical toys	✓ Electronic toys
✓ Toys for pretend	✓ Puzzles, games,
(dolls, trucks, puppets)	and manipulatives
✓ Tape player and tapes	

Age ranges are purposely broad; products need to be selected on the basis of your child's particular needs. Many basic toys reviewed in the Preschool and Early School Years chapters will be of interest and need no special adaptation. Here we have focused on products that lend themselves to adaptation.

Manipulatives, Puzzles, and Tracking Games

■ Puzzle Totes   *2005*

(Lauri $8.99 ●●○○) Rather than having the traditional puzzle tray, these double-thick seven- and eight-piece puzzles have a handle just right for travel and carrying about. Two-toned pieces are able to stand up for dramatic play. New for *2005*, **Big Shapes.** Past favorites: **Marine Life, Earthmovers, Dinosaurs,** and **Work & Play.** (800) 451-0520.

■ Beginner Pattern Blocks   *2005*   SNAP AWARD

(Melissa & Doug $19.99 ●●●●●) Ten wooden scenes are ready to fill with triangles, circles, squares, rectangles, and ovals. Part puzzle, part shape sorter, all beautifully crafted with wooden storage box. A good talking toy for developing language and visual discrimination. This company sells great sound puzzles, but with tiny handles that are harder to lift. **Activity:** Put all 30 shapes in a bag. Player One calls the shape that Player Two needs to find by touch—no looking! Winner is first to feel and find five pieces. (800) 284-3948.

■ Fridge Farm Magnetic Animal Set
2005 SNAP AWARD

(LeapFrog $14.95 ●●●●●) Comes with five ani-
mals that are done in two pieces; match them up
and put them on the farm-board, and you'll hear
the names of each animal. But what's really fun is if you put a horse
head with a pig back, it will say, "horsepig." We love an electronic toy
with a sense of humor! (800) 701- 5327.

■ Plan Toys Shape Sorter 2005

(Brio $20 ●●●●) A handsome curved wooden plat-
form holds four shapes in place. Cut-out shape
boards are fitted over the circle, square,
rectangle, and triangle. Boards can be
used to reinforce color, shapes, or fractions. Also see **Plan Toys' Shape & Sort** ($20 ●●●●)
with three shapes that drop in and slide out—Abracadabra!—when
platform is touched. (888) 274-6869.

■ Puzzibilities Sound Puzzles 2005 SNAP AWARD

(Small World Toys $15.95 each ●●●●●) Six raised pieces are easy to
lift and when they are put back in the puzzle board each makes a rip-
roaring sound. Choose **Wild Animals, Dinosaurs,** or **Under
Construction.** 2½ & up. Also for finer dexterity and knowing and
naming, Puzzibilities nine-piece puzzles have small red knobs and
three themes: transportation, wild animals, and community vehicles.
Puzzibilities also uses big, easy-to-grasp pegs on their three-piece puzzles with shape, numeral, vehicle, and
animal themes. **Activity:** Use the animals to play a memory game. Put three
or four in a row. Have child close eyes
and take one away. What is missing?
Variation: Rearrange the placement of
two. Play "Guess what I moved?" (800)
421-4153.

Lacing Games

Kids dive right into lacing activities without
knowing they're a great way to develop the
fine-motor skills they'll need for writing.
While stringing beads, they can also sort by

color and make patterns, learning to see likenesses and differences. Three favorites: **Lacing Beads in a Box** (Melissa & Doug $15 ●●●●) Thirty handsome painted wooden shapes come with colorful patterns. Comes with two long laces, and all are neatly contained in a wooden box with a plexiglass sliding top for storage. (800) 284-3948. Also fun, **Lacing & Tracing Cinderella** (Lauri $6.99 ●●●●) is made of sturdy chipboard punched with holes that kids "sew" with colorful laces. 4 & up. (800) 451-0520. Also, **Friendly Bugs Sewing Cards** (eeBoo $14.95 ●●●●)—illustrator Melissa Sweet designed these five sturdy cards with happy-looking bugs ready for sewing. 4s & up. (212) 222-0823.

■ Rip Rolling Fun

(Small World Toys $25 ●●●●●) We've seen a lot of these, but often the cars have wheels that might come off, or they move so fast kids can't track them. This one is a winner! Five wooden triangles travel down the wooden track. Designs on triangles create optical illusions as they move. Fun for making something happen and tracking. **Activity:** Use the color words as the pieces are put in place. Talk about them rolling down, down, down. With older kids, see how high you can count together before they all get down. SNAP AWARD '04. (800) 421-4153.

■ Rollipop Starter & Advanced Sets

(Edushape $19.95 & $24.95 ●●●●●) These are among our favorite toddler toys. Toddlers love to drop the oversized colorful plastic balls into the starter set, a tower, and track them as they go down. The balls also travel slowly down the advanced set, a bridge, making it an ideal toy for developing visual tracking. SNAP AWARD '04. (800) 404-4744.

Games:
Matching, Memory, and Language Games

Games are entertaining ways for kids to develop social skills as well as counting, matching, and color concepts. You'll find other good choices in the Preschool, Early School, and Computer chapters.

■ Letter Factory Game 2005 SNAP AWARD

(LeapFrog $24.99 ●●●●●) The first level of play is really a color matching game. Once you pick the color card the electronic voice asks for, it then identifies the letter on the card. The electronic voice then asks you to move your game piece a certain number of spaces. Once you move along, it magically tells you what color space you're on. Level 2 asks kids to find specific letters. There is a little "Chutes and Ladders"-style going backwards built in to the game play. (800) 701-5327.

■ 4-Way Countdown 2005

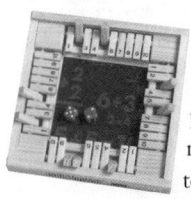

(Cadaco $19.95 ●●●●½) This PLATINUM AWARD-winner just got more interesting. Now designed for 2–4 players, each player has 10 wooden pegs that flip. The object is to be the first player to turn over all your pegs by rolling dice. Players may add, subtract, multiply, or divide the numbers they roll in order to get the number they need. 6 & up. (800) 621-5426.

■ Talking Clever Clock

(Learning Resources $34.95 ●●●●½) Here's a wonderful tool for teaching kids how to tell time. Our nine-year-old tester had given up on ever learning how to tell time—but within minutes he was having fun using the clock that has self-checking features with both digital and analog clock faces. He liked moving the hands of the clock to match the digital read-out. There are buttons that will tell you the time out loud, along with quiz and answer buttons. The same company's nonelectronic clock is still a great choice, but hearing the time out loud is a plus. **Activity**: Set the clock for typical times when you eat, rise, go to bed, leave for school. (888) 800-7893.

"Name That Shape" Games

Games that develop the sense of touch are especially important for kids with visual disabilities. These products are similar, but offer alternative ways of providing sensory feedback. Most come with more pieces than kids can handle, so start with a few and gradually add more.

■ Paz's Memory Game

(Discovery Kids $14.95 ●●●●●) This classic matching game with 50 wooden tiles has images of pigs, penguins, dogs, and rabbits with different colored backgrounds. Follow the game rules for three levels of matching games, or use the tiles for sorting and counting games. **Activity:** *Make a*
stack: Put all the playing pieces face up on a table. Players find all the birds they can find, while the other player finds all the dogs. Who has the taller stack? This little game involves classification, and visual and dexterity skills. Also top rated, **Paz's Feel & Find Challenge** ($14.95 ●●●●) Put shapes in the bag and have players take turns touching (without looking) to find a playing piece that matches one of the playing boards. Winner is the one with the most boards with matching pieces. SNAP AWARD '04. (800) 938-0333.

■ Ryan's Room Get-a-Grip Sorter

(Small World Toys $15 ●●●●) Our tester was truly pleased with himself when he shape-sorted the colored wooden pieces into the triangular sorter that has a handle and forgiving openings. Beautifully crafted and a good parent-child toy. (800) 421-4153.

ABCs and 1, 2, 3s

Most kids learn to read with a mix of approaches; these products give kids playful practice with sounds and letters and things to count.

■ Balloon Lagoon *2005* SNAP AWARD

(Cranium $19.99 ●●●●●) Turn on the musical merry-go-round timer as players take turns fishing for magnetized letters to spell a word, spin wheels to get four parts of an animal lined up, collect matching dice as they fall through the roof of the snack hut, or "tiddly-wink" four frogs into the pond. The first to collect 15 mini balloons is the winner. A lively game that's fun and develops sequencing, dexterity, matching, and simple spelling skills. Also top rated, **Cranium Hullabaloo**—shapes, colors, letters and active play all in one! SNAP AWARD '04. (877) 272-6486.

■ Design & Drill Activity Center

(Educational Insights $39.95 ●●●●●) Here's a new spin on a "working" drill with colorful pegs. Several bits fit into the battery-operated "drill," which works in forward and reverse. Bits can also fit in a hand-powered screwdriver handle when the batteries go dry. **Activity:** Give kids a few days to experiment with

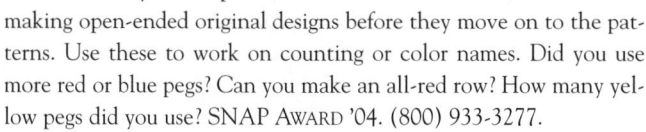

making open-ended original designs before they move on to the patterns. Use these to work on counting or color names. Did you use more red or blue pegs? Can you make an all-red row? How many yellow pegs did you use? SNAP AWARD '04. (800) 933-3277.

■ Fridge Phonics Magnetic Letter Set *2005*

(LeapFrog $17.99 ●●●●●) A set of uppercase letters that not only stick to the fridge, but they can be felt, heard, and seen—a lot of sensory opportunities here! Put the "magnetic phonics reader" onto the fridge and play one capital letter at a time. They say and sing the letter's name and sing the sound they say. Letters are raised to give kids the feel for their shapes. New for *2005*, **Fridge Farm Magnetic Animal Set** ($14.95). Five animals each in two pieces; match front and back, and they say their names. SNAP AWARD '04. (800) 701-5327.

■ Leap Pad Plus Writing Learning System *2005* SNAP AWARD

(LeapFrog $39.99 ●●●●●) We were delighted with the many Dr. Seuss classics such as *Fox In Socks* and *One Fish Two Fish Kids* that have been adapted for this platform for the Leap Pad. In addition, kids who are learning to write their letters and numbers will like this electronic workbook with stylus that really writes. More books and innovative games are slated for this platform, but were not ready for testing. We'll

add them to our website as they arrive. Marked 3 & up, the skills are more appropriate for 5 & up. (800) 701-5327.

■ Story Reader 2005 SNAP AWARD

(Publications International $19.99 ●●●●●) We were happy to find that we could hear and read along with a set of Beatrix Potter's classics: *The Tale of Peter Rabbit*, *Jemima Puddle-Duck*, and *Tom Kitten*. The original art has been used, as well as the language. This platform is less complex than other electronic book readers on the market. Simply plug in the cartridge, and no touching or stylus is needed. The "reader" turns the pages and follows along. Other books for the series are more licensed properties such as **Dora, Scooby Doo,** and **Bambi.** Still recommended, last year's SNAP winner, **Active Pad** ($24.95 ●●●●●). This looks a lot like so many talking book platforms. Touch the pictures with a stylus and it says the name of the object. It's a knowing-and-naming book with lots of familiar objects to talk about. Look for the shape and counting book for this, too. (800) 454-9006.

■ Ryan's Room Around the Blocks 2005

(Small World Toys $26.99 ●●●●½) A high-quality set of 26 blocks with upper- and lowercase letters, plus images to match. All store in a big cloth bag. **Activity:** Use these blocks for playing sound games. Put blocks with three distinctive sounds in sight. Ask child to find the block that has the same sound as the word you say. (800) 421-4153.

Construction Toys

Building invites creative thinking and decision making. Color, counting, and size concepts are built in (we couldn't resist). Best of all, blocks offer a win-win opportunity because there is no right or wrong way for them to be used. Kids with visual challenges can learn their shapes by rubbing the textured blocks on cheeks or hands. For shopping info about classic and new blocks sets, see the Toddlers, Preschool, and Early School Years chapters.

How to adapt blocks:

Add strips of sticky-backed Velcro tape to standard wooden unit blocks or Mega Blocks for a more stable base for building. To increase two-handed skills, have child play at pulling blocks apart and putting them together.

Use colorful plastic Lego Primo, Duplo, and standard Lego building blocks for developing color-matching, counting, and size-discrimination concepts for a child with learning disabilities. **Activities:** Provide containers and play size-, shape-, and color-sorting games to reinforce concepts. Put the toys away by playing a singing color game: To the tune of "Where Is Thumbkin?" Sing, "Where is red? Where is red? Here it is! Here it is!"

Props for Blocks
■ **Gears! Gears! Gears!**

(Learning Resources $20/$40 ●●●●●) Fitting gears together not only develops dexterity; it's a challenging way to promote problem-solving skills as kids make moving "machines." Motors can be added, but start with hand power. SNAP AWARD '99. Stick with the open-ended sets—most of the theme machines get in the way of the play. **Activity:** Play a game of "Keep It Going!" Players take turns adding one gear at a time, but every gear added must connect and keep the motion going. (888) 800-7893.

Pretend Play

Pretend play is not just great fun, it's the way kids develop imagination and creative thinking skills, and try out being big and powerful. Pretending also brings the world down to the child's size and understanding. It's a way to develop communication skills and is an outlet for expressing feelings and fears.

Housekeeping Equipment
Playing with replicas of real household equipment is a safe way

for kids to step into new roles. Add real ingredients to play kitchens, such as water for pouring, playdough, and dry cereal. Kids love the messiness of it all, which motivates ample touching and exploration that strengthen fingers and hands as well as encouraging language and motivating curiosity. For descriptions of toy kitchens, plates, and other pretend props, see reviews in the Toddlers and Preschool chapters.

■ Five Alarm Fun Center

(Step 2 $159.99 **oooo**) This big red fire truck doesn't move, but will provide lots of pretend play opportunities. Comes with two steering wheels (a plus), a pretend CB radio, and emergency light and siren! (800) 347-8372. **Activity:** Sudsy water and a sponge make for great fun and a clean fire engine!

■ Super Saver Teaching Bank 2005

(LeapFrog $19.99 **oooo**½) What we loved about this interactive bank is that your child can set a saving goal. The bank helps keep track of how far you've gone in reaching that goal. As you add coins, it identifies them by name and gives a running total. An engaging way of becoming familiar with coins and their value. 4–8. (800) 701-5327.

■ Teaching Cash Register

(Learning Resources $44.95 **ooooo**) A marvelous tool for pretend and math skills for kids. Kids can use built-in calculator, make change, use coupons and charge cards, and even check the customer's credit! You can even use real coins—very useful for teaching money concepts. The screen tallies, and kids press "Enter" to self-correct. SNAP Award '04. Still recommended, the quiz-free, solar-powered **Pretend & Play Calculator Cash Register** ($39.95). (888) 800-7893.

■ Pretend & Play Teaching Telephone

(Learning Resources $39.95 **ooooo**) For learning functional use of a phone, important numbers, and the concept of 911, this is a gem! Even the concept of taking messages is built into the play. You can program in any phone number and leave a message. When your child calls that number she hears your message. SNAP AWARD '00. (888) 800-7893.

■ Plan Toys Fruit & Vegetable Play Set

(Brio $15.99 **oooo**) Wooden fruits and veggies can be "cut" apart with wooden knife that seems to cut the Velcro-ed segments. Comes with lemon, orange, pear, mushroom, carrot, and tomato, plus board and wooden knife. **Activity:** Use fraction words when you ask child to cut you a half of one fruit or a quarter of something else. (888) 274-6869.

■ Wooden Cook Top Stove

(Alex $50 **oooo**) For tabletop or wheelchair table, this wooden stovetop takes up less room than a standard play kitchen. It has dials and burners and lifts to store utensils. (800) 666-2539. **Activity:** For sniffing, tasting, and touching, present real fruits in parts or wholes. Put pieces in a bag. Child must name fruit without visual cues.

COMPARISON SHOPPER
Doctor's & Vet's Kits

For kids who visit the doctor more frequently than most, playing doctor gives them a chance to take charge, even if it is only pretend. Almost all kits come with cases that are hard to re-pack. Learning Resources' **Doctor Kit** SNAP Award '04 ($24.95 **ooooo**), is the exception to the rule, with tons of props and roomy case. (888) 800-7893. Also, for playing veterinarian, **Let's Pretend Veterinarian** (Small Miracles $29.99 **oooo**½) has a child-sized jacket, puppy, and stethoscope and other medical tools. Also from the same maker, a **Doctor** kit with white coat & stethoscope. (888) 281-1798.

Sounds and Sights Toys

■ Lollipop Drum

(Woodstock Percussion $25 ●●●●●) This lollipop-shaped drum makes a pleasing sound and is ideal for games. **Adaptation:** For kids who can't grasp the handle, tape the handle to a tabletop with drumhead hanging off. **Activity:** One person hits the drum and the other person must change positions with every beat. When you are moving, use exaggerated goofy motions and freeze into funny poses. Switch roles—kids love the power of making you move. Also top rated, **Chick-itas Maracas** ($6.50 ●●●●), small maracas that have a great sound and a perfect fit for little hands. (800) 422-4463.

■ Lynn Kleiner Rhythm Sets

(Remo $24.95 & up ●●●●●) Many instruments for young kids make noise instead of music. Strike up the rhythm band with these kits that are well crafted with sound in mind. **Babies Make Music** includes jingle shaker, wrist jingle, and a small drum and scarf (safe enough for kids who still mouth their toys); **Kids Make Music** includes a 7" tambourine, triangle, wrist bell (with big jingles), rhythm sticks, and one maraca. SNAP AWARD '00. **Activity:** Use drum or rhythm sticks for a math game. Make a stack of cards labeled with numbers 1–10. Put them face down. As a player, you draw a card and tap that number. Other player must guess the number on your card. If she gets it, give her the card. At the end of the game, switch parts. Now the other player does the reading and tapping. (800) 397-9378.

■ Wacky Walk

(Small World Toys $30 ●●●●) Six funny sounds and some lights are set off as tots walk on this long narrow footprint mat. Use it for motivating kids to get moving. This is a fun toy for developing gross motor skills and, for older tots, a budding awareness of right and left. Use this for reinforcing color concepts and counting. **Adaptation:** For older kids, mark the footprints from 1–12 with a permanent marker. **Activity:** Mark a die with "0", "1," and "2" dots. Roll the die and child moves that number of steps. How quickly can he get to the end? (800) 421-4153.

Transportation Toys

Trains

See Preschool chapter for latest wooden train sets. For kids who can't fit tracks together, adapt by mounting to a play board. A tabletop makes this toy accessible to a child in a wheelchair.

■ Duplo

(Lego Systems $10 & up ●●●●●) Chunky plastic BLUE CHIP **Duplo** building bricks are basic gear for working on developing fine motor skills. The idea is to have a plentiful supply for original creations. Bringing home a themed set is also a good idea. **Activity Tip:** Sort the Duplo bricks by color and line them up. How many yellow do you have? Blue? This is a hands-on experience with color. (800) 233-8756.

■ Little People Beep the School Bus

(Fisher-Price $14.99 ●●●●½) Like so many new toys, this classic now comes with lights, sound, and action. Four Little People bounce up and down as this jaunty yellow bus with googly eyes rolls along. It has a wheelchair ramp and a talking bus driver; it also plays "The Wheels on the Bus." We think kids could have done with less talk, but this is likely to make a hit. **Activities:** Play "Who Got Off?" Have child look at the four Little People. She closes her eyes and you remove one passenger. Can she tell who got off the bus? (800) 432-5437

■ Little People Ramps Around Garage

(Fisher-Price $37.95 ●●●●●) Updated with electronic sounds, this two-story garage has ramps, elevator, car wash, and lots of gateways and surprises. It closes for compact storage. This type of toy gives you plenty of opportunities for developing language: colors and position words (*up, down, into* the car wash)—all important concepts that are best understood when experienced. See Preschool and Early School Years chapters for other pretend settings. SNAP AWARD '04. (800) 432-5437.

Puppets

Few toys provide a better way to get kids to express their feelings. Without the need to move themselves, kids in wheelchairs or beds can take on pleasingly active roles through the use of puppets. For top-rated puppets and stages, see the Preschool and Early School Years chapters.

How to Adapt a Puppet

Fill the puppet with a Styrofoam cone. Push a wooden dowel into the cone, and your puppet is ready for action!

Place puppets over big plastic soda bottles that can be moved around like dolls.

Attach a magnet to stuffed finger puppets or Little People-type figures and use them on a metal cookie sheet.

For a kid who can't grasp a rod, attach the puppet to the child's arm with Velcro straps. Her hand may not go inside the puppet, but the child can activate the whole puppet by moving her arm.

■ Animal Puppets *2005*

(Gund $16 each ●●●●) Good news! Gund has re-introduced their beautifully made hand puppets. Choose from some of their favorite bears **(Manni)** or other animals such as **Luke the Lion** or **Bamboo Panda.** (800) 448-4863.

■ Dr. Seuss Hand Puppets

(Manhattan Toy $16 each ●●●●) Fans of *The Cat in the Hat* are going to love this puppet! Or be on the lookout for the **Grinch,** the **Lorax,** and **Horton.** (800) 541-1345.

Dolls, Dollhouses, and Garages

Many wonderful dolls, soft animals, and dollhouses are described in the Toddlers, Preschool, and Early School Years chapters.

Mail Order Dolls

The dolls below will be especially interesting for children with special needs, since they are available with adaptive equipment such as walkers, wheelchairs, and braces. All collections include boy and girl dolls, and are also available in multiethnic variations. We suggest requesting catalogs from several before you buy:

- Lakeshore ($30) 16" vinyl dolls and various special needs equipment. (800) 421-5354.

- Pleasant Company ($84 doll/$30 wheelchair only). (800) 845-0005.

Other Notable Dolls

■ Bendos

(Kid Galaxy $6 & up ●●●●●) Bendable action figures are perfect for dramatic play. Available as athletes, community workers, and nonlicensed male and female action figures, they stand up with blocks, fit into vehicles, and satisfy young collectors. The latest additions are zany-looking **Safari** and **Farm** animals with skinny legs. A word of warning: Remove hats and other small details that may be a choking hazard for kids who are still mouthing their toys. (800) 816-1135.

■ Groovy Girls/Boys & Supersize Groovy Girls

(Manhattan Toy $10 & $50 ●●●●●) These all-fabric 13" multi-ethnic dolls continue to be a big hit. Still top rated, **Supersize Groovy Girls** ($50 each ●●●●●), a 40" child-sized fabric doll that's like a pretend play pal. **Activity Tip:** Give kids real clothing with buttons and zippers that they can dress Supersize Groovy in. Helps develop dressing skills needed for independence. SNAP AWARD '02.(800) 541-1345.

■ Feltkids Felt House & Easels 〈2005〉

(RC2/Learning Curve $19.99 ●●●●●) The play house playmat with four rooms comes with a boy, a girl, staircase, doors, and a few other props. Furnishings are sold separately. Multicultural families are available. Technically not a 3-D dollhouse, it goes places (like Grandma's) a traditional dollhouse can't. A good language tool for telling stories and enlarging vocabulary. New for 〈2005〉, **Kickin' It** (with a multicultural soccer team), and last year's **Jumpin' Gymnasts** ($14.99 each). Also top rated, **FeltKids Easel Feltboards** ($9.99 & 14.99 ●●●●), which can be used with any story pieces. **Activity:** Put some of the big felt pieces out and give "clues": "I'm thinking of something you can sit on. It is red. Can you find it?" (800) 704-8697.

> **ADAPTATION IDEA FOR FABRIC TOYS:** Make your own play board by gluing colored felt on the lid and sides of a sturdy box. Use board for sticking on cutout shapes, letters, and animals. Box can be used to store pieces.

■ Woodkins *2005* SNAP AWARD

(Pamela Drake $11.95–$25 ●●●●●) For kids who don't have the dexterity to sew, cut, or paste, this wooden doll frame has fabric choices that stay in place with a "frame" that closes over the edges of the doll. Dolls have four faces for changing moods. SNAP AWARD '00. Available as a boy or a girl, and in several ethnic variations. New for *2005*, a **Fairy** collection with glittery fabric choices. (800) 966-3762.

> **ADAPTATION IDEA FOR MAGNETIC TOYS:** Put pieces on a cookie sheet so that players can see the choices and reach for a change easily.

Art Supplies

Art materials are more than fun. They provide a great way to motivate kids to develop dexterity and express feelings without words, and they give tons of sensory feedback. Creative exploration without lots of rights, wrongs, or rules also gives kids a wonderful sense of "can do" power.

Special Art Tools

Crayon Sticks (Elmer's $2.99 ●●●●) These oversized crayons are softer than most and will be easier to grasp. These will be fine for encouraging big sweeping arm motion and tracing or free-form drawing. (888) 435-6377.

Crayola Window Mega Markers (Binney & Smith $4.99 ●●●●), washable wide markers that kids can use to draw on windows. (800) 272-9652.

Chubby Colored Pencils (Alex $10 ●●○●●) These pencils have thicker "lead" and an easier-to-grasp hexagonal shape, and they are especially wonderful for kids who cannot grasp traditional pencils. (800) 666-2539.

Beginner Paintbrushes (Alex 3 for $6 ●●○●●) Extralarge brushes with handles shaped like bulbs help kids with fine-motor difficulties to paint. Also, **Sponge Painters** now come with color-changing wands. (800) 666-2539.

Chunkie Markers (Bluepath $10 & up ●○●●) Bypass brushes altogether! Washable paint in easy-to-grasp bottles with sponge applicators. (800) 463-2388.

Stamp Kits and Stencil Kits. Although we like kids to create their own pictures, stampers and stencils can be extremely satisfying for older kids who want realistic results. To adapt stampers for kids with fine-motor difficulties, glue a dowel handle to the back of each stamp.

Crayola Dough (Binney and Smith $1.99 & up ●○●●) Super-soft modeling dough. Buy a six- or eight-pack. (800) 272-9652.

Modeling Dough Pattern Rollers (Alex $8 ●○●●) interchangeable patterned rollers snap between the rolling pin-style handles. (800) 666-2539.

ADAPTATION IDEA: Adapting Crayons, Markers, Glue Sticks, and Brushes. For an easier grip, use a foam hair curler over the drawing tool. Or wrap a crayon with a small piece of Velcro and then have the child wear a mitten. The Velcro will stick to the mitten, allowing the child to color without dropping the tool.

■ **Crayola Color Wonder Paper, Markers & Learning Book: Opposites**

(Binney and Smith $7.99 & up ●○●●) Spiral activity books have been added to this line of mess-free products. The **Opposite** book is the best and develops language skills while giving kids immediate self-correcting pay-offs. Pre-readers may need an adult to reinforce the pairs of opposites. They color the page with their no-mess markers and then can enjoy re-"reading" the pairs. Still recommended, **Color Wonder** blank paper and markers, ideal art materials because the markers are colorless and won't stain anything. They have a "magic" quality and turn color as kids draw on the special paper. **Activity:** Draw letters or a heart of dots and have your child connect them. SNAP Award '01. (800) 272-9652.

■ Crunch Art

(Hands On Toys $7–$25 ●●●●●) An innovative art kit that develops hand power as well as creativity. Kids simply place a small piece of fabric on the foam board, push down on the "crunch-er/puncher" (which is not sharp), and the fabric is in place. They can make designs or draw pictures filled with colorful fabric, mylar squares, or chenille stems. Open-ended and mess-free. SNAP AWARD '03. (888) 442-6376.

■ Doodle Pro *2005*

(Fisher-Price $14 ●●●●) A no-mess magnetic drawing tool, that works just like the old Magna Doodle. Tied-on "pen" and shapes are perfect for drawing, tic-tac-toe, and even writing letters and numbers. Also available in smaller model ($8). 3 & up. (800) 432-5437.

■ Crayola Model Magic Character Creator

(Binney and Smith $10 ●●●●½) Here's a good toy for developing vocabulary along with dexterity. It's a lot like your old Mr. Potato Head with a new twist. You get three bags of Model Magic and plastic hats, facial features, arms, feet, and clothing to press into ever-changeable figures. Takes time to figure out how big the body bases must be in order to fit with body parts. (800) 272-9652.

■ Scratch-Lite Sketcher

(Scratch Art $19.99 ●●●●½) This is a light box on which kids place scratch art paper and draw or write with one of two fancy-tipped drawing tools. Finished art looks nice on windows. Kit comes with stencils and 10 sheets of special paper, so bring home a refill pack. A good quiet-time toy that develops dexterity needed for writing. Takes 3 C batteries. **Adaptation:** Use the light box for tracing activities that can reinforce the shapes of letters and numerals and motivate children to develop dexterity. Still highly recommended, **Scratch Magic Activity Kits** ($4.99 & up). Look for the various kinds of scratch-art paper with colors and foil effects. 5 & up. (800) 377-9003.

Craft Kits

As always, we look for craft kits that are quick and easy and create satisfying results. For more kits see Preschool and Early School chapters. Here are our favorites:

■ Ceramic Allowance Bank *2005*

(Creativity for Kids $14.99 **oooo**) A chubby white ceramic pig ready to paint and hold spare change or allowance. It has an easy-to-pull-out rubber stopper, so they don't need to break the bank when they want to spend some of their savings! Includes a "chores" booklet with star stickers... the idea being that they earn their allowance. We have mixed feelings about paying kids for chores, but we do like the idea of encouraging them to save their pennies, nickels, and dimes! Also new for *2005*, **3 Ceramic Frames** (7 & up. (800) 311-8684.

■ Finger Painting Party *2005*

(Alex $20 **oooo**½) Finger paints allow kids to explore color directly with their whole hands and big sweeping arm movements. For reluctant explorers, this kit comes with chunky-handled tools that make squiggles, swirls, and other delicious patterns. Also ideal for open-ended art exploration, **Collage Party** ($17 **oooo**), a bucket chock-full of buttons, pom-poms, wiggly eyes, scissors, stickers, feathers, and paper. (800) 666-2539.

Q **ACTIVITY TIP: Smelly Art.** Add a few drops of scented oil or spices to homemade dough for extra sensory stimulation. Play a "smelling matching" game: Make pairs of matching balls of putty in paper cups and cover with foil. Punch small holes in foil for sniffing. Players take turns smelling cups to make matching pairs. Add more pairs as child develops the ability to make matches.

Dab-a-Dab-a-Do Sponge Art: Sponges are easy to grab and they motivate artistic and messy art explorations. Cut your own sponges or buy a premade set.

Marble Painting: Place a piece of paper in a shallow box. Dip a spoonful of marbles in tempera paint and place them in the box. Tip box to produce a marvelous marble masterpiece. Great for kids with limited motor control.

Make a Slanted Play Board: For kids who need a slanted surface to work on, cut the sides of a cardboard box at a slant and it's all ready for coloring and other projects.

■ Make-Your-Own Cards 2005

(Made By Hands $17.95 ●●●●) There's no need to cut, and pasting is a snap with the glue stick and precut shapes. There are several sheets of "pop-out" shapes that can be used to decorate pre-folded cards. Kit includes 20 envelopes for mailing finished art work. Store all the goodies in this kit in a neat box with velcro closure. This comes two ways, with pastel colors that are no doubt designed to appeal to girls, and a primary color kit that is likely to appeal to both boys and girls. We go for the latter! **SNAP:** Making their own cards will be fun and easy as well as motivate kids to use fine motor skills and create "mail" they can send to family and friends. No right or wrong way to use this open-ended craft kit. (800) 839-7369.

■ Garden Pinwheel Activity Kit 2005

(Alex $9.99 ●●●●) Here's a kit that you will want to use in the garden. Testers loved painting the oversized flower and bug pinwheels. The center pinwheel easily attaches to the larger frame, and makes a cheerful decoration that is fun to watch spin in the wind. Comes with waterproof paint and paintbrush. While marked 8 & up, our younger testers also had great fun painting their pinwheels. (800) 666-2539.

Easels

There are a number of great stand-alone or tabletop easels on the market. **Portable Easel** (Battat $21 ooo●) is a double-sided magnetic easel that will fit easily on a tabletop. One surface can be used as a chalkboard, the other is a white wipe-off board. Storage holds magnetic letters, numerals, markers, and chalk and eraser. (800) 822-8828. **My Drawing Station** (Alex $40 oooo) has a chalkboard surfaced slant-board with a 100' roll of paper and three cup holders for supplies. Still top rated, Alex's **Tabletop Easel** ($45 ooooo) has a magnetic side to use with magnetic games. SNAP Award '00. (800) 666-2539.

Big Muscles/Physical Play

Toys that challenge children to use their big muscles help them develop gross motor coordination, a sense of their own place in space, independence, and self-esteem.

■ Crayon Balance Beam

(Artistic Coverings $199 oooo½) A pricey but neat piece of equipment that will be a hit with preschoolers and early school-age kids who love the challenge of walking on a beam (with the safety of knowing that they're only inches off the ground). The crayon is 6' long, 10" wide, and has a 4" beam surface. (877) 599-9343.

■ Crawl N Fun 2005

(Playhut $25 ooooo) Testers giggled their way through this 6'-long tunnel as they crawled along! Also top rated: longer and more spacious **Yellow School Bus** and **Red Fire Engine** and a blue **Deluxe Train** engine. These each easily accommodate two kids for pretend fun. 3 & up. (888) 752-9488.

■ Gertie Balls

(Small World Toys $6 & up ooooo) These gummy inflatable balls are soft enough for kids who may be scared of big heavy balls coming toward them. We particularly like the "magical" color-changing Gertie. Put in a cold place, it turns pink; toss it and your handprints show up in blue! SNAP AWARD '02. **Activity:** Start out with a cold ball and count how many catches back and forth it takes to turn the ball to another color. An active counting game. Also top rated, **Jungle Gertie Balls** with fun zebra and tiger stripes; **Nobbie Gertie** with bumps that make it easier to catch; and **Loopies** ($7–$15 ●●●●), six loops of soft fabric-covered foam that are easy to catch. (800) 421-4153.

■ Little Tikes' Patrol Police Car

(Little Tikes $44.99 ●●●●●) Here are more bells and whistles (literally!) for on-the-go adventures. Comes with "lights" on top, siren, and other reasonably quiet electronic sound effects. This foot-powered vehicle is a better choice for developing big muscles than battery-powered ride-ins. (800) 321-0183.

> 🛍 **SHOPPING TIP:** Battery-operated ride-in cars that can be activated with a touch of a button may be a good choice for kids who are unable to pedal. Such toys, however, require constant supervision, regular battery recharges, and a hefty investment.

Trikes and Bikes

Your child may be able to ride a trike or bike with few or no adaptations. You'll find our guidelines for buying and descriptions of top-rated wheeled toys in the Preschool and Early School Years chapters.

How to Adapt a Wheel Toy

Adapting a bike may involve adding an easily made belt of Velcro. Other kids may need a trunk-support seating system or foot harnesses, or a hand-driven trike. Two companies that specialize in adapted riding toys and supplies are Sammons-Preston Corp. (800) 323-5547, and Flaghouse Inc. (800) 221-5185.

Sand Fun

For kids who can't get down on the ground to play in the sandbox, why not bring the sand up to them? Put a small sandbox on a picnic table and, voilá!, a child in a wheelchair can now dig in. Also great, see the **Naturally Playful Sand & Water Table** (Step Two) in the Preschool Chapter.

Books

For years, children with special needs were essentially invisible in picture books. Today publishers are issuing more books that reflect the feelings of, and issues faced by, children who are physically or mentally challenged.

Friends and Family

■ ABC for You and Me

(by Meg Girnis/photos by Shirley L. Green, Whitman $15.95 ●●●●) Full-color photos capture school-age kids with Down syndrome playing with familiar toys and each other. There's a lot to talk about as you look at the upbeat photos of this alphabet book with your child and perhaps make another book with A–Z photos of your child.

■ How About a Hug?

(by Tricia Taggart, Jason & Nordic $8.95 ●●●●) A sweet story that follows a girl with Down's syndrome from wake-up, to school, and home again. Each of the people in her world gives her encouragement as well as a loving hug. 4 & up. (814) 696-2920.

■ What Happens Next?

(by Cheryl Christian/photos by Laura Dwight, Star Bright Books $3.95 ●●●●) There's a baby on the left page and a tub on the facing page. What happens next? Open the sturdy flap page and see the baby taking a bath. A series of sequencing events is caught in photos with the "answer" in the foldout. Photos include a child with Down's syndrome. (800) 788-4439.

Siblings

■ Big Brother Dustin

(by Alden R. Carter/photos by Dan Young with Carol Carter, Albert Whitman $14.95 **oooo**) Dustin, a boy with Down's syndrome, prepares with his parents and grandparents for the arrival of his baby sister. Beautifully told and marvelously illustrated with photos that capture the ups, downs, and wonder of expectanthood—across generations. 3 & up.

■ Ian's Walk: A Story About Autism

(by Laurie Lears/illus. by Karen Ritz, Albert Whitman $14.95 **oooo**) Ian, who has autism, hears, tastes, and sees things differently from his two sisters. So a simple walk to the park to feed the ducks is anything but simple. Told in the first person by his sister, this tender tale captures the ambivalent feelings that a sibling must deal with as she also deals with her brother's special ways of experiencing the world. A reassuring tale for siblings. 5 & up.

■ Way to Go, Alex!

(by Robin Pulver/illus. by Elizabeth Wolf, Albert Whitman $14.95 **oooo**) When Carly helps her brother (who has mental retardation) train for the Special Olympics she forgets to prepare him for running through the blue ribbon at the finish line! This touching story reflects the ache and the pride and affection siblings have for their sibs with disabilities. 6–8.

Kids Coping in Mainstream Classrooms and the World

■ Let's Talk About It: Extraordinary Friends

(by Fred Rogers, Putnam $15.99 **oooo**) Newest in an excellent series, this book is ideal for opening a dialogue about how kids without disabilities feel and interact with kids who have disabilities. Photos and simple text raise issues about feeling shy, and concerns about what to say and do. Mr. Rogers reinforces the idea that we are all special. 4–8.

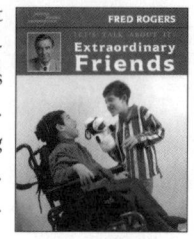

■ Seeing Things My Way

(by Alden R. Carter/photos by Carol S. Carter, Albert Whitman $14.95 **oooo**) Amanda goes to a mainstream class, but gets a lot of extra help with her schooling with special equipment and teachers.

This firsthand account tells how the world looks to Amanda and other kids with severe visual impairments but optimistic and determined outlooks. 6–9. Also by the same team, **Stretching Ourselves: Kids with Cerebral Palsy,** about three kids with very different degrees of cerebral palsy and how they "stretch" themselves physically, socially, and intellectually. 5 & up.

Inspirational Books
■ We Go In a Circle *2005*
(by Peggy Perry Anderson, Houghton Mifflin $15 **oooo**) When a racehorse hurts his leg, running in the circle of a track is no longer possible. But in this story, the horse heals and finds a new circle where he carries those who may not be able to walk, talk, or see, but instead ind joy in "hippo therapy," which is rewarding for the riders as well as the horses.

■ Franklin Goes to the Hospital
(by Paulette Bourgeois/illus. by Brenda Clark, Scholastic $4.50 **oooo**) Franklin is injured and needs an operation. He's very brave until he has to have an x-ray. Then he fears people will be able to see that he's not brave inside. A good story along with a glimpse at what it's like to be a hospital patient. 4–7.

■ Howie Helps Himself
(by Joan Fassler/illus. by Joe Lasker, Albert Whitman $13.95 **oooo**) Howie, a boy with cerebral palsy, wants to be able to move his wheelchair on his own. A book that reinforces a positive sense of "can do." 4–8.

■ Zoom!
(by Robert Munsch, Scholastic $13.99 **oooo**) Kids with wheelchairs will get the over-the-top humor of this fantasy. Lauretta needs a new wheelchair and she wants the one that zooms! 5 & up.

Coping with Visual Challenges
■ Looking Out for Sarah
(by Glenna Lang, Charlesbridge $15.95 **oooo**) Perry, a black lab guide dog, plays a central role in Sarah's busy day. They go to the post office, on the train, to a classroom to sing, and even to the park for a romp. 6 & up.

■ The Night Search

(by Kate Chamberlin, Jason & Nordic $8.95) Heather, who is blind, does not want to carry the white cane her teachers have taught her to use. On a camping trip she discovers how important it is to her. Available in Braille. ($24.95). (814) 696-2920.

■ Private and Confidential: A Story About Braille 2005

(by Marion Ripley/illus. by Colin Backhouse, Dial $16.99 ❍❍❍❍) Laura soon discovers that her Australian pen pal is visually impaired. Up for the challenge, Laura learns how to write in Braille so that he can read her letters by himself. The book comes with a Braille chart so that kids can try their own hand at Braille writing.

■ The Right Dog for the Job 2005

(by Dorothy Hinshaw Patent/photos by William Muñoz, Walker $16.95 ❍❍❍❍) Ever wonder how dogs are trained to become seeing eye dogs? Follow the puppy Ira as he prepares for his special job. 5 & up.

■ Sarah's Sleepover

(by Bobbie Rodriguez/illus. by Mark Graham, Viking $15.99 ❍❍❍❍) Sarah's cousins have come for a sleepover. When the power goes out, it's Sarah, who is blind, who is able to keep them calm and take the lead.

> **SHOPPING TIP:** A neat novelty for a child learning to read Braille is a plastic placemat with the Braille alphabet imprinted on it. From Straight Edge.

Coping with Hearing Impairments and Introducing Sign Language

Every day more than 500,000 Americans use American Sign Language to communicate. You'll find great choices here for kids of every age.

■ The Handmade Counting Book

(by Laura Rankin, Dial $15.99 ●●●○) Painterly images of toys, seashells, and flowers help readers learn to sign numbers 1–20, 25, 50, 75, and 100 in American Sign Language. All ages. Also: **The Handmade Alphabet.**

■ Moses Goes to School

(by Issac Millman, Farrar, Straus & Giroux $16 ●●●○) An upbeat slice-of-life book that follows Moses throughout the day in the special public school he attends, where all the kids are deaf or hard of hearing. This is a sequel to the even more remarkable **Moses Goes to a Concert,** which features a deaf percussionist and shows how Moses and his friends "feel" the music. SNAP AWARD '01.

Previously recommended signing books: Handsigns (by Kathleen Fain, Chronicle), all ages; **Handtalk Zoo** (by George Ancona & Mary Beth, Aladdin); **More Simple Signs** (by Cindy Wheeler, Viking); **Opposites** and **Happy Birthday!** (by Angela Bednarczyk & Janet Weinstock, Star Bright Books).

Audio

■ Alex, Ben & Co. BLUE CHIP

(Kid'n Together $9.98 tape/$14.98 CD ●●●●○) Inspired to sing songs to help his son Matthew (who has Down's syndrome) learn concepts such as body parts, the ABCs, counting, and more, Alex Meisel and his brother created this collection of classics and original music with dollops of humor and upbeat flavor. (800) 543-6386.

■ Come Outside to Play

(Makin' Music $14.99/$9.99 ●●●●○) A mix of 26 lively traditional and original get-up-and-move songs designed for active participation. Lyrics for action songs, finger play, and chants are included in the booklet with entertaining ideas for enlarging upon the songs. Also available separately, a set of rhythm sticks and egg-shaped shakers with a wonderful feel and sound! 3 & up. SNAP AWARD '03. (877) 236-1984.

■ Ella Jenkins' Nursery Rhymes BLUE CHIP

(Smithsonian Folkways $9.50 ●●○○○) A good choice for working on memory and language skills. Jenkins sings familiar rhymes and cues kids to repeat and join in.

■ Songames for Sensory Integration

(Belle Curve $24.99 ●●○○○) Here's a collection of playful musical activities for developing motor, language, and listening skills in child-appealing ways. Both CDs and a booklet full of ideas for sensory integration were developed by occupational therapists. SNAP AWARD '01. (888) 357-5867.

■ Time to Sing

(Center for Creative Play $16.99 ●●○○○) Developed by Dave Hammer, a speech-language pathologist from Children's Hospital of Pittsburgh, this collection of traditional songs has been arranged at a slower pace and sung with greater clarity to enable all children to sing along. CD features musicians from the Pittsburgh Symphony as well as adult and child singers. SNAP AWARD '02. 2–6. (800) 262-8052.

For electronic equipment, see Audio chapter.

Resources

Books: Most bookstores will order any books listed here from major publishers. Here are the phone numbers for several smaller publishers they may not regularly deal with: Jason & Nordic (814) 696-2920; Albert Whitman (800) 255-7675; Woodbine House (800) 843-7323.

Videos: Many of the titles in the Video chapter will be enjoyed by all children. In fact, many are closed-captioned. Descriptive Video Service (DVS), for visually impaired audiences, adds between-the-scenes narrations to TV and videos. For information about DVS television or videos, write to DVS, WGBH, 125 Western Ave., Boston, MA 02134. DVS video titles include *The Lion King* and *Anne of Green Gables*.

■ Healthy All Over

(Healthy All Over $24.95 each ●●○○○) These two tapes, made especially for kids with disabilities, feature 'tween/teens with Down syndrome doing exercises with a pleasant exercise coach leading the fun.

In **Let's Have Fun,** the boys and girls do stretching and aerobic exercises. The video reinforces what the leader is saying with images. So when she suggests they are walking up steps, half the screen shows a flight of steps. On **Let's Get Strong,** the leader and kids use weights. SNAP Award '03. (631) 864-9173.

Additional resources: A number of useful catalogs are targeted directly for the special needs market. Many contain useful adaptation devices. Browsing the catalogs below can help you find some great products as well as ideas for adapting more widely available toys.

- Achievement Products (800) 373-4699
- Lighthouse, Inc. (800) 829-0500
- Crestwood Communication Aids (414) 352-5678
- Constructive Playthings (800) 832-0572
- Enabling Devices (800) 832-8697
- Environments (800) 342-4453
- Flaghouse Inc. (800) 221-5185
- Funtastic Learning Catalog (800) 722-7375
- Lakeshore (800) 421-5354

Online sites of interest:
- www.disabilityresources.org
- www.familyvillage.wisc.edu
- www.autism-resources.com
- www.geocities.com/heartland/plains/8950
- www.ericec.org

Two national organizations provide toy lending library services and play-centered programs for children with special needs and their families. To locate the center nearest you, contact:
- National Lekotek Center, 2100 Ridge Avenue, Evanston, IL 60201, or call (800) 366-7529.
- USA Toy Library Association, 2530 Crawford Avenue, Suite 111, Evanston, IL 60201, usatla.deltacollege.org, or call (847) 920-9030.

Top-Rated Mail-Order Catalogs/On-Line Sites

For busy families, mail-order catalogs and on-line services are a time-saving way to shop. This list includes companies that feature many of the products we recommend.

Children's Catalogs

These catalogs offer a variety of toys, puzzles, games and outdoor equipment. Some also have selected books, videos and audios.

Back to Basics Toys	**(800) 356-5360**
Constructive Playthings	**(800) 832-0572**
Grand River Toy Co.	**(800) 567-5600**
Grandparent's Toy Connection	**(800) 472-6312**
HearthSong	**(800) 325-2502**
Imagine the Challenge	**(888) 777-1493**
Sensational Beginnings	**(800) 444-2147**

School Catalogs of Interest

Community Playthings	**(800) 777-4244**
Environments	**(800) 342-4453**
Learning Resources	**(800) 222-3909**

Specialty Catalogs

American Girl	(800) 845-0005
Asia for Kids	(800) 888-9681
Chinaberry (books)	(800) 776-2242
Educational Insights	(800) 933-3277
Lego Shop at Home	(860) 763-4011
My Twinn (dolls)	(800) 469-8946
National Geographic	(800) 638-4077

Audio, Video, & Music Catalogs

Big Kids	(800) 477-7811
Music for Little People	(800) 409-2457
Signals WGBH Educational Foundation	(800) 669-9696

On-Line Sites

amazon.com
asiaforkids.com
babycenter.com
barnesandnoble.com
buildabear.com
grandrivertoys.com
kbtoys.com
rightstart.com
toysrus.com

Safety Guidelines

Many people assume that before toys reach the marketplace they are subjected to the same kind of governmental scrutiny as food and drugs. The fact is that although the government sets specific safety standards, there is no agency like the FDA that pretests and approves or disapproves products.

The toy industry is charged with the responsibility to comply with federal safety standards, but they are self-regulating, which means it's not until there are complaints or reports of accidents that the Consumer Product Safety Commission (CPSC) enters into the picture. The CPSC is the federal government agency charged with policing the toy industry—but not until the products are already on the shelf!

What does all this mean to you as a consumer? Basically it means "Let the buyer beware!" Both small and large manufacturers have run into problems with small parts, lead paint, strangulation hazards and projectile parts.

The CPSC releases useful recall warnings that are posted in most major toy stores, and manufacturers are required to release recalls to the wire services. The CPSC has a hotline if you want further information about a recalled product or want to report one that perhaps should be recalled; you can call (800) 638-CPSC. The CPSC also publishes a safety handbook that you can request.

To protect your child, here is a safety checklist to keep in mind when you're shopping for playthings:

For infants and toddlers:

- **Dolls and stuffed animals.** Select velour, terry or non-fuzzy fabrics. Remove any and all bows, bells and doo-dads that can be swallowed. Stick to dolls with stitched-on features rather than buttons and plastic parts that may be bitten or pulled off.

- **Crib toys.** Toys should never be attached to an infant's crib with any kind of ribbon, string, or elastic. Babies and their clothing have been known to get entangled and strangled by such toys.

- **Soft but safe.** Be sure that soft toys such as rattles, squeakers and small dolls are not small enough to be compressed and possibly jammed into a baby's mouth.

- **Heirlooms.** Antique rattles and other treasures often do not meet today's safety standards and can be a choking hazard.

- **Wall hangings and mobiles.** Decorative hangings near or on the crib are interesting for newborns to gaze at but pose a safety hazard once a child can reach out and touch. They need to be removed when an infant is able to touch them.

- **Foam toys.** Avoid foam toys that can be chewed on and swallowed and present a choking hazard.

- **Push-and-straddle toys.** If you're looking for your child's first push toy, make sure it's stable and your child can touch the ground when sitting on the toy.

- **Toy chests.** Old toy chests with lids that can fall do not meet today's safety standards. They can severely injure and even entrap small children. New chests have removable lids or safety latches. We recommend open shelves and containers for safe and easy access instead of the jumble of a deep toy chest.

- **Age labels and small parts.** When you see a toy labeled "Not for children under 3," that's a warning signal! It usually means there are small parts. Such products are unsafe for toddlers—no matter how smart they may be! They are also unsafe for some threes and fours who frequently put things in their mouths.

- **Batteries.** Toys that run on batteries should be designed so that kids cannot get to the batteries.

- **Quality control.** Run your fingers around edges of toys to be sure there are no rough, sharp or splintery, hidden thorns. Check for products that can entrap or pinch little fingers.

For older children:

- **Eye and ear injuries.** Avoid toys with flying projectiles. Many action figures come with a number of small projectile parts that can pose a safety hazard if pointed in the wrong direction and that certainly pose a danger if there are younger children in the house.

- **High-power water guns.** Doctors report many emergency room visits from children with eye and ear abrasions caused by the trendy high-powered water guns.

- **Burns.** Avoid toys that heat up when used. Many of the toy ovens and baking toys become hot enough to cause burns.

- **Safety limits.** Establish clear rules with kids for sports equipment, wheel toys, and chemistry sets.

- **Adult supervision.** Avoid toys labeled "Adult supervision required" if you don't have the time or patience to be there.

For mixed ages:

Families with children of mixed ages need to establish and maintain safety rules about toys with small parts.

- Older children need a place where they can work on projects that younger sibs can't get hurt by or destroy.

- Establishing a work space for the older sib gives your big child the privilege of privacy along with a sense of responsibility.

- Old toys need to be checked from time to time for broken parts, sharp edges, or open seams. Occasionally clearing out the clutter can foster heightened interest in playtime. It also brings old gems to the surface that may have been forgotten.

Safety Standard for Bike Helmets

We applaud the federal safety standard that all bike helmets had to meet by February 1999. Do little kids really need helmets? Look at the data and you decide:

About 900 people, including more than 200 children, are killed annually in bicycle-related incidents; about 60% of these deaths involve a head injury. Data shows that very young bike riders incur a higher proportion of head injuries! More than 500,000 people are treated annually in U.S. emergency rooms for bicycle-related injuries. Research indicates that a helmet can reduce the risk of head injury by up to 85%!

New helmets must adequately protect the head, and have chin straps strong enough to prevent the helmet from coming off in a crash, collision, or fall. Helmets for children up to age five will cover more of the head to provide added protection to the more fragile areas of a young child's skull. New helmets will carry a label stating that they meet CPSC's new standards, to eliminate confusion about which certification mark to look for on helmets.

CPSC offers the following tips on how to wear a helmet correctly:

- Wear the helmet flat atop your head, not tilted back at an angle.

- Make sure the helmet fits snugly and does not obstruct your field of vision.

- Make sure the chin strap fits securely and that the buckle stays fastened.

Noisy Toys

In addition to all the above criteria, we have always considered the noise level of products. Loud toys are more than just annoying—they can actually pose a risk to your child's hearing. Recently, with the generous assistance of Nancy Nadler of the League for the Hard of Hearing, we tested the sound level of many new toys. In doing so, we discovered that many ordinary rattles and squeakers produce sounds measured at 110 to 130 decibels. Yet experts say that sustained exposure, over time, to noise above 85 decibels will cause hearing damage. Because current regulations allow manufacturers to make toys which produce sounds up to 138 decibels at a distance of 25cm, parents must be informed consumers. We suggest that you:

- consider noise levels of toys before purchasing them.

- remember that musical toys, such as electric guitars, drums, and horns, emit sounds as loud as 120 decibels.

- stop and listen before purchasing a toy that makes a noise. If it sounds too loud for your ears, it probably is! Don't buy it.

- be very careful with toys designed to go next to the ear (such as toy phones and toys with headsets).

- remember that noisy floor toys are best listened to at a distance... teach your child not to place his ears on the speaker of the toy.

These guidelines have been prepared in conjunction with the League for the Hard of Hearing.

Subject Index

Brand Name and Title Index

NOTE: Toys and equipment are listed under manufacturer or distributor. The following codes are used for titles of works: (A) = Audio tape; (B) = Book; (C) = Computer software/CD-ROM; (V) = Video.

Visit our website.

www.toyportfolio.com Updates, reviews of award winners, media listings, and parenting articles.

Are you in a parenting group or play group?

Contact us about special rates available for fundraisers and bulk orders.